AMBITION AND BEYOND:
Career Paths of
American Politicians

AMBITION AND BEYOND:
Career Paths of
American Politicians

Shirley Williams and
Edward L. Lascher, Jr., editors

Institute of Governmental Studies Press
University of California, Berkeley
1993

Library of Congress Cataloging-In-Publication Data

Ambition and beyond : the career paths of American politicians / edited by Shirley
    Williams and Edward L. Lascher, Jr.
        p. cm.
    Includes bibliographical references.
    ISBN 0-87772-338-9
    1. Politicians--United States. 2. Politics, Practical--United States. I. Williams,
    Shirley, 1930- . II. Lascher, Edward L.
    JK1726.A43 1993
    324.2'2'0973--dc20   93-9860
                                                              CIP

145145

DEDICATION

In memory of our fathers, George Edward Gordon Catlin and Edward L. Lascher, who loved and studied politics.

CONTENTS

Acknowledgements

Shirley Williams
Edward L. Lascher, Jr.
Harvard University

The interest of the Institute of Politics at the Kennedy School of Government, Harvard University, in the career paths of elected politicians, goes back to its founding in 1966. Among Institute of Politics Fellows, who spend a semester at Harvard, are many elected politicians from both parties and from all three levels of government (federal, state, and local) as well as some from overseas. The Institute of Politics has conducted, since 1974, a biennial conference for newly elected members of Congress and another conference, biennially since 1975, for newly elected mayors. The Institute's objective, to educate and involve undergraduates in the commitment, excitement, and challenge of political life, has been triumphantly achieved.

But there has been a dearth of academic research into the career paths of elected politicians. So in December 1987, the then Director of the Institute, Jonathan Moore, together with the Institute's first Director, Professor Richard Neustadt, convened a meeting to exchange ideas on how research and teaching on elected politicians might best be promoted. Two years later, a seminar was arranged at which a number of young scholars submitted papers on the career paths of American politicians.

This book owes its existence to that seminar. It was held at the Institute of Politics, Harvard University, in December 1989, and chaired by Professor Dick Fenno of Rochester University. Shirley Williams then was Interim Director of the Institute, having replaced Jonathan Moore's successor, Dick Thornburgh, who had become Attorney General of the United States and, subsequently, Under-Secretary at the United Nations. Several of the papers presented at that seminar were revised to take account of later developments in American politics and were rewritten to become chapters of this book.

x

Professor Williams and Professor Edward Lascher as co-editors would like to express gratitude to Professor Dick Fenno and to Professor Nelson W. Polsby who have supported the project throughout; to Shirley's husband, Dick Neustadt, whose enthusiasm for the study of elected politicians is undimmed; and to Edward Flood and Anne Doyle Kenney, to whom we owe much for their help and assistance in preparing the book for publication.

Finally, we would like to express gratitude to Jerry Lubenow, Maria Wolf, Pat Ramirez, and Catherine West at IGS Press and to Bruce Cain of the Institute of Governmental Studies at the University of California, Berkeley, for encouraging and wise advice in producing this book.

ABOUT THE AUTHORS

Susan Carroll is Associate Professor of Political Science at Rutgers University and Senior Research Associate at the Center for the American Woman and Politics (CAWP) of the Eagleton Institute of Politics. She is the author of various works on women's political participation including *Women as Candidates in American Politics* (1985), and she has conducted research on women candidates, voters, elected officials, and political appointees. Her most recent research focuses on the impact of women in public office. Carroll received her Ph.D. in political science from Indiana University.

Linda L. Fowler is Professor of Political Science at Syracuse University, where she has taught since 1975. She is the author of *Political Ambition: Who Decides to Run for Congress*, with Robert D. McClure (1989) and a recently completed manuscript, *Candidates, Congress, and the American Democracy*, to be published by the University of Michigan Press, as well as numerous articles on congressional politics in a variety of scholarly journals and edited volumes. Fowler is former chair of the Legislative Studies Section of the American Political Science Association and represented the American Political Science Association in Japan in 1991. She has twice received awards for outstanding undergraduate teaching at Syracuse; she received her Ph.D. and M.A. from the University of Rochester.

Fernando J. Guerra is Assistant to the President for Faculty Resources at Loyola Marymount University. Prior to this appointment, he served as Associate Dean of the College of Liberal Arts. Guerra is also chair of the Chicano Studies Department. He has written several articles including "Ethnic Officeholders in Los Angeles County," *Sociology and Social Research* (January 1987); "The Emergence of Ethnic Officeholders in California," in *Racial and Ethnic Politics in California* (1991); and "Conditions Not Met: California Elections and the Latino Community," in *From Rhetoric to Reality: Latino Politics in the 1988 Elections* (1992). Guerra received his Ph.D. and M.A. in political science from the University of Michigan.

John R. Hibbing is Professor and Chair, Department of Political Science, University of Nebraska-Lincoln. His research has centered on legislatures, legislative elections, and legislative careers. Most of it involves the United States Congress although he has also studied the British House of Commons and the new Hungarian National Assembly. His articles have appeared in the *American Political Science Review*, the *American Journal of Political Science*, the *Journal of Politics*, the *British Journal of Political Science*, among other journals, and he is co-editor of the *Legislative Studies Quarterly*. Current research interests are citizens' perceptions of their national legislatures both in the new democracies of Central Europe and in the United States.

Edward L. Lascher, Jr., is Assistant Professor of Public Policy at Harvard University's Kennedy School of Government, specializing in elective politics. His publications include articles on congressional voting, nonpartisan elections, and the attractions of local legislative office. He is currently engaged in research on deliberation in legislative bodies. Prior to his graduate studies he served as a staff member for the California State Legislature. A native Californian, Lascher received his A.B. from Occidental College in Los Angeles and his M.A. and Ph.D. from the University of California, Berkeley.

Timothy Prinz is Assistant Professor of Government and Foreign Affairs at the University of Virginia, where he teaches courses on Congress and the media in politics. He received his bachelor's degree in political science and philosophy from the University of Dayton and went on to earn an M.A. and Ph.D. in political science from Harvard University. He has published articles on congressional elections and congressional careers, and his current research examines the influence of the media on elections to the House of Representatives.

Peverill Squire is Associate Professor and Chair of the Department of Political Science at the University of Iowa. He has been a visiting professor at Meiji University, Tokyo, Japan. Squire is the editor of *The Iowa Caucuses and the Presidential Nominating Process*, and his articles on various aspects of American politics have appeared in *American Political Science Review*, *Journal of Politics*, *Public Opinion Quarterly*, *Legislative Studies Quarterly*, and other scholarly journals. He received his Ph.D. from the University of California, Berkeley.

Shirley Williams is Public Service Professor of Electoral Politics and Director of *Project Liberty*, a project to assist democracy in East Central Europe, at the Kennedy School of Government at Harvard University. She teaches courses on the European Community, electoral and advocacy politics, and women in politics. Williams serves in Britain's House of

Lords. She was elected to the House of Commons 1964-79 and again from 1981-83. She cofounded the Social Democratic Party in 1981 and was elected to serve as president from 1982-88. She served in several cabinet posts including Paymaster General and Secretary of State for Education and Science (1976-79). In 1974 she was made a Privy Counsellor. Williams' publications include "Sovereignty and Accountability in the European Community," in *The New European Community: Decision-making and Institutional Change* (1991); *Politics is for People* (1981); and *A Job to Live* (1985). She attended Columbia University as a Fulbright Scholar; is an Honorary Fellow of Newnhan College, Cambridge, and Somerville College, Oxford, and was Visiting Fellow of Nuffield College, Oxford.

Introduction

Shirley Williams
Harvard University

Any politician whose career has unfolded within the British parliamentary system, as mine has done, cannot be other than amazed by the complexity and variety of political career paths in the United States. This book addresses that complexity and variety; it is a collection of essays by some of the ablest young American political scientists on that subject, a subject surprisingly neglected until recently.

The federal system offers several levels of government in which politicians can serve and an abundance of elected offices of all kinds. The variations among the regions of this vast country, and among the states within each region, offer different structures of opportunity, which in turn shape politicians' career paths. The separation of powers enforces a separation of careers, legislative, executive, and judicial. The paths followed by ambitious men and women, although intersecting now and then, will diverge on sectoral lines.

In the British parliamentary system, political career paths offer only a limited number of choices. Because politics is more subject than most callings to chance and circumstance, the career path of any politician will twist and turn, rise and fall. But for a British politician the goals are limited, and the direction is plain. Once elected to the House of Commons, the possible career paths are few, and one dominates all the others. Most members of Parliament aspire to become ministers or shadow ministers (the term for Opposition spokespeople), in short, members of the executive, which is largely recruited from their ranks. Some will seek to become chairs of important committees or of Parliamentary Party committees, though for many MPs these are at best compensation for failing to achieve ministerial office or for having achieved and then lost it. Finally, a few MPs move up the narrow ladder to contend for the Speaker's chair, via the Speaker's panel (an appointed group of MPs who chair debates).

Members of Parliament are almost always recruited by way of active membership in a political party. Potential candidates for Parliament will have worked as volunteers in local and national election campaigns, been elected to party offices or sometimes to local government positions as councillors or county councillors. Max Weber, in his famous essay "Politics as a Vocation" says: "There are two ways of making politics one's vocation; either one lives 'for' politics or one lives 'off' politics," though the contrast is not, he declares, an "exclusive" one.[1] These men and women may not have a "vocation" for politics in Weber's sense of grasping its moral imperatives, but only at the parliamentary level are they able to "live off" politics in the sense of actually earning a livelihood from it. With the exception of a few hundred organizers, known as party agents or campaign managers, political offices in Britain at the subnational level do not attract salaries, though expenses and loss of work time may be reimbursed.

Still, many of the men and women referred to above, potential candidates for national office, are career politicians in Anthony King's sense of the term.[2] They live for politics. Their spare time is devoted to it, and the time they spend on their formal, paid jobs is reluctantly and grudgingly conceded. Their ambitions and aspirations are defined in political terms. For some, those ambitions have as their objective a mayoralty, or chairmanship of a county or regional council. Even if achieved, those objectives will not mean that they live *off* politics, though their time will be largely consumed by politics. For many, the goal is to move from living *for* politics to living *off* politics as well as *for* it, in other words being elected to a paid position as an MP.

Recruitment of candidates for Parliament takes place in the United Kingdom at several levels. Potential candidates emerge at the local level; local party officers or the local agent encourage promising young party activists to try their hand at fighting for a council seat, or even a parliamentary one. Others attract the attention of national party officials, or of party leaders or senior members. Speeches at annual party conferences

---

[1] Max Weber, "Politics as a Vocation," translated by H. H. Gerth and C. Wright Mills, Social Ethics Series, Facet Books, Fortress Press, Philadelphia, 1965, from *Max Weber: Essays in Sociology* (Oxford University Press: Oxford, 1946).

[2] Anthony King, "The Rise of the Career Politician and its Consequences," *The British Journal of Political Science*, July 1981.

are a useful way to attract the attention of national leaders. The history of recruitment of parliamentary candidates is dotted with the names of politicians who were great mentors and patrons: R. A. Butler, Hugh Dalton, Herbert Morrison, Willy Whitelaw, and Anthony Crosland are some who come to mind.

Obviously many potential candidates are self-starters, in the sense of attracting attention to themselves, but they have no chance of selection as candidates without the support of their party. Indeed, formally it is party activists elected to a local executive or management committee who choose the candidate to represent their party at the general election, though in some parties now their choice is subject to ratification by the local membership as a whole. The fierceness of the competition to become a party's candidate will depend on whether the constituency is safely in that party's hands (a "safe seat"), marginal among the parties, or solidly held by another political party.

The outcome of the general election will, with rare exceptions, be determined by the electorate's opinion of the contending parties rather than of the contending candidates. (By-elections, the equivalent of a special election in the United States, offer much more scope for candidates to mobilize personal votes). Electors will be swayed by the record of the government in power, the national campaigns mounted by the main political parties, especially on television, and the state of the economy, rather than by the personality or promises of individual candidates. Most of the money for the national campaign is raised by the political parties. No television or radio time can be purchased for the purposes of promoting a candidate, and, if a program is made about a particular constituency, all the candidates' names must be mentioned. The allocation of broadcasting time among the parties, both during general elections and between them, is done by a committee on party political broadcasts chaired by the Government Chief Whip, on which all parties with an official party group in Parliament are represented. It broadly reflects electoral support at the previous election.

The restriction on party political advertising and the system of allocating broadcast time between nationally (or at least regionally) established political parties inhibits individual entrepreneurship. Politics in Britain remains a team game. New teams can, at their peril, enter the playing field, but individuals, however gifted, will not get far without the support of a substantial party. Recent British political history is littered with the broken hopes of brilliant "men of destiny": Enoch Powell and David Owen spring to mind.

Local government, though important as a recruiting ground for national elected office, does not play as significant a role as in the United States. Neither at local nor at county level do subnational governments in Great Britain today have much autonomy or much power. They are closely controlled by central government as to the revenues they can raise and the expenditures they can incur. Yet despite these limited powers and the absence of remuneration other than modest expenses, thousands of men and women seek election as councillors every year. Few of them are motivated by "progressive ambition," since as noted above, few will advance to the parliamentary level. What does actually motivate them remains a fascinating question. It is a question that "ambition theory," the dominant theory in explaining and interpreting career paths in politics, does not adequately address. Nor is the answer relevant only to Britain. The United States, too, possesses what Peverill Squire calls in this volume "dead-end legislatures." "Dead-end legislatures" offer neither attractive remuneration, nor professional staff nor good opportunities for advancement. Yet they too attract men and women whose modest ambitions do not go beyond serving the community and achieving the status of elected representative.

The United States offers aspiring politicians a rich choice of career paths: city and county office, state senates and assemblies, statewide office including governorships, the House of Representatives, the Senate, and the presidency. In addition, a huge array of posts from the federal and state cabinets to upper ranks of agencies are filled by political appointment. Furthermore, many elected officials at the state level and above carry their own complement of personal staff, as do committees in many legislatures.

In the United States, regional and interstate differences account for some of the discrepancies in the opportunity structures ambitious politicians confront. As Squire points out, state legislatures differ in terms of the opportunity they offer for advancement. They also differ in terms of the path advancement many take. Some are "springboard legislatures," where members have a relatively good chance to advance to higher office in a different institution; in other words, the prospects of external progress are good. Others are professional legislatures, offering reasonably good remuneration and attractive working conditions, in which an elected lawmaker can pursue a satisfying career; the internal incentive structure is more promising than the external incentive structure. Still others are dead-end legislatures, where none of these characteristics are found. But what seems to be generally true, as John Hibbing points out, is that a period of office as a state legislator is becoming a more frequently chosen path to federal office. Term limits, discussed in the conclusion to this book, may have a significant impact on the frequency of this choice.

The electronic media's domination of the American political scene is often cited as the main reason for the candidate-centered, personalized politics Linda Fowler identifies in her chapter as typifying contemporary American politics. Certainly the scope for individual entrepreneurship in politics is far greater in the U.S. than in western European democracies and appears to be growing as the influence of the parties weakens. The explanation, however, cannot be found only in the dominance of television and radio as communicators of political personalities, images, and ideas. It is the interaction between weak political parties, the electronic media, and the free market in political advertising that produces candidate-centered politics in the U.S. Television and radio are powerful media in European politics too, but in the regulated systems of Britain and of several other western European countries, the electronic media actually enhance the power of party leaders, who decide which candidates will appear on the party's television and radio broadcasts.

Political career paths can tell us much about the role of the parties and the role of the media in democracies. Career paths also tell us a great deal about the structure of opportunities for minorities, for women, and for politicians from different states. To take one example from this book, the thousands of paid posts, as committee staff, legislative aides, and local district aides constitute a relatively new and increasingly significant recruiting ground for future elected politicians. Fernando Guerra in his chapter shows how important they may be in the early stages of a political career for certain underrepresented minorities. It is therefore surprising that more scholarly effort has not been devoted to their study.

In one way, of course, political biography sheds light on career paths by tracking the course of a single outstanding individual. But the enterprise is a different one from research into career paths in general. Biographers usually write after the event; few have studied their subjects as they work, campaign, and project themselves. Most try to capture personal character rather than examining one career path compared to others.

If the study of political career paths had been more assiduously done, the theories on political motivation that now dominate political science might carry more conviction with those of us who are practitioners of politics. As a practitioner at every level of politics from that of local activist to Cabinet minister, I find some of the theories oversimplified and therefore unsatisfactory. In pursuit of a scientific basis on which to construct models capable of yielding quantifiable results, political men and women are presented as rational actors making choices abstracted from the challenges, strokes of fortune, serendipity, and vision that make politics the most exciting and unpredictable of careers.

Ambition theory has for a generation dominated this area of political science. Joseph Schlesinger defined the behavior of the politician as "a response to his office goals." Political ambition fell into three categories: (1) progressive ambition, the ambition to achieve higher office than the one now held; (2) static ambition, the ambition to retain the office now held; and (3) discrete ambition, which is satisfied by a single term in office. In this book, several of the contributors point to certain weaknesses of ambition theory, while not denying the contribution it has made to understanding what motivates politicians. To begin with, only one of the categories, progressive ambition, properly describes what most of us call ambition in everyday language, namely the desire to advance to a higher office. Static ambition and discrete ambition, the other categories, are oxymorons; ambition is neither static nor discrete. Furthermore, the attempt to define progressive ambition excludes ambition to move to higher responsibilities and status while holding the same elected office. To become chair of the House Committee on Ways and Means, or on Armed Services, is at least as lofty an ambition for a freshman representative as to become a senator. Internal career paths—careers *within* the House of Representatives or the Senate or a state legislature—are not adequately taken into account in ambition theory.

Linda Fowler in her chapter argues that ambition theory fails to grasp the complex and unpredictable nature of politics, the way in which political environments change and individuals relate to these changes. Candidates are recruited from a large pool of potential politicians: little study has been done of the reasons why able and qualified people decide not to enter a political contest. As Peverill Squire aptly points out, "although many may express progressive ambitions, only a few act on that desire." Ambition theory does not help us to decide who, out of a large and promising field, will actually enter the race.

The theory that politicians behave in ways that will maximize their political opportunity for higher office, while capturing the motives of many, also fails to explain just those political actions that best embody the excitement, the risk, the heroism, and the tragedy of politics.

Ambition theory cannot tell us why Senator Albert Gore, Sr. in 1968 continued to advocate opposition to the war in Vietnam although all his leading advisors told him (correctly) that it would cost him reelection in Tennessee. Ambition theory does not explain why in 1968 Hubert Humphrey refused to disassociate himself from President Johnson at the Democratic convention, although his advisors told him that he would benefit politically from doing so. Ambition theory does not shed light on the resignations in Britain of Edward Boyle over the Suez expedition or of Roy Jenkins over membership of the European Community, from secure Cabinet and party positions widely regarded as launching pads for yet higher office.

Political resignations in Britain admittedly involve very different considerations from resignations in the United States. In Britain, most ministers have their own political base, in the constituency and in the party. Well-timed resignations (like those of Harold Wilson and Aneurin Bevan in 1951) may even enhance a politician's standing in his party and thereby his chances of achieving higher office. In the U.S., executive appointees are the creatures of the president or the governor. If they resign, few can expect to be backed by a multitude of activists, or a party faction ready to declare them its leaders. Members of Congress enjoy far greater autonomy then do members of the House of Commons, but Cabinet members in the U.S. enjoy far less autonomy then their opposite numbers in Britain.

The autonomy of members of Congress is indeed great and becoming greater. Reforms in campaign financing have been circumvented or vetoed; attempts to limit paid access to the electronic media have run afoul of the First Amendment to the Constitution. Incumbency has become a way of life. Incumbents determine the rules of the game and those rules protect them from serious challenge. Incumbents have a significant influence on the redrawing of congressional districts. Incumbents decide on the staffing and on the level of communication to their constituents the taxpayer shall finance, a privilege made much more valuable by the development of direct mail and targeting techniques.

But as incumbents entrench themselves in their separate fiefdoms, so a frustrated electorate turns to call them to account. Its weapons are crude and undiscriminating. Chief among them are term limits, which cut short the careers of dedicated public officials and political crooks alike. Others deprive representatives of their powers, for instance the proposed constitutional amendment to enforce a balanced federal budget. All of them reflect a disturbing antagonism to politics and politicians.

It is an antagonism fed not only by the media, but by politicians themselves. The executive lambasts the legislature, the legislature excoriates the executive, and even the judicial branch is intermittently sucked into the political maelstrom. It is not surprising that sections of the electorate conclude that no politician can be trusted and that everyone must be shackled or cut short.

These new pressures may radically reshape the career paths of future U.S. politicians. Restrictions on their powers will make politics a less challenging profession. Term limits will make a political career profoundly frustrating. But they will provide fascinating subject material for those young political scientists who will write the next volume on career paths.

The essayists in this book have been selected from among the most promising young men and women working in this field of political science. Learning from practitioners as well as from theorists, they do not simplify. The book is divided into three sections, following a review of the literature and research by Timothy Prinz. The first section looks at Congress. Linda Fowler discusses how candidates are recruited, the significance of personalized campaigns, the importance of incumbency, and the diminution in the number of seriously contested races. As incumbents strengthen their position, recruitment is concerned more with succession than with challenge, and that alters the dynamics of the system. John Hibbing explores the consequences of low turnover in Congress and of long careers: progressive ambition finds its outlet not always in office seeking but sometimes in position seeking. Ambition theory is more valuable as a theory of opportunities, Hibbing says, than as a way of measuring the psychological motivations of individual politicians.

The second section of the book is concerned with the subnational levels of government and lawmaking from which so many national politicians are recruited. In his chapter, Peverill Squire distinguishes between those state legislatures (which he calls "professional legislatures") that offer levels of renumuration and staffing that amount to a reasonably attractive career that conforms to "static ambition" in Schlesinger's terminology; those that provide rich opportunities for advancement ("springboard legislatures," satisfying "progressive ambition"), and finally those that offer neither ("dead-end" legislatures). Edward Lascher, using the findings of industrial and organizational psychologists, argues that ambition theory does not adequately explain what motivates politicians, and that work satisfaction is a major factor in determining whether politicians remain in their chosen field.

Susan Carroll and Fernando Guerra, in the third section of the book, explore recruitment patterns for women and minorities and seek to explain why certain sectors of the population are so seriously underrepresented in federal political office. Guerra shows that the system of legislative aides has become a recruiting ground for African Americans, Latinos, and other minorities in southern California's polyglot politics. Carroll weighs the various factors that help explain the underrepresentation of women, such as socialization, conflicting family demands, the professionalization of state legislatures, and the financial barriers to candidates for national office. She hopes that women's networks will go some way to offset women's traditional handicaps.

My own view is that, in the U.S., systemic factors have taken over from socialization as the main constraints on the advance of women; in particular incumbency, the tiny number of open races, the first past-the-post voting system, the single-member constituency, and the rising costs of campaigns at federal or statewide level, which I suspect inhibit many women from seeking elected office in the first place.

The opportunities for research in this richly rewarding field are legion. I have mentioned some emerging new areas above. In addition, the Senate has been little studied. Internal career paths open up whole new areas for inquiry: the interrelationship between career paths and different kinds of state legislature; the career paths of politicians whose ambitions are encompassed within a state; the factors, other than personal ambition—work satisfaction, patriotism, idealism, call it what you will—that motivate politicians. The study of career paths offers an exciting opportunity to cast light upon the complex, contradictory, confusing, and fascinating calling known as politics, a calling that matters to us all.

Such studies are not only of academic interest. They concern those who work with elected officials, and those thousands of men and women who at some point in their lives contemplate a political career. The quality of a democracy is determined by the quality of those who run for elective office, so it is important for all of us to know how they are recruited and what factors shape their subsequent careers.

Chapter 1

The Career Paths of Elected Politicians: A Review and Prospectus

Timothy S. Prinz
University of Virginia

"Early in his career, the fledgling political scientist learns that his discipline is ill-defined, amorphous, and heterogeneous" (Greenstein and Polsby 1975; vii). The persistently amorphous character of political science can especially plague the researcher working in a field that crosses many of the standard categories of the discipline. The literature on careers and career paths is disparate and far-flung, and mastering the diverse results found in the fields of political recruitment, political elites, personality and politics, political biography, legislative studies, and the numerous other bits and pieces scattered elsewhere presents something of an organizational nightmare. There is little sense of logical flow or orderly progression to the study of careers or career paths.

Moreover, the study of career paths is heavily influenced by the prevailing approaches to the study of political science. The discipline has undergone a marked change in approach and method in the last three decades, and a sense for this change is important in any assessment of the literature on careers and career paths. In 1954 Donald Matthews wrote

> . . . a major gap in the facts concerns the political career patterns of decision makers. For the United States, especially, it would be useful to know the usual pattern or sequence of public offices leading to the Presidency or Congress and whether or not there are differences between political career patterns in one-party or two-party areas, between the career patterns of Democrats and Republicans, and so on. Questions such as these have yet to be systematically explored (Matthews 1954, 59).

These questions retain much of their relevance almost 40 years later. Scholars have answered Matthews' call, but the effort has been intermittent and unsystematic.

Some, if not most, of this inattention to careers and career paths may be explained by the sheer difficulty of the task. Defining and identifying political careers and career paths in politics is no easy task. One student of political careers has noted both the "theoretical difficulty" and empirical impossibilities associated with the study of career paths (Wahlke, Eulau et al. 1962, 73). Another author has described politics "as one of the most unpredictable of careers" (Willson 1959, 222), and without some predictability studying career paths is a pointless endeavor.

In general, political careers do not possess the regularized patterns of advancement found in business or the professions. Moreover, the diverse character of the American political system, with its federal structure providing numerous points of entry into politics and manifold different routes to higher office, makes such a study difficult. On the one hand, it is likely that no two career paths will be exactly alike; on the other hand, the sheer size and scope of the system make it empirically difficult to obtain the overarching perspective necessary to discover the regular patterns that might occur. Finally, it is difficult to grasp the unique mixture of ambition and opportunity that combine to produce a political career. Both institutional factors (i.e., an open seat, a supportive party, the opportunity for future advancement, etc.) and individual attributes and experiences (i.e., a desire to run, timing, the right political connections) must come together in just the right fashion. The serendipity prevalent in political careers renders any attempt at generalization about career paths risky indeed.

DEFINING THE POLITICAL CAREER

A necessary first step in overcoming these obstacles to the study of the career paths of elected politicians is defining precisely what one means by a political career. At an early point in the study of politicians and their careers, Lasswell ridiculed the notion that politics had any resemblance to a career.

> In American politics the escalator to the top is not a regimented, orderly lift, but a tangle of ladders, ropes, and runways that attracts people from other activities at various stages of the process, and leads others to a dead end or a blind drop (Lasswell 1960, 303).

Lasswell's comment echoes the difficulties in identifying a political career described above. From an objective standpoint, it is difficult to develop a comprehensive perspective on the various entry points and opportunities for advancement prevalent in the contemporary political career. It may be the case that like Justice Stewart's observation on pornography, we know a political career when we see it, but it is difficult to identify in advance the empirical characteristics essential to the definition of a political career.

Eulau answered Lasswell by arguing that the important point is that "political careers may be subjectively conceived as real and, because they are so conceived, they have real consequences for the taking of political roles and behavior" (Wahlke, Eulau et al. 1962, 74). Eulau goes on to bemoan the fact that we know so little about the careers of politicians, and in the process offers a useful working definition of a political career.

A political career, like careers in other pursuits, is a more or less typical sequence of events, a developmental pattern in the life histories of politicians moving into positions made available by the framework of institutions (71).

Although this is a rather imprecise definition of the political career, it emphasizes one aspect of the political career that will be an important theme throughout this paper: the structure of opportunity. As Eulau notes, a political career is not simply determined by the politician's desire for advancement or skill in obtaining office, but is influenced by opportunities and limitations structured in the political system. In many ways "the structure of opportunity" captures that combination of ambition and serendipity that is so crucial to the advancement of a political career.

Leonard Ruchelman (1970) also emphasizes the structure of opportunity in his study of the careers of New York state legislators. He defines a political career "as a pattern in the lives of individuals moving into different positions made available by the governmental framework." Despite the fact that careers are fundamentally influenced by the availability of positions, Ruchelman maintains that opportunity can be studied systematically. "Important [in the study of political careers] is the fact that career paths are not necessarily the result of chance; nor are they determined entirely by the skills of the politician. Rather, there is good reason to believe that given certain conditions, career lines show important uniformities" (Ruchelman 1970, 27). Unfortunately, neither Ruchelman nor any of the other early students of political careers specified what these regularities might be. Though the political career may possess certain regular patterns of entry and advancement, these paths have not been clearly identified nor even well illustrated.

An intriguing alternative to defining what constitutes a political career is identifying the career politician. In his discussion of politics as vocation, Weber (1946) presents a distinction between the person who lives for politics and one who lives off politics. This distinction was largely an economic one—those who live for politics make politics their life, either through the possession of power or through some commitment to a cause, and those who live off politics gain their livelihood from politics and the political career. This difference was important for Weber because it largely determined who would enter politics and why. In order for those who desire to live for politics to enter the realm at all, they must be independently wealthy, or possess the means to make their living elsewhere, else only those who live off politics will seek office.

Weber's essentially economic distinction still retains its relevance. For instance, the fact that politicians are now able to earn their living in politics is an important explanation for the emergence of the contemporary political career. Indeed, the prevailing distinction between amateur and professional legislators is fundamentally rooted in (among other things) the notion that representatives serving in professionalized legislatures no longer must practice law or some other profession in order to support themselves. Being a legislator can now be a full-time job, a description that certainly applies in the larger states (California, New York, Massachusetts, Michigan, and Ohio readily come to mind). The emergence of such professionalized legislatures has in many ways made the pursuit of a political career—and identifying such a career—much easier.

Admittedly, there is something of a chicken and an egg problem here; nonetheless, the distinction between those who live for politics and those who live off politics can be quite useful in identifying political careers. In most cases, the professional politician is the one who lives off politics, who actively pursues a political career—he or she *is* the career politician. The amateur politician, in contrast, is more difficult to distinguish. Usually attracted to politics by a concern for an issue or issues, politics becomes a vehicle for advancing a particular set of concerns—for expressing a particular conception of the public interest. Admittedly, the progress of such amateur politicians can come to look much like a political career. The distinction can blur with the emergence of numerous legislative and other political positions in which an amateur or professional politician can remain for some time if he or she chooses.

Moreover, it may no longer be the case that the amateur politician views politics as a sidelight and is increasingly attracted to the idea of making politics a career (Wilson 1962; Loomis 1988; Canon 1989). Anthony King (1981) observes a number of changes along these same lines in Great Britain. He finds that "career politicians" are replacing their noncareer counterparts in British politics. King describes career politicians as those committed (presumably of their own free will) to politics. They regard politics as their vocation, they seek fulfillment in politics, they foresee their future in politics, and they would be upset if they could not continue in politics. The obvious difficulty with this definition is distinguishing the career politician from the noncareer type. The only factor separating the two types is a subjective sense of commitment that is rather difficult for the political analyst to observe. Even further, one might well argue that all politicians are in one sense or another committed to politics, either as their vocation or avocation, and the problem is differentiating between the two. (King is able to distinguish between the two types relatively easily in British politics, relying on biographies, memoirs, diaries, etc. Such an approach may work in Britain, but it appears to be much less useful in the American context where all politicians tend to be lumped in one category.)

The virtue of the more economic interpretation becomes readily apparent by comparison. When political scientists think of the career politician, they most often have in mind those who live off politics, seek to remain or advance in office, and pursue politics because it is their livelihood. On this view, questions of commitment or motivation for public service are relegated to secondary importance.

As this discussion illustrates, defining the political career is no simple task. The notion of a career implies a series of regular advancements, a succession of steps up the ladder from office to office. Unfortunately, it is difficult to identify the ladder of advancement in the American political system. The myriad opportunities to pursue elected office means that there is not one clearly defined path, but a number of alternative paths for advancement that the ambitious politician seeking a political career may follow.

To the extent that political careers can be identified at all, two factors emerge as particularly important. First, the numerous points of entry and opportunities for advancement mean that political careers are heavily dependent on the structure of opportunity; careers are in many ways shaped by a unique mix of ambition and opportunity, of subjective and objective factors. Second, the economic perspective on political careers offers a useful vehicle for locating ambition in politics, and for understanding the drive to enter and remain in political office. As Alan Ehrenhalt's (1991) recent book makes clear, the foremost factor separating contemporary politicians from their predecessors is their transparent sense of ambition, a situation that has been facilitated at least in part by the emergence of politics as a means for earning one's living.

THE STAGES OF THE POLITICAL CAREER

Despite the difficulties associated with identifying the political career or the career politician, there are some useful ways to characterize political careers that simplify the task somewhat. One is to divide the political career into identifiable stages: recruitment, advancement, retirement. The first stage, recruitment, is concerned with the initial decision to enter politics. Studies of recruitment focus on questions concerning who enters politics and why; the social and psychological background of politicians; the community and partisan networks that encourage entry into a political career, and the influence that political institutions and structure have on the entry of potential candidates into politics.

While getting into politics is the necessary first step, advancing in politics is the key to a political career. Studies of advancement in politics are perhaps the most amorphous part of the literature on the career paths of elected politicians. They begin with studies dedicated specifically to the examination of the career paths of politicians, but also include a wide variety of works on the career within specific political institutions (most notably the legislature in the case of elected officials). The roles that institutions and the structure of opportunities play in shaping the career path receive close scrutiny here. Given its amorphous and far-flung nature, advancement within the career is perhaps the area most in need of systematic research.

Retirement is the final stage of the career, and studies of the decision to leave politics can tell us much about the current state of politics and the political career: the costs of running for office, the demands of public service, the attractiveness of other pursuits, and the compensations available upon leaving political office. While this subject has only recently been studied, answering questions of who decides to leave politics and why can say much about the nature of the political career and also about the political system more generally.

The stages of the political career are a useful point of departure for this review of the literature. The discussion is organized around two themes: political recruitment and political ambition. The literature on political recruitment is an obvious place to begin this examination. Political ambition is important for the structure it lends to the study of careers, and the emergence of ambition theory marks an important landmark.

Finally, the study of career paths has been heavily influenced by the prevailing approaches to the study of political science. The discipline has undergone a marked change in approach and method in the last three decades, and a sense for the changes wrought by the advent of the behavioral revolution and the emergence of rational choice approaches to politics is important in any assessment of the literature on careers and career paths. Thus this review weaves an historical sense for the development of the discipline into the discussion of recruitment and ambition. While this approach cannot be comprehensive, it does help to integrate the various approaches to the study of careers and the disparate findings on careers and career paths. In an effort to provide yet another view of the literature, following this review of the literature on political careers and career paths are two case studies on the careers of members of Congress and of women and minority politicians.

POLITICAL RECRUITMENT

Studies of political recruitment are fundamentally concerned with who enters politics and how they enter. The motivations of those who enter politics as well as the ways that the political system shapes the opportunities for entry into politics are crucial subjects for study. In the context of political careers, recruitment here refers largely to legislative recruitment, since the legislature is so often the focal point of elected officials seeking a career. While politicians also seek other elected offices—the county or city council, the mayor's office, or the governor's chair—in many cases these offices are much less amenable to career aspirations and sometimes are viewed as stepping stones to higher office. In addition, scholars have given much less attention to these other offices. Focusing on career paths, then, requires attention to legislative recruitment, since entry and career advancement in elected politics takes place largely in and through the legislature.

The Social Background Approach

Early studies of recruitment compared the backgrounds of those who enter politics to the rest of the populace, and researchers learned rather quickly that the opportunity to seek elected office is unevenly distributed in society. These studies found that the typical politician is better educated, works in higher-status occupations, and has a more privileged background than those he or she represents. Matthews' study (1954) of political decision makers is probably the seminal work in this field, and this study and those that followed soon produced a fairly complete portrait of the American politician. The typical candidate for elective office about to embark on a political career in the 1960s and 1970s was a well-educated, metropolitan, middle- or upper-class, middle-aged, white Protestant professional man who was both occupationally and socially mobile and had a better than average income (Schwartz 1969).

While providing a fairly clear picture of the backgrounds of politicians, this research offered few other insights into the decision to enter politics or the pattern of the political career. Nevertheless, the early, social background approach to recruitment was still prominent as late as 1975, as witnessed by one of the leading summaries of recruitment studies:

> The purpose of recruitment studies is to explain the processes
> which result in a differentiation between political elites and
> masses, and between political and other social elites (Czudnowski
> 1975, 156).

The prominence of the social background approach is explained in part by the ready availability of data—survey after survey generated a wealth of background information on politicians. The vast majority of these early studies were very much rooted in the social systems approach to politics. As one author noted, the importance of recruitment studies "consists in the expectation that recruitment patterns can explain certain characteristics in the orientations and role performance of office holders and political elites" (Czudnowski 1975, 156). In other words, recruitment is important because of the ways in which the social backgrounds of politicians can influence their outlook and behavior in politics. By now this description of the typical politician is accepted as standard lore in American politics, but it might do for students of careers and career paths to reflect on whether this description has changed over time, and how and why it has changed. One of the widely accepted truisms of American politics is that anyone can run for office; an individual does not have to come from a particular background or social class in order to enter politics. Yet the standard portrait drawn by Matthews and others belies this possibility. Which view is correct? Does the standard description still apply, or does it need modification? The answers to these questions are of fundamental importance, since they tell us much about those who can and do ultimately pursue an elective political career.

In spite of the wealth of information, the social background approach to explaining recruitment into politics often fell short of the mark. As one reviewer noted, there are sufficient holes in the social background evidence "to suggest that a demographic profile is not the most fruitful tool for identifying those who have a proclivity for politics" (Prewitt 1965, 109). Due in part to dissatisfaction with the limits of this approach, scholars began to turn their attention to other aspects of politicians and the political system that might be important in determining who runs for office. Among the alternatives were the personalities of politicians, political socialization, and certain structural aspects of the political system that influenced entry into politics.

The Political Personality

Do politicians possess a distinctive personality type that differs from the rest of us? One of the first to answer this question with a resounding yes was Harold Lasswell, who argued that politicians are more likely to be aggressive seekers after power. Laswell sought to connect the individual's approach to politics to "the whole personality system." Laswell's hypotheses dominated the early literature, and since that time excursions into the relationship between personality and politics have (not surprisingly) generated a large literature, but only those works closely tied to the study of career paths will be examined here.

First, however, several practical and methodological problems plague the study of personality and politics. On the one hand, it is difficult to obtain measures of personality differences sufficiently sensitive to demonstrate the connections between personality and political behavior. Researchers have struggled for some time to make explicit the connections between personality characteristics and political responses, with little success. Second, it is difficult (if not impossible) to develop research designs that isolate and adequately measure the personality characteristic of interest. Unique situations and other environmental factors intervene, so that it is difficult to distinguish the influence of personality in shaping political behavior. Finally, it is difficult to measure politicians in general; not surprisingly, many are loathe to take personality tests.

These difficulties are well illustrated in relevant samples of the literature. In one of the earliest tests for a political personality type, McConaughy (1950) administered a battery of personality and opinion tests to 18 state legislators in South Carolina and to two small control groups of nonpoliticians. The results were mixed at best: the legislators were less neurotic and less introverted, more self-sufficient, dominant, and lacking in feelings of inferiority than the control groups. A similar study (Browning and Jacob 1964) administered thematic apperception tests to both politicians and nonpoliticians, and found that "being a politician does not entail a distinctive concern for power, or achievement or affiliation." Individuals were just as likely to pursue these goals in the economic realm; however, in communities where politics was the center of attention and interest, individuals attracted to politics were likely to score higher on these measures than nonpoliticians.

An intriguing attempt to connect personality differences to political behavior (and political careers) is Barber's (1965) study of 27 first-term state legislators in Connecticut. Through interviews and responses to questionnaires Barber identifies four types of legislators, based on their level of activity in the legislature and their desire to return to the legislature.

	Willing to Return	Unwilling to Return
Active	Lawmakers	Advertisers
Inactive	Spectators	Reluctants

Obviously, Spectators and Lawmakers are the important categories from the perspective of political careers. Usually recruited from noncompetitive small towns, Spectators enjoy the camaraderie and excitement associated with the game of politics but do not actively participate in legislative business. Barber identifies Lawmakers as those highly active and motivated individuals who make the legislature work. These are the people most likely to seek a political career. Barber finds that these differences in political types are fundamentally rooted in personality differences: lawmakers tend to have a much greater self-concept and higher levels of self-esteem than those in the other three categories.

James Payne and his associates (1984) present a slightly different perspective on the motivation to seek political office. They argue that politicians are motivated by an emotional drive—they label it a compulsion—to accept the rigors of political life. From extensive interview data, Payne and his colleagues have gleaned a number of different types of these motivations, though most politicians possess only one of the types:

Status—the need for prestige or public recognition

Program—the need to work on public policy

Conviviality—the need to please others, gain approval
Obligation—the need to follow one's conscience
Game—the need to compete in challenging interactions

According to Payne, these motivations provide the emotional drive that explains active participation in politics. In an interesting parallel, Michael Maccoby (1976) found in his study of corporate executives that interview respondents could be categorized in types that correspond quite well with the Payne incentives.

Unfortunately, Payne and his colleagues do not say where these motivations come from, nor how they come to be activated in the political realm. In short, the theory of motivation in its current state has little predictive value, and as such contributes only marginally to the study of political careers or career paths. Following Barber, it might be interesting to discover if, for example, a particular personality type is more likely to seek a career in politics, and, if this is the case, to explain why it might be so.

Later studies have maintained that the decision to enter politics largely depends on socialization. Browning (1968) identifies a distinctive personality "syndrome" closely connected to efforts to achieve success. The choice of politics as the arena in which to seek power and achievement "hinges on perceptions acquired during intensive and prolonged socialization." Schwartz (1969) conducts a test similar to Browning's, and his results also seem to indicate a personality structure "distinctive to politics."

> In sum, the individual who is predisposed to political activity is likely to differ . . . in the following ways: he is higher in needs achievement, autonomy, aggression, and dominance, and lower on needs abasement, change, succorance, and order. . . . (561)

The question is whether these personality differences have any important implications for politics, or, in this case, the political career.

These later studies call attention to the ways in which personality interacts with a given context to produce behavior. As Greenstein (1987) notes, analysts of the connections between personality and politics need to pay greater attention to the way political context and environmental factors intervene between psychological factors and behavior. This point is especially important for the study of careers, since it may be the case that some personalities are disposed to careers in some situations and not others, but this point has never been systematically studied. Further, this attention to the connection between personality, context, and behavior is in many ways an important prelude to ambition theory.

The personality and politics literature has produced a rather mixed bag of results. The numerous difficulties associated with this field compelled one scholar to observe that "along the path of motivational analysis lies madness" (Davies 1963, 59). Two basic problems remain. First, it is extremely difficult to assess the precise connections between personality and politics. A number of studies claim to have identified a distinctive political personality type, but the evidence points to relatively modest differences between politicians and ordinary people. Politicians are slightly more power-oriented and a little more secure than the average individual, but this hardly constitutes a firm foundation for building a theory of political careers. A more serious problem is how to connect these findings to the study of career paths. Presumably, it would be good to know whether a particular personality type predisposes an individual towards a political career, or if personality is somehow an important factor in shaping how an individual pursues a political career. Despite some rather isolated examples (like Barber's work or the Georges' biography (1956) of Woodrow Wilson), these are issues about which we still know very little, and may never know very much.

Political Socialization

While the personality and politics literature focuses on whether politicians are self-starters, the study of political socialization is concerned with whether social influences play any role in the decision to enter politics. Generally speaking, political socialization refers to the formal and informal social, psychological, and cultural mechanisms that in one way or another shape an individual's attitudes toward (and behavior in) the political system. The social background literature uncovered the connection between social status and entry into politics but left unanswered the question of motivation. Do social factors have any role to play in the decision to run for office? Do different socialization experiences have any connection to political recruitment? In recent years, socialization has become particularly important as an explanation for the decision to seek political office (see Carroll, this volume).

Not surprisingly, the same sorts of problems that plague the attempt to connect personality and political behavior also affect the study of political socialization. For one, it is difficult to study the effects of socialization directly, or to isolate these effects, since social factors are just one of any number of influences on political attitudes and behavior. Another fundamental problem with these types of issues is the fact that they cannot be tested directly; "whether the politician-to-be internalizes the norms of society and . . . acquires orientations towards [politics] that distinguish him from age cohorts cannot be directly examined" (Prewitt 1965, 96).

The connection between socialization and recruitment to politics is a major issue in the literature. Prewitt explores whether those more heavily socialized to politics—individuals exposed to politics at an early age, who grew up in a family or social environment that encouraged involvement in political issues—are more likely to enter politics and pursue a political career. The family connection has always had a prominent place in American politics—the Adamses, LaFollettes, Lodges, Roosevelts, Tafts, and Kennedys are only a few examples. In addition, the available evidence seems to indicate that if family or authority figures are actively involved in politics, they tend to pass on that involvement to the next generation. Wahlke, Eulau, and their colleagues find that primary groups (family, teachers, and friends) exerted strong socialization influences on the legislators in their four-state study. Moreover, whereas most people cite adolescence as the time that they first became aware of and interested in politics, these legislators were more likely to mention childhood and grammar school as the time they first became interested in politics. Thus, there appears to be substantial evidence for a socialization effect in political recruitment.

The difficulty is that the evidence is all one-sided. Data for those who enter politics are readily available, but not for those who are heavily exposed to politics and did not pursue politics. Nevertheless, though the data are limited, "we do know from several studies that the percentage [of politicians] which come from politically active families is higher than chance alone would explain" (Prewitt 1965, 107).

What these findings suggest is that in some cases, social background and personality make little difference in the decision to enter politics and pursue a political career. Instead, a person can be drawn to politics solely because he or she inherited an interest. Later studies have sought to combine the effects of personality, background, and socialization, and have found that socialization retains its prominent role in the decision to enter politics (Prewitt 1965, 4; Eulau 1969).

These issues have received renewed interest in recent attempts to explain why so few women enter politics. Kirkpatrick concluded in her study of U.S. state legislators that

The principal constraints that impede women's full participation in the power processes in society appear to be rooted in prevailing role distributions rather than in anatomy, physiology, male conspiracy, or even in the basic values of society. Education, occupational experience, place of residence, average age of entry into a legislative career are all products of the sex role system (1974, 239).

In short, just as previous studies concluded that inheriting a disposition towards politics was important for explaining the decision to enter politics, the opposite is also true: those who are socialized not to consider politics or a political career are much less likely to enter the political arena.

Political Structure

The preceding discussion might leave one with the impression that students of recruitment were interested only in studying individuals, or that the individual decision to run is the only factor important for entry into politics. But the decision to enter politics is also conditioned by the opportunities available to do so, so students of recruitment began to focus on a number of features of the political system that shaped the decision to enter politics (Tobin and Keynes 1975).

For example, scholars soon recognized that not all individuals who might be inclined to run for office did in fact pursue a political career, and so sought to understand the factors responsible for winnowing the field from potential office seekers to actual candidates. Seligman et al. (1974) divided the process of narrowing the field of candidates into three stages: certification, selection, and role assignment. Prewitt (1970) compared the process to a Chinese box puzzle, with smaller and smaller boxes nesting inside each other.

The early studies also stressed the importance of party in political recruitment. Sorauf (1963) found that party dominates candidate selection in Pennsylvania. Seligman and his colleagues (1974) examined the nomination process in Oregon in great detail and found that, although a variety of groups are involved in the selection process, parties lack influence. In a four-state study, Tobin (1975) noted that institutional variations in the nomination system tend to influence the patterns of partisan (and other groups') influence on recruitment. Parties are much more influential in the recruitment process in closed primary systems, and they tend to emphasize prior political experience, while open primary systems are much more fluid.

Patterson and Boynton (1969) present a similar distinction in their analysis of legislative recruitment in Iowa. On the one hand, recruitment can occur in an environment in which parties dominate political life and exert direct control over the opportunities for office. In other situations, parties still compete for office and in this sense organize the competition for seats, but recruitment is much more a matter of personal ambition and self-recruitment. Wahlke and his colleagues concur: "political career patterns and orientations are likely to be shaped by that structure of the party system—[in this case by] the degree of party competition found in a given [political] system." In short, parties tend to narrow the scope of conflict and in turn manage the recruitment process in order to control outcomes, which imposes a sort of career perspective on political offices.

The role of parties in structuring the opportunities for office remains a critical issue today. Political science has yet to describe adequately how parties structure the contemporary political career in either the entry or advancement state. Of particular interest is how the two parties are changing, especially given the recent rise of a two-party South. How exactly do partisan considerations combine with ambition to produce political careers? Do self-starting politicians choose a party and then choose the career path, or do ambitious politicians choose the party most likely to advance their political career? It is not difficult to imagine that this is the case in some parts of the country, which may go a long way to explain why Republicans continue to lag behind Democrats in the Congress and many state legislatures (Ehrenhalt 1989). Such a perspective on careers may also help explain the resurgence of the GOP in the South—given increasing evidence that Republican candidates can win, a larger number of eligible candidates may seek minority party affiliation.

Conclusion

Despite a wealth of information, political scientists are still unable to specify in detail how and why the people who enter politics and pursue a political career differ from other individuals in important ways: social background, political socialization, or the psychological motivations to seek office. Perhaps the best way to summarize the early study of political recruitment is to borrow from a critique of these studies:

too little research has concerned itself with the whole of the recruitment process; instead, we have excellent descriptions of isolated fragments: a handful of investigations of psychological factors, a substantial number of studies of the social backgrounds of political leaders, and numerous investigations of the political institutions which mark the final phase of the recruitment process . . . (Jacob 1962, 703).

The early history of the study of recruitment is one of intensively focused fragments. Moreover, there is little relationship between what we know about recruitment and the career paths of elected officials. As Matthews has noted,

If students of legislative recruitment and legislative careers are to progress beyond providing "interesting" descriptive material they must do a better job of demonstrating how recruitment matters (Matthews 1985, 18).

Fortunately, some of the later works on political recruitment that focused on political ambition and the structure of opportunities within the political system were able to accomplish some of these tasks.

POLITICAL AMBITION

The study of political ambition is the central theme in the more recent study of political careers and career politicians. Ambition for office lies at the heart of any understanding of careers in politics, and the development of ambition theory marks an important turning point in the study of political careers and career paths.

Schlesinger's seminal work on ambition opens with a simple yet elegant description of the importance of ambition for the study of political careers. "Ambition lies at the heart of politics. Politics thrive on the hope of preferment and the drive for office" (1966, 1). The usefulness of this perspective for the study of political careers cannot be overstated. The central premise of ambition theory is that a politician's behavior is a response to the desire for advancement. Thus, ambition theory literally assumes the idea of a political career. The crucial question is whether ambition theory can tell us anything about the career paths of politicians.

Schlesinger identifies three types of ambition: *discrete* ambition refers to those officials who seek a particular office for a given term and then choose to retire from public life; *static* ambition refers to those politicians who seek to remain in the office they currently hold; and *progressive* ambition defines those who seek an office higher than the one they currently hold. Schlesinger suggests that most politicians have progressive ambitions and that the urge for higher office is suppressed only when circumstances dictate that it is unreasonable.

Given that all, or at least most, politicians seek to advance, how in fact do they advance? As Schlesinger notes, ambition theory makes sense only if there is some order to the opportunities for political careers, if political ambition is channeled in straightforward ways. The structure of opportunities is thus a key component of ambition theory; the seats available and the hierarchy of positions for advancement give shape and definition to the political career. Ultimately the structure of opportunities interacts with ambition to determine whether a political career begins and the likely path that career might take.

For Schlesinger the most notable characteristic of the structure of opportunities is its openness; there are innumerable outlets for political ambition. From the point of view of ambition, however, the electoral system is also full of risks, providing some initial structure to the system since risk tends to foster some ambitions and deter others. Similarly, the costs of a political career provide some structure to the system. Running for office and pursuing a political career entail certain sacrifices in terms of time, privacy, family life, and the opportunity costs associated with other careers (i.e., job security, financial security, and the like).

The other source of structure is the party system. For almost any office of consequence a candidate must compete as a Democrat or a Republican, requiring an additional calculation for the ambitious politician concerning the competitive chances of each party.

> Together the two-party system and the differential risk factor provide stability for the American opportunity structure, which in turn contributes to the stability of the American political system. Few politicians can have any direct or purposeful impact on the range of opportunities available to them. Each politician must work within an opportunity structure that he cannot alter. This is not to say that he cannot improve his own chances, but rather that the conditions he must cope with are not his to create. A politician makes decisions which affect his own ability to advance. He must choose his party, time his entry into politics, select his constituency, decide which offices to run for. The sum of these decisions by politicians everywhere certainly affects the general character of the system, but the individual politician . . .
> is unable to affect the general structure of opportunities (19).

This conclusion probably needs some modification now. Politicians, particularly those in legislatures, have somewhat greater control over the structure of opportunities today than they did at the time Schlesinger wrote this. For one, the opportunities to remain in their current office are much greater (and more attractive) for many politicians, affording them a much greater opportunity to pursue a political career. But despite these changes, Schlesinger's essential point remains intact, particularly for those seeking to enter politics.

The remainder of Schlesinger's study is a meticulous and extensive examination of the structure of opportunity for political offices in the United States. He finds that, although there is variation from state to state, an identifiable structure of opportunity exists in the American political system: there is a logical order of recruitment and progression in office. The standard pattern is one with which we are all now quite familiar. The ambitious politician usually begins with a seat at the local level, in either county or city government, and advances to a position in the state legislature or state administrative hierarchy, and from there seeks national office.

Schlesinger finds no one career path, only certain central tendencies within the system. For instance, he identifies 11 states that possess clearly marked paths to the Senate or the governor's chair. Located mainly in New England or the Midwest, each of these states manifests "a strong tendency to keep distinct the career lines." Most of the politicians in these states begin as state legislators and advance to higher office by regular steps. Most of the states' senators come from the House of Representatives, while the governors come either from statewide elective office or the state legislature (112).

While Schlesinger's study is a landmark in the study of career paths, it is not without its limitations. One is Schlesinger's narrow focus on the state as the unit of analysis; he is interested in political careers as they occur within the state. This means that the governorships and Senate seats are the only high offices that receive close scrutiny. We know very little about the local career path, except to the extent that it is part of the career sequence to the governorship or the Senate; nor does Schlesinger much consider the path to the House of Representatives.

A number of scholars have sought to build on Schlesinger's work in ambition theory, though as one student has noted, "the structure of opportunity and the structure of ambition have proved extremely difficult to link empirically" (Fishel 1971, 25). One of the earliest efforts is Black's (1970) attempt to formalize the ambitious politician's decision calculus. As Black notes, Schlesinger presents a strong case for the importance of political ambition, but provides "little evidence of how it develops" (144).

Black's theory of political ambition "rests on the idea that office seekers attempt to behave in a rational manner in selecting among alternative offices; that rather than being driven by excessive ambition, they tend to develop ambition slowly as a result of their changing circumstances" (145). In other words, when a politician is confronted with a decision to seek higher office or remain in his or her current position, he or she will examine the alternatives, evaluate them in terms of the likelihood of their occurrence and the relative value they hold, and select the alternative that yields the most desirable outcome. Black develops a simple decision calculus to formalize this approach to political ambition:

$$u(O) = pB - C$$

where u(O) represents the utility of office for the politician prior to the election, p is the candidate's estimate of probability of winning the office, B is the subjective measure of benefits that the individual will receive from winning the office, and C is the cost required to campaign and obtain the office. Black maintains that given this relatively simple calculus, a potential candidate will seek office if (1) the benefit (B) of officeholding and the probability of winning (p) are greater than the costs (C): [pB > C], and (2) the utility of officeholding [u(O)] is more valuable than other pursuits. Black admits that these are obvious conditions that tell us little about the actual calculations of politicians. What is of interest to Black are the costs attached to seeking political offices, particularly those costs that are determined in part by "the structural characteristics of the political system" in which the candidate decides to seek office (146).

As the remainder of Black's paper demonstrates, these costs (as well as the other aspects of ambition theory) are difficult to measure empirically. His examination of 435 city councillors in San Francisco develops hypotheses and measures that at best provide indirect support for the theory. Black's analysis does produce an intriguing finding, however, one that might be labeled the capture theory of political careers. He finds that once a candidate enters the political arena, the costs of progressive ambition relative to other pursuits decline at a continuous rate. In other words, once the proverbial hat is thrown in the ring, in many instances this very fact opens the door to static and progressive ambition, since it

is in some ways more costly for an individual to quit politics and return
to private life. Moreover, as a political career ages—as more time is
invested—the option of foregoing a career becomes relatively less
attractive. In a sense, the initial investment tends to pull the candidate
further and further along the career sequence. Thus the pursuit of higher
office may have less to do with being bitten by the political bug than we
might expect, and more to do with the fact that the initial decision to run
in a sense commits the politician to ambition and a career.

The other notable descendant of Schlesinger is Rohde's (1979) study
of the political ambition of members of the House of Representatives.
Rohde makes two important contributions to the study of political careers.
First, he presents a more concrete theoretical approach to the study of
career paths for House members, and second, Rohde offers a number of
tests of hypotheses generated by the expanded theory.

Rohde begins by noting that Schlesinger's classification of ambition
is largely retrospective: a representative who serves only one term and
leaves displays discrete ambition, one who runs for reelection manifests
static ambition, and those seeking higher office exhibit progressive
ambition. A difficulty with this approach is that it does not lend itself
well to prospective analysis, for predicting the kind of ambition a
politician has. Rohde resolves this difficulty in much the same way
Schlesinger did: by assuming all politicians have progressive ambition
and that circumstances dictate that actual choice of ambition. In this
view, then, static ambition is not a consciously chosen strategy, but a
behavior pattern manifested because of the risks associated with
progressive ambition and the representative's unwillingness to accept
those risks. Such an assumption works reasonably well when considering
the House of Representatives.

Following Black, Rohde develops a simple calculus to capture the
decision situation facing members of the House where the expected value
of running for office is a function of the probability of winning, the value
of the office and the costs of running. Not surprisingly, a politician will
run if the expected value of the higher office exceeds that of the one
currently held. This approach underlines the importance of the opportunity structure central to the political career. In large measure, the
probability of winning office and the costs of running are determined by
the opportunity structure. The benefits of office for the most part remain
constant, and politicians simply respond to the situation in which they are
placed: the greater the risk of running for higher office, the less likely it
is that the politician will run.

Rohde derives several sets of hypotheses from this generalized theory of political ambition. The first set concern the value of higher office; he infers that Senate seats are more desirable than the governorship, and thus House members are more likely to run for Senate seats than for the governor's chair. A second set of hypotheses concerns the probability of winning higher office. Obviously, House members are more likely to seek a Senate seat when the incumbent is not seeking reelection. In addition, House members are more likely to seek higher office when the partisan balance in the race is in their favor. Rohde also hypothesizes that the greater the degree of overlap between the member's present constituency and the prospective constituency, the more likely it is that he or she will seek higher office. A final set of hypotheses focuses on the present value of the House seat. We would expect that less senior members of the House are more likely to make a run for higher office than those with greater seniority, since more senior members are more likely to value their present office.

Not surprisingly, the data from 1954 to 1974 confirm these predictions. Members of Congress are more likely to seek a Senate seat than a governorship and more likely to run for a four-year governorship than a two-year term. Members are also more likely to run for higher office when the probability of winning is higher and are more likely to seek the Senate from a small state (where constituencies are more likely to overlap) than from large states. Members who leave the House for a Senate run also tend to do so early in their House career.

Rohde's exploration of ambition in the House illustrates the usefulness of ambition theory for the study of political careers. And it underlines the importance of the structure of opportunity in ambition theory and in development of the career path. Brace's (1984) follow up to Rohde's study also stresses the importance of the structure of opportunity—whether a seat is open or highly competitive, the nature of the partisan division, the amount of constituency overlap—as well as the present value of the House seat in the decision to run for higher office.

A number of other studies have confirmed the basic tenets of ambition theory. Prewitt and Nowlin (1969) find that ambitious city councillors—those who said they were interested in seeking higher office—differ from those who lack ambition in two important respects: the ambitious tend to have much greater breadth of view, and they tend to favor expanding the prerogatives and responsibilities of higher offices. Hain (1974) finds that age can greatly affect ambition: the older a politician is, the less likely he or she is to seek advancement. Finally, several studies of Senate voting behavior confirm many of our suspicions rooted in ambition theory. Senators with static ambition tended to demonstrate a great degree of variation in their roll call voting behavior, while those with progressive ambition—for either party leadership posts or the presidency—tended to moderate their voting behavior to bring it in line with the larger constituency (Van Der Slik and Pernacciaro 1979; Abramson, Aldrich, and Rohde 1987; but compare Hurley 1989).

The usefulness of ambition theory for the study of political careers is by now readily apparent. But while a number of studies have sought to build upon the foundation of ambition theory or to verify its predictions, little effort has been made to present descriptive studies of career paths and the structure of opportunities since Schlesinger's work. Mezey (1970) published a rather straightforward examination of the structure of opportunities for the Congress, but his results are now largely dated.

A preliminary examination of one narrow aspect of the structure of opportunity for the House reveals several interesting patterns. In his examination of members of the House from 1948 to 1966, Mezey discovered some 20 different paths to the chamber that accounted for over 96 percent of all legislators. A glance at the Congress in 1980 reveals the same variety of paths, but with some interesting changes (see Table 1.1).

While the data are too limited to draw firm conclusions, they do tend to indicate substantial changes in career paths to the House. The most obvious is an increase in the number of state legislators reaching Washington. In 1980, over 36 percent of all House members came to Congress from their respective state legislatures, as compared with an average of 29 percent for the period from 1948 to 1966. And by 1980, a slight majority of all members elected to the House had some prior political experience at the local level, either in some local office or the state legislature. When all types of political experience are taken into account, 7 in 10 had prior experience before entering Congress. Another change is the virtual disappearance of the judiciary as an avenue to Congress. Also, the decline in the number of members coming from the local attorney's office urges collapsing that office with other local elective offices—there now appears no distinctive career path here, and little to distinguish it from other local offices.

Finally, Table 1.1 also indicates that amateurism is alive and well in congressional elections (Canon 1989, 1990). Almost 30 percent of the class of 1980 held no elective office prior to entering the House of Rep-

Table 1.1. *Penultimate Office Prior to Election to House of Representatives*

	Mezey (1948-1966)	1980
State Legislature	29.3%	36.8%
Local Office	10.6	10.6
D.A. or Prosecuting Attorney	6.3	4.6
Judicial	6.3	—
Administrative/	5.9	
Federal Executive		4.6
Congressional Office/	3.4	
Legislative Aide		4.6
Higher Office/	1.8	
State Executive		6.4
Law Enforcement	0.7	
Party Ranks	—	3.0
No Prior Political Experience	35.8%	29.5%
Business		10.8
Attorney		10.1
Academia		3.2
Media/Publisher		2.5
Local Political Organization		1.1
Doctor		
School Teacher/Principal		
Union		all less than 1%
Widow		
Minister		

Source: Mezey 1970, 568; Barone and Ujifusa, *The Almanac of American Politics 1982*.

resentatives. These figures persist throughout the decade. Fowler and Maisel (1989) note that "roughly 40 percent of the first time members in the last four Congresses have neither campaigned for the House before nor held elective office prior to taking their seat in the chamber." Banks and Kiewiet (1989) report a similar figure, 32 percent, for the period 1970 to 1984. It would appear, then, that there is still a place for the political amateur within the halls of Congress.

Admittedly, this analysis is preliminary, but a strong case can be made that research such as this can make an important contribution to the understanding of career paths. As a necessary first step, research at the state and local level could tell us a great deal about the opportunities and obstacles for careers. Further research at the national level would contribute much to the identification of specific career paths to the House and Senate. There are additional questions to be answered as well. Are there distinct career paths within the individual states or in particular regions of the country? What are the important factors that shape these career paths? These and other topics deserve extended attention.

The importance of ambition theory for political careers lies in its usefulness for studying careers and career paths. Ambition theory provides a basic structure, a framework for examining the career and the career politician that in turn generates testable hypotheses on the nature of careers and career paths as well as generalizations about political careers. Admittedly, not all politicians display ambitious office-seeking at all times, but generally these "profiles in courage" are the exceptions that prove the theoretical rule. Moreover, the true test of ambition theory is whether one can use it to say anything substantive about the nature of careers and career paths, and here the theory has already made a substantial contribution. Ambition theory and its focus on the structure of opportunities provide a ready means for exploring both the limits and possibilities of political careers and the shape and pathways they take.

Thus far, political recruitment and ambition theory have dominated the discussion of political careers. The central place of each of these two perspectives is well illustrated in the following case studies. The first examines the voluminous literature on the emergence of careers in Congress, and the second focuses on the political careers of women and minority politicians.

THE CONGRESSIONAL CAREER

Perhaps the single best place to study the career paths of elected officials is the United States Congress. As the preceding discussion indicates, Congress was often the first laboratory for studying political recruitment and testing the tenets of ambition theory. As a result, more is known about the careers and career paths of senators and representatives than any other elected office. Moreover, a seat in the House of Representatives is a the first step on the national ladder of career advancement in the American federal system, and for this reason aspiring career politicians often set their sights on advancement to Congress. Studies of recruitment to Congress thus make an important contribution to our understanding of the first stages in the career paths of elected politicians.

The emergence of a congressional career also helps illustrate the dynamics driving political careers generally. The increasing tendency of representatives to view their service in Congress as a career has been well documented (Bullock 1972; Fiorina et al. 1975; Kernell 1977; Fiorina and Prinz 1992). Price (1971, 1975) observes a growing membership stability in the Senate after the Civil War and a similar trend in the House at the turn of the century. In addition, the institutionalization and professionalization of the legislature that began at about the same time made both the House and the Senate more attractive places to work (Polsby 1968; Polsby et al. 1969; Price 1971; Kernell 1977). Together, the two processes provide a persuasive explanation as to how long and continuous service in the Congress became both possible and desirable. Kernell's (1977) examination of turnover at the turn of the century buttresses this point. He finds that the increasing attractiveness of careers in the House is largely responsible for the secular decline in turnover that occurs during this period. Finally, the adoption of seniority as the basis for awarding committee and subcommittee chairs and ranking minority positions ensures that those who remain will enjoy significant power and prestige. The expanding scope and responsibility of the federal government in the twentieth century provides the contemporary member of Congress with numerous influential areas for the exercise of power. These developments mean that career paths follow a predictable pattern in the House and Senate, one that has been closely studied due to its intrinsic importance to congressional politics.

The House and Senate also offer an opportunity to study the final stages of the elected career. Why and under what conditions do members leave their positions in the House to try for the Senate, or to seek some other office? Why do members choose to retire from a career in elected politics and return to private life? Research on retirement from Congress offers crucial information concerning the final stages of the career path. This examination of the literature on congressional careers will review works in all three stages of the career: recruitment, advancement, and retirement.

Congressional Recruitment

Due to its importance for congressional politics (Swenson 1982) and for issues of representation, congressional recruitment has always been a topic of scholarly interest. As with the more general studies of political recruitment, scholars began by trying to capture the influence of social structure on recruitment to Congress. Candidates for Congress tend to be better educated, hold higher-status occupations, and come from more privileged backgrounds than their constituents. Early studies of winning and losing candidates for Congress found that winners tend to be of higher social status than losers (Huckshorn and Spencer 1971; Fishel 1973), which suggests that voters may prefer candidates of higher social status—or that higher status individuals have better access to the resources (time, money, connections) that make them successful candidates. Scholars have sought to explain why some political elites choose to pursue elective office rather than some other political position, but these efforts have met with only mixed success (Patterson and Boynton 1969).

The prevailing explanations for these differences in social backgrounds tend to be less than satisfying. Aberbach, Putnam, and Rockman's comparative study of bureaucrats and elected officials in Western Europe (1981) concludes that unequal access to education is the primary reason, though the United States possesses a much more egalitarian educational system *and* a wider gap between citizens and their elected officials. Clearly, other factors appear to be at work in the United States, and scholars have examined a wide variety of explanations. Prewitt's study (1970) of recruitment to the city council emphasizes the importance of self-selection and prior political interest and activity for those who plan to seek higher office.

The literature on congressional recruitment follows the same path as recruitment studies generally. Scholars soon turned from the social background approach to political structure. The process of getting nominated to run for Congress and the structure of opportunities are important factors for explaining entry into politics at the congressional level.

Many of the earlier studies of congressional recruitment focused on the role of party in the nomination process. Snowiss' (1966) case study of Chicago suggests that party structure plays a critical intervening role in congressional recruitment, and other studies have confirmed this view. Tobin (1975) found that parties tend to dominate closed nomination systems; moreover, where political parties tend to control the nomination, career advancement is likely to depend on having previously held office. In short, political parties tend to impose a career perspective on the ambitious politician, creating the closest thing to a regular career path found in politics. Fernando Guerra discovers a similar sort of pattern in his examination of the career paths of minority politicians in this volume.

While the early results are largely time-bound, it would be interesting to discover whether similar structural differences appear in a more candidate-centered era in the initial decision to run. How important are parties or other political groups in influencing the decision to run, either by actively seeking nominees to run or by providing the resources necessary to make the decision a serious one? In short, how do the political parties currently shape the structure of opportunities for seats in the national legislature? Given recent changes in the role of parties in congressional elections (Herrnson 1988) and the increasing importance of money in these races, these are topics that deserve further research.

Another topic for further study is the connection between state legislative positions and the decision to run for Congress. For some time, the conventional wisdom has suggested that state legislative seats are an important springboard to Congress, though the precise process of moving from one seat to the other has never been systematically studied. The results presented in Table 1.1 provide some confirmation for the conventional wisdom, and Schlesinger argues that the often similar constituencies between the two offices makes the move a natural and relatively easy one, but this is about as far as this examination of the structure of opportunities has gone. Early studies concluded that more professional legislatures tended to produce more (and better) candidates for Congress, but Fowler and McClure (1989) have recently suggested that state legislative service may now be a more attractive alternative, indicating that the state legislative career may be emerging in some states as a viable career path in its own right.

With the possible exception of Fowler and McClure's admirable study, it is surprising how little attention political scientists have given to the initial decision to run for Congress. Fishel (1971, 1973) and Huckshorn and Spencer (1971) examine congressional challengers in some detail, but neither considers the question of why challengers choose to run in the first place. Instead, these works focus on the social backgrounds of challengers, the political contexts of challenger campaigns, and the career perspectives of challengers.

Kazee (1980) focuses on the challenger's decision to run in the face of adverse electoral circumstances: given the almost overwhelming advantages accruing to incumbents, why does anyone run against them at all? He finds that objective electoral circumstances have little to do with the challenger's decision to run, that most challengers decide to run based on subjective perceptions of the situation and find the experience a positive personal one despite defeat (compare Maisel 1986). While there may be some obvious rationalization going on here, Kazee's study sheds some light on the fact that the decision to run for Congress may not be as difficult as objective circumstances indicate.

Jacobson and Kernell (1983) explore the influence of national forces on candidates' decisions to run for Congress, arguing that national political conditions are important to the extent that they affect the decisions of local political elites either to enter the race or to support a particular candidate. Quite simply, "more and better candidates appear when signs are favorable; worse and fewer when they are unfavorable" (1983, 34).

Fowler and McClure's detailed examination of the race to replace Barber Conable in New York's 30th congressional district integrates a number of perspectives on recruitment to Congress. In seeking to explain who did and did not decide to enter the race for the open seat vacated by Conable, their study sheds light on the decision to run and the factors that are involved in that decision. As their findings indicate, it takes much more than an open seat to attract quality candidates; the conventional wisdom concerning political ambition and career aspirations does not always apply. In the case of the 30th New York district, those politicians most expected to compete for the seat declined to run, and then, two years later, one of them chose to challenge the freshman incumbent. Understanding these events requires attention to how aspirations mesh with opportunities to forge a political career. Fowler and McClure demonstrate in considerable detail how individual decisions and favorable political conditions must coalesce to create the opportunity to pursue a political career.

Like the majority of studies of congressional recruitment, Fowler and McClure emphasize the importance of the structure of opportunities in the decision to run for Congress. Political context—local political conditions such as an open seat, a favorable partisan split in the district, and good national conditions such as a growing economy—is a crucial factor in the decision to seek a House seat. Yet there is still a great deal more to be learned concerning the precise influence of the various factors associated with the structure of opportunities. Political science has yet to specify precisely how and under what conditions factors such as incumbency, party structure, campaign finance, and other variables influence the decision to compete for a seat in Congress.

The Internal Career

The question of who eventually gets to Congress is interesting because, once there, an ambitious politician can expect to stay for some time if so inclined. The growing professionalization of the institution combines with the emergence of the incumbency advantage (Mayhew 1974a; Cover and Mayhew 1977) to produce a ready-made career path for politicians. John Hibbing's chapter in this volume provides convincing evidence of the emergence of the internal career; this discussion presents a more general overview of the literature on this topic.

An examination of the internal career in Congress draws attention to the institutional factors that affect the career paths of elected politicians. Much like the influence of incumbency and party division in the decision to run for Congress, seniority, retirement benefits, party cohesiveness, and other factors impose a real structure to the career within the chamber. With a few notable exceptions, members are adverse to taking the risks associated with advancing before their time, which means that advancement possesses a regular pattern.

The basic structure of the internal career path within the House is readily identifiable. Fenno (1962) observes two paths to influence within the House: the committee system and the party hierarchy. While the two overlap to a certain extent, each is a separate path to power within the chamber. Thanks to the division of labor and specialization across committees, most of the power within the House resides in the committee system, and that power flows to committee leaders. More importantly, members rise to committee posts via the seniority system, so the system builds in incentives for individual members to seek reelection and pursue a career in the chamber. The party system works in a similar fashion, although there is less of an emphasis on careers since members of the House are for the most part elected by their colleagues to party leadership posts. Within the party leadership, however, there is a clear progression of offices, again usually awarded on the basis of seniority. The incentives to pursue a political career thus play an important (if not overriding) role in both of the primary avenues to influence within the House.

Loomis' (1984) study of the structure of opportunities in the House presents a good summary of the career paths available to the current member of Congress. He finds a relatively stable career pattern in the House, with members advancing much more quickly than they did 15 years ago (a point John Hibbing also confirms in this volume). The expanded number of committee and subcommittee positions gives representatives access to power rather quickly; in addition, the leadership has responded to the problems of integration created by the decentralization of power by expanding the number of leadership positions open to junior members. Interestingly, the long-term consequences of these trends may inhibit or deter the development of careers. "An expanded structure of opportunities [produces] the illusion of career advancement without providing for adequate leverage to turn nominal leaders into actual legislators" (Loomis 1984, 200). In other words, with more power brokers on the playing field, the currency of power is diluted, and the frustration of actually trying to get something accomplished may ultimately convince some members to leave the game. The recent spate of members retiring in 1992 due to frustration with the institution provides some impressionistic evidence for this point.

The implications of the emergence of the congressional career are legion; Mayhew's (1974) speculative essay is only one familiar case in point (see also Fiorina 1989). Mayhew argues that the career orientations of members of Congress are a crucial factor in all aspects of legislative behavior. To cite the best-known case, members advertise themselves, claim credit for good things that happen in their districts, and take positions on public policy issues all with an eye to getting reelected and continuing their career in the House.

The emergence of the congressional career has other consequences as well. The recruitment of members to the legislature has obvious implications for representation (Snowiss 1966; Olson 1971; Arnold 1990). Further, scholars have only begun to examine the connections between congressional careers and public policy. Loomis (1987) highlights the connections between the emergence of the internal career and policy change. In the same vein, King and Seligman (1976) present an intriguing discussion of the connections between critical elections, career paths, and policy outcomes. David Brady's (1988) recent study of critical elections also underscores the connection between electoral changes and policy change. Though often overlooked in the examination of the internal career, these are issues that deserve greater examination.

Retirement

The emergence of an internal career has solidified another trend in Congress: voluntary retirement. Since the mid-1960s, voluntary retirement from the House and Senate has increased, and explanations for this change are varied. Cooper and West (1981, 1981-82) examine the traditional explanations for retirement from Congress—age, political vulnerability, and higher political ambition—and find that none of them can account for the new trend. They settle on a growing dissatisfaction with House service as the primary explanation—one that might have been captured had they chosen to examine retirements by party, since we might expect the bulk of dissatisfied members to come from minority Republicans who have seen little prospect of majority power.

Frantzich (1978a, 1978b) examines the careers of 358 members of Congress between 1965 and 1974 and reaches the same conclusion. While the causes of retirement are numerous, job dissatisfaction is the prevailing explanation. Hibbing's interviews with retirees from the 1978 House find that the direct costs and opportunity costs of congressional service have increased in recent years. The recent internal reforms that have spread power to more junior members have also reduced the benefits of long service in the House, dampening political ambition and confirming Loomis' speculation noted above. Nowadays, a member is as likely to have as much power in his or her third term as in the eighth or ninth, reducing the incentive to retain the seat. In addition, several changes in the pensions awarded to retiring members probably have some connection to the decision to retire. Hibbing's chapter in this volume examines these points in much greater detail.

Studies of legislative retirement have focused almost exclusively on the U.S. Congress. In an earlier generation, scholars have noted the relatively high turnover rate in state legislatures (Hyneman 1938), which resulted in some applied research in how service might be made more attractive. More recently, scholars have speculated on the growing power and responsibility of state legislatures (Fowler and McClure 1989; Fowler and Maisel 1989), resulting in increased attractiveness of state legislative careers, but much more research remains to be done in this area.

Conclusion

The study of congressional careers is in many ways a microcosm of the typical political career. From recruitment to retirement, many of the

same issues and concerns over the decision to run and the structure of
opportunities that confront the contemporary member of Congress are
faced by politicians at other levels throughout the Republic.   Thus,
knowledge of the limits and possibilities for a career in Congress is
readily transferable to the study of political careers generally.

THE CAREERS OF WOMEN AND MINORITY POLITICIANS

The political careers of women and minorities provide a unique
opportunity to examine the factors that affect career paths.   The vast
majority of these careers are in the nascent stages, enabling the researcher
to study first-hand the development of the political career from its first
steps and to examine in detail the behavioral and institutional variables
that influence career paths.   In addition, many of these careers occur at
the local level, requiring attention to the dimensions of the local career
path rather than the standard progression from local to state to national
office.   To the extent that political science can learn more about the
aspirations and motivations of women and minority politicians seeking to
make public office a career, as well as the structure of opportunities and
political contexts facing their candidacies, the more that knowledge can
be applied to political careers generally.

The central question in much of the contemporary scholarship on
these two groups focuses on why there are not more women and other
minorities in public office.   The result is a rather large literature on
women's entry into politics.   In contrast, there are relatively few studies
of minority politicians or their career paths.   This paucity of information
is perhaps best exemplified by the fact that one of the leading texts on
blacks in American politics does not contain a chapter on black politicians (Barker and McCorry 1980).   This lack of attention can be
explained by the fact that those who have studied minorities in politics
often have had an agenda other than careers.   With only a handful of
minority officials in positions of power, issues such as discrimination,
obstacles to election, and the overall representativeness of the political
system have received the most attention.

Recruitment

A common element in the studies of recruitment is the peculiar set
of constraints women and minorities face as politicians.   To begin with,
much of the contemporary scholarship on women in political office has

emphasized how difficult it is for women (and men, for that matter) to get started in political careers. Incumbents are difficult to unseat. The high costs of campaigning and the lack of adequate funding mean that only those candidates capable of using their own funds or generating a large pool of financial support are able to run credible campaigns. In addition, the structure of the American political system makes it difficult for women and minority candidates to become self-starters. Weak political parties, the entrepreneurial nature of nomination politics, candidate-oriented campaigns, and single-member district elections all tend to work against the candidacies of women and minority politicians (Matthews 1985).

Racial and ethnic divisions also place peculiar constraints on the ambitious pursuit of a political career for the minority politician. Banfield and Wilson (1967) note that "those who are elected generally find it necessary to be politicians first and Negroes second. If they are to stay in office, they must often soft-pedal the racial issue that is of most concern to Negroes as Negroes." Frazier (1962) puts the issue more forcefully, arguing that the Negro politician must serve two masters—his or her constituency and the white propertied class that is the basis of government. Another observer describes the difficulty as one of dual validation: the potential minority candidate must find legitimacy within his own constituency and also within the wider society dominated by the white propertied class (Merton 1968; Baird 1977).

Some researchers have speculated that socialization has biased the playing field against women and minorities. Family concerns, job concerns, concerns over the role of women in society, and lack of self-confidence all affect women more than men (Carroll 1983, 7). Darcy et al. present a rather convincing case that a substantial part of the reason for the underrepresentation of women in public office is their underrepresentation in the eligible pool of candidates—in the business and professional occupations from which a vast majority of public officials are recruited (1987, 96). Traditionally, women's occupations and activities simply have not provided the same sort of gateway to political office as prestigious male occupations. Data from the 1970s indicate that women's occupations and educational status account in large measure for their absence from state legislatures. Further research designed with reference to these findings would make an important contribution to this aspect of women's entry into politics.

Socialization has been an important concern in studies of black politicians as well. In one of the first large-scale studies of the backgrounds, motivations, beliefs, and expectations of black elected officials, Conyers and Wallace (1976) found that black and white officials differed markedly in their motivations for seeking government office. Blacks were more likely to give high priority to correcting social injustices and low priority to serving the nation, while whites were more likely to reverse these priorities. Cole's (1976) in-depth study of black local officials in New Jersey found that the typical black elected official emerged from a social and political milieu sharply different from that of whites. Most white officials came from a background of civic or party participation; blacks entered politics with a sense of social injustice nurtured by participation in the civil rights movement.

A final obstacle to a political career flows from the fact that most women and minority politicians are serving in their first office; that is, their political careers, if they have begun at all, have only just begun. Yet, experience in one public office is a stepping stone to higher office—it is the very foundation of the political career. Given the small number of women and minorities in office, it is not surprising, then, that so few are currently pursuing elected political office as a career. However, while members of both these groups are currently much less likely to have climbed that ladder of successive elective positions, this may well be remedied by time. In addition, Carroll (1983, 33) has shown that women are more likely to have held appointive positions prior to their elective offices, indicating that women may pursue slightly different paths at the outset of their political careers. Further research would help to confirm this difference.

Political Structure

A brief review of the literature indicates that the social backgrounds of women and minority politicians do not explain the differences in recruitment or career paths Generally speaking, women politicians do not appear to differ that much from their male counterparts. For most women candidates, running for office is a natural extension of other forms of political activity (Kirkpatrick 1974; Van Hightower 1977). Entry into politics follows a logical progression from voluntary community service or voluntary civic or political activity to candidacy for local public office. An initial interest in political issues and concerns culminates in the decision to run for office. And despite the apparent differences in the social backgrounds and socialization of black politicians, scholars soon turned their attention to aspects of the political system that were more important explanations for entry and advancement in politics.

Considering first women politicians, a number of studies have concluded that women do not appear to face differential treatment in recruitment or campaigning for office (Van Hightower 1977; Carroll 1983, 1985; Darcy et al. 1987; Cf. also Mandel 1981). Moreover, these same studies have emphasized the importance of the structure of political opportunity as the key factor determining the number of women in public office. Some of these barriers—the incumbency advantage, the dearth of open seats, the lack of adequate resources like money and organization—are faced by all prospective candidates, although some have maintained that women are disadvantaged *vis-à-vis* men in many cases (Carroll 1985). Given that existing barriers tend to preserve the status quo—men in office—these barriers tend to slow the progress of women.

Carroll's early study (1985) of women candidates examined their recruitment and electoral activities in some detail. Although she finds some evidence that women candidates are treated differently—women were somewhat less likely to be recruited by party leaders than their male counterparts and were more likely to be recruited for races where they had little chance of winning—she concludes that the structure of opportunity is much more important than gender in explaining their success or failure.

> . . . the electoral success rate of women seems less directly related to their sex than to the structure of political opportunity and the electoral situations they confront. Winning or losing for women candidates seems affected most strongly by factors over which individual women have little or no personal control. In contrast, factors subject to the control of individual candidates exert considerably less influence on election outcomes (Carroll 1985, 48).

Much the same could be said for all candidates generally. These findings were confirmed in Darcy, Welch, and Clark's detailed study of women candidates (1987). As far as local elections are concerned, Darcy, Welch and Clark find that

> . . . women do not suffer from a lack of organizational support. Under most circumstances women may receive more support than men from such groups as neighborhood organizations, single-issue groups, and women's organizations. Political party leaders, traditionally thought to be important barriers to women seeking

office, no longer appear to be so, at least at the local level (Darcy, Welch, and Clark 1987, 58).

At the state legislative level, Darcy et al. find no evidence of discrimination against women. Voters do not respond differently to women candidates, nor are women recruited differently or funded at lesser levels than men. It would appear, then, that the cultural milieu and the political system no longer pose barriers to the election of women: if more women run, more will be elected. The question that remains, however, is why aren't more women running? As noted earlier, this is an area where further research would bear much fruit.

Finally, at the national level, while there has been a marked change in the type of woman who runs for Congress (Kincaid 1978; Gertzog 1984, 45), there is little evidence of voter discrimination against women congressional candidates. In general, women candidates tend to be evaluated *more favorably* by voters, and voters perceive themselves closer to women candidates than their male competitors. "From all angles, women candidates in congressional races are as effective and do as well as similar men candidates. In terms of voter reactions, sex is not relevant to congressional elections" (Benze and Declerq 1985). Nor is there convincing evidence of bias in campaign finance for women congressional candidates. Several studies have found that women do just as well as men in raising money for their congressional campaigns (Declerq, Benze, and Ritchie 1983; Benze and Declerq 1985; Burrell 1985), and that this finding holds across all types of races, whether against a well-funded opponent or not (Uhlaner and Scholzman 1986). However, there is considerable evidence that women are much less likely to be nominated as candidates in open seats or seats where there is a realistic chance of winning.

To conclude, virtually all of the attention to the career paths of women politicians has been focused on the recruitment of women to office. To the extent that we know anything at all about the careers of politicians, it is probably safe to say that we know a good deal about the circumstances surrounding their entry into politics. This observation is not meant to down-play the importance of these questions; it is to emphasize the importance of the other stages of the career. With the exception of some brief biographical efforts (LeVeness and Sweeney 1987), very little attention has been given to women's progress through the traditional hierarchy of career steps.

Political structure has been an especially important factor in the literature on the political careers of minority politicians. Research has generated a serious debate on the role of structural factors in impeding the progress of blacks and other minority politicians in the political career structure, as disparate findings prompt varied conclusions concerning the importance of political structure in minority careers.

To begin, Leonard Cole's (1976) detailed study finds little evidence of any systematic influence of local political structure on the opportunities for black politicians to enter politics or pursue a political career. Cole concludes that structural factors are largely unimportant; that the existence of at-large elections, nonpartisan electoral systems, heavy white majorities, or other structural factors thought to disadvantage black politicians have not precluded their rise to office. In 1966 Wilson argued that the key to black success in urban politics lay in their ability to form alliances with liberal whites, and Cole's results echo this theme. They suggest that the socio-economic characteristics of local populations are essential considerations in the election of black local officials. Browning, Marshall, and Tabb reach similar conclusions. At the local government level in the 1960 and 1970s, they find that "the incorporation of blacks and Hispanics into city government was inextricably bound up with the replacement of conservative coalitions by liberal challenging coalitions" (Browning, Marshall, and Tabb 1984, 18). It would appear, then, that the beginnings of the political career for minority politicians possess a unique character.

While Cole finds little evidence for the influence of political structure, the relative influence of socio-economic factors versus political structure on the entry of minorities to political office has been a topic of some debate in the academic literature. It is important to note that both Cole's study and Browning, Marshall and Tabb's research occurred in the North and West respectively, and the political context in which minority politicians seek office is bound to have important effects on the structure of opportunity.

More importantly, several studies have presented evidence indicating that structural factors such as at-large elections or small city councils tend to disadvantage minority groups at the polls (Karnig 1976; Taebel 1978). Others have maintained that the influence of structural factors is in fact minimal, or at least greatly exaggerated (Jones 1976; McManus 1978). The most recent foray into this dispute maintains that, besides the black proportion of the population, "the single most important factor affecting black electoral prospects is the nature of the elections system" (Cavanagh and Stimson 1983, 20-21). Though the jury may still be out in this debate, its very existence draws attention to the unique set of factors that may influence the career paths of minority politicians. In the context of minority careers, due in part to the local character of these careers, the structure of opportunities takes on a rather unique meaning, one rooted in the nature of constituency and the electoral system, and one that certainly deserves further study.

One can make the case that constituency is the single most important structural factor in the election of minorities. As Williams (1987) has noted, with some exceptions the career paths of black (and, to a lesser extent, Hispanic) elected politicians tend to follow the natural logic of constituency. "The racial composition of the jurisdiction or, to be more specific, the black population as a percentage of the total population is regarded as one of the strongest predictors of black candidates' success" (Williams in Cavanaugh 1983). Black politicians hold few statewide or national offices, since relatively small proportions of black citizens vote in these elections. They are more likely to serve in local politics, as city councillors, county commissioners, or mayors. Given the importance of constituency in minority careers, one can expect that those careers will be maintained by and large at the local level.

Smith's (1981) examination of black House members and their districts presents a different perspective on the role of constituency and offers a glimpse of the career path at the national level. He finds that in terms of their socio-economic characteristics, black congressional districts tend to be atypical of the national black population. Most black congressional districts are in the urban North, while slightly more than half the black population lives in the South. In terms of income, education, and occupation, black politicians tend to be slightly more advantaged than the average black citizen.

However, no one has examined whether these differences pose problems for black representation in Congress. Smith finds that blacks are well placed in the power structure in the House and in many ways are indistinguishable from their white counterparts. Yet, of the 15 black representatives in the House in 1981, only 4 or 5 had effective black majorities in their districts, which raises the interesting question of whether these differences in district constituency make any difference in the representative style or voting behavior of black members of Congress. In 1988, blacks held 23 seats in the house, with 14 elected from black majority districts and only two from districts where whites composed the majority of voters. The other seven came from districts with substantial minority (black and Hispanic) populations.

Party is another factor in the structure of opportunities important in the election of minorities. In an extensive analysis, Karnig and Welch (1980) found that blacks were more likely to run in local nonpartisan election systems, presumably because under such conditions there is no need to cultivate partisan attachments. However, they also find that blacks are more likely to be elected mayor in partisan systems. They explain this result by suggesting that "once on the ballot, blacks benefit from the partisan system" (146). The implications of these results for the careers of minority politicians are very clear. If one can muster enough support to win nomination, a partisan electoral system will work to the benefit of minority politicians, particularly in areas where minorities constitute only a small portion of the voting constituency.

The careers of minority politicians provide an excellent opportunity to examine the structure of opportunities from a different perspective. Almost by necessity, the political careers of minority politicians follow the logic of constituency, which means that to the extent that careers exist at all, they exist at the local level. The standard progression from local to state to national office does not apply here, largely because the structure of opportunities (namely, the logic of constituency) is so dramatically different. Minority careers thus afford ample opportunity to examine careers in an entirely different light; in particular, they offer the chance to examine the influences on the local political career in great detail.

Further, the logic of constituency will not hold sway forever. Changes in the ways minorities are elected to office are forthcoming, and it behooves the student of political careers to be attentive to these changes. Fernando Guerra's chapter in this volume highlights these points nicely. As more minority constituencies are created at the local and congressional level, they provide further opportunities to study the dynamic of political careers in these settings. And as more minority politicians are elected from majority districts, students of careers will be presented with the opportunity to plot these patterns as well.

PROSPECTUS

The twin themes of recruitment and ambition provide a useful framework for examining the vast literature on political careers and career paths in the United States. Clearly, these two concepts are interrelated and contain areas of overlap. But to the extent that they are conceptually distinct, political recruitment is concerned with who enters politics and why. Political ambition, on the other hand, focuses on what happens to the career once it has begun. Issues of career maintenance and advancement come to the fore. Cutting across both of these categories are concerns for political structure. Structure and context shape the opportunities for entry into politics in important ways and affect the possible paths the career might take.

Each of these broad conceptual categories contains questions and areas that deserve further research, but the difficulties associated with defining and identifying a political career raise an initial set of questions. Some of these questions have to do with the appropriate method(s) for studying careers and career paths. Many of the answers to these questions will be fundamentally connected to what students of careers seek to learn about the political career; nevertheless, students of careers would do well to ask themselves precisely how political careers and career paths ought to be studied. How can analysts grasp the rare combination of personal and institutional factors, the unique mix of ambition, opportunity, and good fortune that produces a political career? The wide range of opportunities for entry in the American political system make it difficult to identify careers and career paths. Can students of careers find systematic ways of identifying and describing political careers and career paths? Can one find meaningful data and appropriate methods of measurement that adequately define and describe the career and produce meaningful generalizations about political careers? Much work has been done under the rubric of ambition theory, but much more remains to be done. Previous studies have been somewhat narrowly focused—and perhaps for good reason. It may not be time to attempt to answer these large questions. Nevertheless, they are important guides both for this review and for future research on political careers.

Entry into politics is perhaps the most obvious place to begin asking questions about the political career, and the initial decision to enter politics deserves further study from political scientists. Why do politicians decide to run in the first place? Recent efforts have emphasized how ambition interacts with the structure of opportunity and other political factors to promote or deter entry into politics. More work needs to be done on identifying the factors that shape the decision to run for political office. From the standpoint of political psychology, there may be more to learn about how ambition for politics emerges and blossoms into a political career. Understanding the motives for seeking office can make a significant contribution to ambition theory, which up to this point has focused solely on those players already competing in the political game. Finally, with more women and minority politicians entering the fray, an understanding of how the standard description of the American politician has changed over time and an examination of the barriers women and minority politicians face would make an important contribution to the understanding of contemporary political careers.

A second area for further research is the structure of opportunity and other political factors that affect the political career. By now it is readily apparent that ambition theory and its emphasis on the structure of opportunities—the various openings and barriers that deter and promote a political career—provide a useful vantage point for examining career paths and political careers. Ambition and the structure of opportunity combine in unique ways, and students of careers need to give greater attention to the ways individual motivations combine with the structure of opportunities to produce a political career. To cite but one prominent example from this review, how do political parties currently structure the opportunities for office? To return to the questions raised by Matthews, are there important regional or partisan differences in the patterns of political careers? Are there other important institutional features of the political system that affect the decision to run for elected office? A politician can have all the ambition in the world, but without the opportunity to pursue that ambition, the political career is an empty phrase. Thus, we need to know much more about the factors that are important in determining the opportunity for a career and the shape of the career path.

In addition, more research is needed on the patterns of political career paths. Both identification and description of career patterns and standard paths can assist greatly in further theory building concerning political careers. In the same vein, students of political careers would do well to learn more about how advancement occurs in the political career. The political careers of members of Congress, women politicians, and minority politicians provide diverse settings in which to examine the structure of opportunities and other factors that influence the development of political careers. Given close scrutiny, one should be able to generalize in a systematic fashion about the ways in which political structure and political institutions affect career paths. The chapters in this volume highlight the varying approaches that can be taken to study the effects of structure and other factors on both the emergence and development of the political career.

The study of political careers and the career paths of elected officials is still very much in its nascent stages. A great many questions still need to be answered. These questions provide exciting opportunities to break new ground on important issues critical to our understanding of politicians and politics.

REFERENCES

Aberbach, Joel D., Robert D. Putnam, and Bert A. Rockman. 1981. *Bureaucrats and Politicians in Western Democracies.* Cambridge: Harvard University Press.

Abramson, Paul R., John H. Aldrich, and David W. Rohde. 1987. "Progressive Ambition Among United States Senators: 1972-1988." *Journal of Politics* 49:3-35.

Andersen, Kristi, and Stuart Thorson. 1984. "Congressional Turnover and the Election of Women." *Western Political Quarterly* 37:143-56.

Arnold, R. Douglas. 1990. *The Logic of Congressional Action.* New Haven: Yale University Press.

Baird, Frank L. 1977. "The Search for a Constituency: Political Validation of Mexican-American Candidates in the Texas Great Plains." In *Mexican-Americans: Political Power, Influence or Resource*, ed. Frank L. Baird, Lubbock, Texas: Graduate Studies, Texas Tech University, no. 14.

Banfield, Edward C., and James Q. Wilson. 1967. *City Politics.* Cambridge: Harvard University Press, Ch. 20.

Banks, Jeffrey S., and D. Roderick Kiewiet. 1989. "Explaining Patterns of Candidate Competition in Congressional Elections." *American Journal of Political Science* 33:997-1015.

Barber, James David. 1965. *The Lawmakers.* New Haven: Yale University Press.

Barker, Lucius J. 1989. *New Perspectives in American Politics.* New Brunswick, N.J.: Transaction Publishers.

_____, and Jesse J. McCorry, Jr. 1980. *Black Americans and the Political System*, 2d ed. Boston: Little Brown.

Benze, James, and Eugene Declerq. 1985. "The Importance of Gender in Congressional and Statewide Elections." *Social Science Quarterly* 66:954-63.

Black Elected Officials: A National Roster. 1988. Washington, D.C.: Joint Center for Political Studies.

Black, Gordon S. 1972. "A Theory of Political Ambition: Career Choices and the Role of Structural Incentives." *American Political Science Review* 66:144-59.

Bogue, Allan G., Jerome M. Clubb, Carroll R. McKibbin, and Santa A. Traugott. 1976. "Members of the House of Representatives and the Process of Modernization, 1789-1960." *Journal of American History* 63:275-302.

Brace, Paul. 1984. "Progressive Ambition in the House: A Probabilistic Approach." *Journal of Politics* 46:556-71.

Brady, David. 1988. *Critical Elections and Congressional Policy Making.* Stanford: Stanford University Press.

Browning, Rufus P. 1968. "The Interaction of Personality and Political System in Decisions to Run for Office." *Journal of Social Issues* 24:93-109.

_____, and Herbert Jacob. 1964. "Power Motivation and the Political Personality." *Public Opinion Quarterly* 28:75-90.

_____, Dale Rogers Marshall, and David H. Tabb. 1984. *Protest is Not Enough: The Struggle of Blacks and Hispanics for Equality in Urban Politics.* Berkeley: University of California Press.

Bullock, Charles S., III. 1972. "House Careerists: Changing Patterns of Longevity and Attrition." *American Political Science Review* 66:1295-1305.

_____. 1975. "The Election of Blacks in the South: Preconditions and Consequences." *American Journal of Political Science* 19:727-39.

Burrell, Barbara. 1985. "Women's and Men's Campaigns for the U.S. House of Representatives, 1972-1982: A Finance Gap?" *American Politics Quarterly* 13:251-72.

Canon, David T. 1989. "Political Amateurism in the United States Congress." In *Congress Reconsidered*, 4th ed., ed. Lawrence C. Dodd and Bruce I. Oppenheimer, Washington, D.C.: Congressional Quarterly Press, 65-87.

_____. 1991. *Actors, Athletes, and Astronauts: Political Amateurs in the United States Congress.* Chicago: University of Chicago Press.

Carmines, Edward G., and James A. Stimson. 1989. *Issue Evolution: Race and the Transformation of American Politics.* Princeton: Princeton University Press.

Carroll, Susan J., and Wendy Strimling. 1983. *Women's Routes to Elective Office: A Comparison with Men's.* New Brunswick, N.J.: Center for American Women, Rutgers University.

_____, and Wendy Strimling. 1983. *Women's Routes to Elective Office: A Comparison with Men's.* New Brunswick, N.J.: Center for American Women, Rutgers University.

Carroll, Susan J. 1985. *Women as Candidates in American Politics.* Bloomington: Indiana University Press.

Cavanagh, Thomas E. 1983. *Race and Political Strategy: A JCPS Roundtable.* Washington, D.C.: Joint Center for Political Studies.

_____, and Denise Stockton. 1983. *Black Elected Officials and Their Constituencies.* Washington, D.C.: Joint Center for Political Studies.

Christopher, Maurice. 1976. *Black Americans in Congress.* New York: Thomas Y. Crowell.

Cole, Leonard A. 1976. *Blacks in Power: A Comparative Study of Black and White Elected Officials.* Princeton: Princeton University Press.

Conyers, James E., and Walter L. Wallace. 1976. *Black Elected Officials: A Study of Black Americans Holding Governmental Office.* New York: Russell Sage Foundation.

Cooper, Joseph. 1981-82. "Voluntary Retirement, Incumbency, and the Modern House." *Political Science Quarterly* 96:279-300.

_____, and William West. 1981. "The Congressional Career in the 1970s." In *Congress Reconsidered,* 2d ed., ed. Lawrence C. Dodd and Bruce I. Oppenheimer, Washington, D.C.: Congressional Quarterly Press, 83-106.

Cover, Albert, and David Mayhew. 1977. "Congressional Dynamics and the Decline of Competitive Congressional Elections." In *Congress Reconsidered,* ed. Lawrence C. Dodd and Bruce I. Oppenheimer, New York: Praeger, 54-72.

Czudnowski, Moshe M. 1975. "Political Recruitment." In *Handbook of Political Science,* vol. 2, ed. Fred I. Greenstein and Nelson W. Polsby, Reading, Mass.: Addison-Wesley Publishing Co., 155-242.

Darcy, Robert, and Sarah Slavin Schramm. 1977. "When Women Run Against Men." *Public Opinion Quarterly* 41:1-12.

_____, and James Choike. 1986. "A Formal Analysis of Legislative Turnover: Women Candidates and Legislative Representation." *American Journal of Political Science* 30:237-55.

_____, Susan Welch, and Janet Clark. 1987. *Women, Elections and Representation.* New York: Longman.

Davies, James C. 1963. *Human Nature in Politics.* New York: John Wiley & Sons.

Declerq, Eugene, James Benze, and Elisa Ritchie. 1983. "Macha Women and Macho Men: The Role of Gender in Campaigns Involving Women." Paper presented at the meeting of the American Political Science Association, Chicago, September.

Diamond, Irene. 1977. *Sex Roles in the State House.* New Haven: Yale University Press.

Ehrenhalt, Alan. 1991. *The United States of Ambition: Politicians, Power, and the Pursuit of Office.* New York: Times Books.

Elliot, Jeffrey M. 1986. *Black Voices in American Politics.* San Diego: Harcourt, Brace, Jovanovich.

Elshtain, Jean Bethke. 1981. *Public Man, Private Woman.* Princeton: Princeton University Press.

Eulau, Heinz, William Buchanan, LeRoy Ferguson, and John C. Wahlke. 1961. "Career Perspectives of American State Legislators." In *Political Decision-Makers,* ed. Dwaine P. Marvick, Glencoe, Ill.: The Free Press.

Fenno, Richard F. 1973. "The Internal Distribution of Influence: The House." In *The Congress and America's Future,* 2d ed., ed. David B. Truman. Englewood Cliffs, N.J.: Prentice-Hall.

_____. 1989. *The Making of a Senator: Dan Quayle.* Washington, D.C.: Congressional Quarterly Press.

Fiorina, Morris P. 1989. *Congress: Keystone of the Washington Establishment,* 2d ed. New Haven: Yale University Press.

_____, and Timothy S. Prinz. 1992. "Legislative Incumbency and Insulation." In *Encyclopedia of the American Legislative System,* ed. Joel H. Silbey, New York: Charles Scribner's Sons.

_____, David Rohde, and Peter Wissel. 1975. "Historical Change in House Turnover." In *Congress in Change,* ed. Norman J. Ornstein, New York: Praeger.

Fishel, Jeff. 1971. "Ambition and the Political Vocation: Congressional Challengers in American Politics." *Journal of Politics* 33:25-56.

_____. 1973. *Party and Opposition: Congressional Challengers in American Politics.* New York: David McKay Company, Inc.

Fowler, Linda L. 1989. "Local Influences on Congressional Recruitment." Paper prepared for delivery at the annual meeting of the Midwest Political Science Association, Chicago, April 14-15.

_____, and Robert D. McClure. 1989. *Political Ambition: Who Decides to Run for Congress.* New Haven: Yale University Press.

_____, and L. Sandy Maisel. 1989. "The Changing Supply of Competitive Candidates in House Elections, 1982-1988." Paper presented at the annual meeting of the American Political Science Association, Atlanta, August 31.

Frantzich, Stephen E. 1978a. "Opting Out: Retirement from the House of Representatives, 1966-1974." *American Politics Quarterly* 6:251-76.

_____. 1978b. "De-Recruiting: The Other Side of the Congressional Equation." *Western Political Quarterly* 31:105-26.

Frazier, E. Franklin. 1962. *Black Bourgeoisie.* New York: The Free Press.

George, Alexander, and Juliette George. 1956. *Woodrow Wilson and Colonel House: A Personality Study.* New York: The John Day Company.

Gertzog, Irwin. 1984. *Congressional Women.* New York: Praeger.

Greenstein, Fred I. 1967. "The Impact of Personality on Politics: An Attempt to Clear Away Underbrush." *American Political Science Review* 61:629-41.

_____. 1968. "The Need for Systematic Inquiry into Personality and Politics: Introduction and Overview." *Journal of Social Issues* 24:1-14.

_____. 1987. *Personality and Politics: Problems of Evidence, Inference, and Conceptualization.* Princeton: Princeton University Press.

_____, and Nelson W. Polsby. 1975. *The Handbook of Political Science,* vol. 2. Reading, Mass.: Addison-Wesley.

Hain, Paul. 1974. "Age, Ambitions, and Political Careers: The Middle-Aged Crisis." *Western Political Quarterly* 27:265-74.

Henry, Charles P. 1977. "Legitimizing Race in Congressional Politics." *American Politics Quarterly* 5:149-76.

Herrnson, Paul S. 1988. *Party Campaigning in the 1980s.* Cambridge: Harvard University Press.

Hibbing, John R. 1982a. "Voluntary Retirements from the U.S. House of Representatives: Who Quits?" *American Journal of Political Science* 26:467-84.

_____. 1982b. "Voluntary Retirements from the U.S. House: The Costs of Congressional Service." *Legislative Studies Quarterly* 7:57-73.

_____. 1982c. *Choosing to Leave: Voluntary Retirement from the U.S. House of Representatives.* Washington, D.C.: University Press of America.

_____. 1991. "Contours of the Modern Congressional Career." *American Political Science Review* 85:405-28.

Huckshorn, Robert, and Robert Spencer. 1971. *The Politics of Defeat.* Amherst: University of Massachusetts Press.

Hurley, Patricia. 1989. "The Senate, Representation, and Recruitment to the Presidency." Paper presented at the annual meeting of the American Political Science Association, Atlanta, August 31-September 2.

Hyneman, Charles S.   1938. "Tenure and Turnover of Legislative Personnel." *Annals of the American Academy of Political and Social Science* 23:21-31.

Jacob, Herbert.   1962. "Initial Recruitment of Elected Officials in the U.S.—A Model." *Journal of Politics* 24:703-16.

Jacobson, Gary C., and Samuel Kernell.   1983. *Strategy and Choice in Congressional Elections*, 2d ed. New Haven: Yale University Press.

Karnig, Albert, and Susan Welch.   1980.   *Black Representation and Urban Policy.* Chicago: University of Chicago Press.

Kazee, Thomas A. 1980. "The Decision to Run for the U.S. Congress: Challenger Attitudes in the 1970s." *Legislative Studies Quarterly* 5:79-100.

_____. 1983. "The Deterrent Effect on Incumbency on Recruiting Challengers in U.S. House Elections." *Legislative Studies Quarterly* 8:469-80.

Kernell, Samuel. 1977. "Toward Understanding 19th Century Congressional Careers: Ambition, Competition, and Rotation." *American Journal of Political Science* 21:669-93.

Kincaid, Diane D. 1978. "Over His Dead Body: A Positive Perspective on Widows in the U.S. Congress." *Western Political Quarterly* 31:96-104.

King, Anthony. 1981.   "The Rise of the Career Politician in Britain—And Its Consequences." *British Journal of Political Science* 11:249-85.

King, Michael R., and Lester G. Seligman.   1976. "Critical Elections, Congressional Recruitment, and Public Policy." In *Elite Recruitment in Democratic Polities: Comparative Studies Across Nations*, ed. Heinz Eulau and Moshe M. Czudnowski, New York: John Wiley and Sons, Sage Publications.

Kirkpatrick, Jeane. 1974. *Political Women.* New York: Basic Books.

_____. 1976. *The New Presidential Elite: Men and Women in National Politics.* New York: Russell Sage Foundation and The Twentieth Century Fund.

Kohn, Walter S. G. 1980. *Women in National Legislatures: A Comparative Study of Six Countries.* New York: Praeger.

Ladd, Everett Carl. 1969. *Negro Political Leadership in the South.* New York: Atheneum.

Lasswell, Harold D. 1960. *Psychopathology and Politics: A New Edition.* New York: Viking Press.

Latimer, Margaret K. 1979. "Black Political Representation in Southern Cities: Election Systems and Other Causal Variables." *Urban Affairs Quarterly* 15:65-86.

Le Veness, Frank P., and Jane P. Sweeney. 1987. *Women Leaders in Contemporary U.S. Politics*, Boulder, Colo.: Lynne Rienner Publishers.

Loomis, Burdett. 1984. "Congressional Careers and Party Leadership in the House of Representatives." *American Journal of Political Science* 28:180-201.

_____. 1987. "Taking the Queue: Careers and Policy in the U.S. House of Representatives." In *Political Elites in Anglo-American Democracies: Changes in Stable Regimes*, ed. Harold D. Clarke and Moshe M. Czudnowski, DeKalb: Northern Illinois University Press.

_____. 1988. *The New American Politician*. New York: Basic Books.

Maccobby, Michael. 1976. *The Gamesman: The New Corporate Leaders*. New York: Simon and Schuster.

Maisel, L. Sandy. 1986. *From Obscurity to Oblivion: Running in the Congressional Primary*, rev. ed. Knoxville: University of Tennessee Press.

Mandel, Ruth B. 1981. *In the Running: Women as Political Candidates*. New York: Ticknor & Fields.

Marable, Manning. 1985. *Black American Politics*. London: Verso.

Marvick, Dwaine. 1976. "Continuities in Recruitment Theory and Research: Toward a New Model." In *Elite Recruitment in Democratic Polities: Comparative Studies Across Nations*, ed. Heinz Eulau and Moshe M. Czudnowski, New York: John Wiley and Sons, Sage Publications.

Matthews, Donald R. 1954. *The Social Background of Political Decision-Makers*. Garden City, N.J.: Doubleday.

_____. 1985. "Legislative Recruitment and Legislative Careers." In *Handbook of Legislative Research*, ed. Gerhard Loewenberg, Samuel C. Patterson, and Malcolm E. Jewell, Cambridge: Harvard University Press, 17-55.

Mayhew, David R. 1974a. "Congressional Elections: The Case of the Vanishing Marginals." *Polity* 6:295-317.

_____. 1974b. *Congress: The Electoral Connection*. New Haven: Yale University Press.

McConaughy, John B.   1950. "Certain Personality Factors of State Legislators in South Carolina." *American Political Science Review* 45:897-903.

Merton, Robert K.   1968. *Social Theory and Social Structure.* New York: The Free Press.

Mezey, Michael L.   1970.   "Ambition Theory and the Office of Congressman." *Journal of Politics* 32:563-79.

Namier, Lewis B.   1929. *The Structure of Politics at the Accession of George III.* London: Macmillan.

Patterson, Samuel C., and G. R. Boynton.   1969. "Legislative Recruitment in a Civic Culture." *Social Science Quarterly* 50:243-63.

Payne, James L.   1984. *The Motivation of Politicians.* Chicago: Nelson-Hall Publishers.

Perry, Robert T.   1976. *Black Legislators.*   San Francisco: R & E Associates.

Polsby, Nelson W.   1968. "The Institutionalization of the U.S. House of Representatives." *American Political Science Review* 62:144-68.

_____, Miriam Gallagher, and Barry S. Rundquist.   1969. "The Growth of the Seniority System in the U.S. House of Representatives." *American Political Science Review* 63:787-807.

Poole, Keith T., and L. Harmon Ziegler. 1985. *Women, Public Opinion, and Politics: The Changing Political Attitudes of American Women.* New York: Longman.

Prewitt, Kenneth.   1965. "Political Socialization and Leadership Selection." *The Annals of the American Academy of Political and Social Science* 361:96-111.

_____. 1970.   "Political Ambitions, Volunteerism, and Electoral Accountability."   *American Political Science Review* 64:5-17.

_____, and Heinz Eulau.   1969. "Social Bias in Leadership Selection, Political Recruitment, and Electoral Context." *Journal of Politics* 33:293-315.

_____, Heinz Eulau, and Betty Zisk. 1966. "Political Socialization and Political Roles." *Public Opinion Quarterly* 30:569-82.

_____, and William Nowlin.   1969. "Political Ambitions and the Behavior of Incumbent Politicians."   *Western Political Quarterly* 22:298-308.

Price, Douglas.   1971. "The Congressional Career: Then and Now." In *Congressional Behavior*, ed. Nelson W. Polsby, New York: Random House, 14-27.

_____. 1975. "Congress and the Evolution of Legislative 'Profes-sionalism.'" In *Congress in Change: Evolution and Reform*, ed. Norman J. Ornstein, New York: Praeger, 2-2

_____. 1977. "Careers and Committees in the American Congress: The Problem of Structural Change." In *The History of Parliamentary Behavior*, ed. William O. Andelotte, Princeton: Princeton University Press, 28-62.

Ray, David. 1974. "Membership Stability in Three State Legislatures, 1893-1969." *American Political Science Review* 68:106-12.

_____. 1976. "Voluntary Retirement and Electoral Defeat in Eight State Legislatures." *Journal of Politics* 38:426-33.

Reed, Adolph L. 1986. *The Jesse Jackson Phenomenon*. New Haven: Yale University Press.

Robinson, Pearl T. 1982. "Whither the Future of Blacks in the Republican Party?" *Political Science Quarterly* 97:207-32.

Rohde, David W. 1979. "Risk-Bearing and Progressive Ambition: The Case of the U.S. House of Representatives." *American Journal of Political Science* 23:1-26.

Ruchelman, Leonard. 1970. *Political Careers: Recruitment through the Legislature*. Rutherford, N.J.: Farleigh Dickinson University Press.

Schlesinger, Joseph A. 1966. *Ambition and Politics: Political Careers in the United States*. Chicago: Rand McNally.

_____. 1967. "Political Careers and Party Leadership." In *Political Leadership in Industrialized Societies*, ed. Lewis J. Edinger, New York: John Wiley and Sons.

Schwartz, David C. 1969. "Toward a Theory of Political Recruitment." *Western Political Science Quarterly* 22:552-71.

Seligman, Lester G., Michael King, Chong Lim Kim, and Roland Smith. 1974. *Patterns of Recruitment: A State Chooses Its Lawmakers*. Chicago: Rand McNally.

Snowiss, Leo M. 1966. "Congressional Recruitment and Representation." *American Political Science Review* 66:627-39.

Sorauf, Frank J. 1963. *Party and Representation*. New York: Atherton Press.

Swenson, Peter. 1982. "The Influence of Recruitment on the Structure of Power in the U.S. House, 1870-1940." *Legislative Studies Quarterly* 7:7-36.

Taebel, Delbert. 1978. "Minority Representation on City Councils: The Impact of Structure on Blacks and Hispanics." *Social Science Quarterly* 59:142-52.

Tobin, Richard J. 1975. "The Influence of Nominating Systems on the Political Experience of State Legislators." *Western Political Quarterly* 28:553-66.

_____, and Edward Keynes. 1975. "Institutional Differences in the Recruitment Process: A Four-State Study." *American Journal of Political Science* 19:667-82.

Uhlaner, Carole, and Kay Schlozman. 1986. "Candidate Gender and Congressional Campaign Receipts." *Journal of Politics* 48:30-50.

Van Der Slik, Jack R., and Samuel J. Pernacciaro. 1979. "Office Ambitions and Voting Behavior in the U.S. Senate: A Longitudinal Study." *American Politics Quarterly* 7:198-224.

Van Hightower, Nikki R. 1977. "The Recruitment of Women for Public Office." *American Politics Quarterly* 5:301-14.

Volgy, Thomas J., John E. Schwarz, and Hildy Gottlieb. 1986. "Female Representation and the Quest for Resources: Feminist Activism and Electoral Success." *Social Science Quarterly* 67:156-68.

Wahlke, John C., Heinz Eulau, William Buchanan, and LeRoy C. Ferguson. 1962. *The Legislative System: Explorations in Legislative Behavior.* New York: John Wiley and Sons.

Walton, Hanes, Jr. 1972. *Black Politics: A Theoretical and Structural Analysis.* New York: J. B. Lippincott.

_____. 1973. *The Study and Analysis of Black Politics: A Bibliography.* New Jersey: Scarecrow Press.

_____. 1985. *Invisible Politics: Black Political Behavior.* Albany: State University of New York Press.

Weber, Max. 1946. "Politics as Vocation." In *From Max Weber: Essays in Sociology,* ed. H. H. Gerth and C. Wright Mills, New York: Oxford University Press.

Welch, Susan. 1985. "Are Women More Liberal than Men in the U.S. Congress?" *Legislative Studies Quarterly* 10:125-34.

_____, and Timothy Bledsoe. 1985. "Differences in Campaign Support for Male and Female Candidates." In *Research in Politics and Society,* ed. Glenna Spitze and Gwen Moore, Greenwich, Conn.: JAI Press.

Williams, Linda. 1987. "Black Political Progress in the 1980s: The Electoral Arena." In *The New Black Politics: The Search for Political Power,* 2d ed., ed. Michael B. Preston, Lenneal J. Henderson, Jr., and Paul L. Puryear, New York: Longmans.

Wilson, James Q. 1960. *Negro Politics: The Search for Leadership.* Glencoe, Ill.: The Free Press.

_____, 1962. *The Amateur Democrat: Club Politics in Three Cities.* Chicago: University of Chicago Press.

Wilson, James Q. 1966. "The Negro in Politics." In *The Negro American,* ed. Talcott Parsons and Kenneth B. Clark, Boston: Houghton Mifflin Co.

Willson, F. M. G. 1959. "The Routes of Entry of New Members of the British Cabinet, 1868-1958." *Political Studies* 7:222-32.

_____. 1970. "Entry to the Cabinet, 1959-1968." *Political Studies* 18:236-8.

Wittmer, Richard T. 1964. "The Aging of the House." *Political Science Quarterly* 79:526-41.

Ziegler, Harmon, and Michael A. Baer. 1968. "The Recruitment of Lobbyists and Legislators." *American Journal of Political Science* 12:508.

Congressional Careers

Introduction

Edward L. Lascher, Jr.
Harvard University

It has become commonplace to emphasize the high level of individualism inherent in the way members of Congress conduct business both in Washington and in their district offices. As the chapters by Linda Fowler and John Hibbing make clear, the importance of individualism for an understanding of Congress is not limited to analysis of how members carry out their duties while in office; it is also important to the study of their career paths. Legislators come to Washington by way of highly personalized electoral campaigns. Once ensconced in the capital, their political careers can take a variety of paths. Members' career decisions are strongly affected by their resources and opportunities and by the context in which their decisions are made, but the choices remain with the individual lawmakers. These choices in turn have ramifications for how members of Congress do their jobs and for how Congress performs as an institution.

Fowler focuses explicitly on the personalized nature of congressional campaigns in her review of the literature on recruitment of congressional candidates. She indicates that congressional candidates are "largely self-starting entrepreneurs, and their decision to run or remain on the sidelines ultimately rests on personal considerations." Reflecting this understanding, the autonomous individual "is now at the core of theoretical and empirical work on recruitment."

While sympathetic to the methodological individualism that underlies the dominant rational choice perspective on candidate recruitment, Fowler contends that cost-benefit analysis has some limitations in assessing the probability of a decision to run. In particular, ambition theory has tended to ignore both the importance of context in the development of ambitions and the dynamic nature of ambition itself. She argues that personal ambitiousness develops in response to a politician's experiences and evaluation of these experiences. For example, she suggests that the praise or criticism of party leaders may dampen or nourish interest in political office. She also offers a useful list of structural factors (e.g., community economic opportunities) that may affect decisions to seek elective positions.

Personalized campaigns have a number of important institutional effects, according to Fowler. For example, in the electoral realm individualized campaigns increase the incumbency advantage because challengers tend to be poorly equipped to overcome officeholders' advantages in name recognition, in ability to project a favorable image of themselves, and in fund raising. The incumbency advantage in turn has a number of effects, such as making it difficult for Congress to become more descriptively representative of the population, as Susan Carroll indicates as well in her chapter. Additionally, Fowler suggests that personalized campaign styles may be linked to the "home styles" (see Fenno 1978) developed by particular members of Congress.

Hibbing also emphasizes the personal nature of career choices in his chapter on the career paths of members of Congress. Because most previous research focuses on the House of Representatives, Hibbing does so as well. Unlike most previous researchers, however, he offers an alternative to viewing members as choosing between simply remaining in the House ("static ambition," in Joseph Schlesinger's term) and seeking election to a higher office such as governor or U.S. senator ("progressive ambition," according to Schlesinger). Hibbing stresses the opportunity for directing ambition toward moving up *within* an institution such as the House. He demonstrates that there are a variety of paths available to the upwardly mobile member while still remaining in the House (e.g., seeking a party whip position, attempting to become a subcommittee or committee chair). He further shows that there has been a shift in the distribution and number of important House positions from the 1950s to the 1980s, and therefore in the contour of congressional career paths. He offers a preliminary exploration of some of the factors that influence whether members can move up within the House.

While drawing on his own research to stress the significance of the internal congressional career, Hibbing summarizes the key findings regarding decisions to leave Congress. Consistent with the rational choice model of legislative behavior, he indicates that choices to seek higher office are influenced by the desirability of such office, the odds of successfully capturing it, and the personality of the representative (e.g., willingness to take risks). Against the argument that members of

Congress deciding to leave politics altogether are motivated by general dissatisfaction with the job of congressional representative, he argues that voluntary retirement from elective office may be prompted by financial considerations, the desire to avoid losing face in a losing election, and similar factors.

In a provocative conclusion, Hibbing challenges the notion that political scientists have developed a theory of political ambition. He argues that instead it is a theory of opportunity that has been developed, and that ambition, a psychological predisposition, remains untested. The implication is that we must either probe deeper into the reasons why politicians might differ with respect to how much they want to move up in the political world, or concentrate more explicitly on expanding our knowledge about the impact of opportunities. Hibbing opts for the latter course of action, but both are ripe for research.

Fowler and Hibbing suggest several topics on which further research is needed. More attention to U.S. senators is needed, both in terms of recruitment and in terms of career paths once in office. Further research is needed into why potentially strong candidates fail to express interest in running for Congress. The notion of the internal congressional career is relatively new, and further refinements would be helpful; this remains an area in which scholars could concentrate their efforts.

REFERENCES

Fenno, Richard F., Jr.   1978.   *Home Style: House Members in Their Districts*.   Boston: Little, Brown and Company.

Chapter 2

Candidate Recruitment and the Study of Congress: A Review Essay

Linda L. Fowler
Syracuse University

Personalized campaigns have long been a hallmark of electoral politics in the United States, but in recent years emphasis on candidates has become even more pronounced, especially in congressional races. Most Americans expect that individuals, rather than parties, will define the alternatives on the ballot and determine the competitiveness of House and Senate contests, yet they take candidates' willingness to run largely for granted. When they do think about who runs, it is usually to disapprove—either of the candidates' abilities or their motives. In faithful adherence to the Jeffersonian tradition, Americans still believe, as Jefferson himself once observed, "that whenever a man has cast a longing eye on offices, a rottenness begins in his conduct" (quoted in Auden 1962, 304).

The indifference to candidate recruitment has been almost as widespread among congressional scholars as it is within the general public. Several reviewers have remarked on the neglect of research on candidates' decisions to seek public office (Jones 1981; Arnold 1982; Lipset 1983; Broder 1989); and in designating political recruitment one of the "undertilled fields" of American politics, Arnold has observed: "It is all very curious that political scientists have devoted so much to the study of citizens' final choices between the two candidates who make it to the general election and so little to the study of how the thousands of potential candidates are winnowed down to two" (1982, 97). Matthews makes the point even more strongly in criticizing legislative specialists for assuming that "who legislators are and how they got there" is important without testing this assertion (1983, 17).

My purpose is to show how assumptions about candidate recruitment permeate our understanding of congressional politics and to suggest ways of examining them empirically. The supply of prospective candidates is itself an important determinant of congressional politics; for candidates not only dominate explanations of election outcomes, their motives and means of attaining office also figure in scholarly analyses of representation and lawmaking. Thus, knowledge of how the candidate pool varies over time and across communities shapes our grasp of the institution's overall performance.

In examining who initially weighs a race for Congress and why some prospective candidates choose to run and others remain on the sidelines, some adjustments will be necessary in the theoretical treatment of ambition at both the micro and macro level. Two important modifications I consider are the development of individual ambition for a career in Congress and the influence of contextual variables on the supply of potential candidates. I also explore conceptual and measurement problems that can affect the research strategies of scholars interested in studying recruitment. Finally, I conclude with an evaluation of promising areas for inquiry. Throughout the chapter, I draw distinctions between recruitment to the House and Senate where they seem appropriate.

RECRUITMENT AND CONGRESSIONAL BEHAVIOR

In an earlier era of congressional research, recruitment seemed to matter more than it does today. Scholars were heavily influenced by sociological perspectives on the institution, notably role theory, and hence they placed a good deal of emphasis on legislators' backgrounds, experience, and paths to office (see Matthews 1983). When scholarly perspectives shifted toward goal-oriented models of legislative behavior in the 1970s, it became more important to know what lawmakers (or prospective lawmakers) wanted, and less necessary to investigate why they brought particular traits and objectives with them into the congressional arena.

Yet several different strands of contemporary research on Congress raise the question of "who lawmakers are and how they got there," to use Matthews' (1983) definition of recruitment. The first is the increasing power of incumbency with its attendant separation of presidential and congressional mandates. The second is the representativeness of the institution and its remarkable stability of membership in the face of recent social change. The third is the significant alteration in the distribution of power within the House and Senate. Implicit in much of this work is the presumption that a new kind of member with a different set of objectives has entered the congressional scene and transformed both its electoral politics and institutional arrangements. From the discussion that follows, it is clear that very convincing evidence supports this argument. But, paradoxically, there is not much analysis of why such shifts took place.

RECRUITMENT AND ELECTION OUTCOMES

Recruitment directly affects the outcomes of congressional elections because of the personalized nature of House and Senate races. As party loyalties have waned, voters have assigned greater weight to the individual attributes of the contestants (Mann 1978; Mann and Wolfinger 1980; Hinckley 1980; Jacobson 1987a; Cain, Ferejohn, Fiorina 1988; Abramowitz 1988). Moreover, as House and Senate contests have grown more complex and expensive, the candidates' skill in overseeing a sophisticated organization of pollsters, fund-raisers, direct mail experts, and volunteers is itself a critical election variable (Herrnson 1989). Both the electorate's choice and the caliber of the campaign thus depend upon who runs.

House Elections

The effect of individual candidates is strongly evident in analyses of the incumbency effect in House elections, which, as everyone knows, has produced reelection rates above 90 percent in the past two decades and over 98 percent in 1986 and 1988. Three trends are noteworthy: (1) greater attention to reelection among representatives elected after the mid-1960s; (2) diminished effectiveness among challengers; and (3) greater insulation of House results from national political tides.

(1) House incumbents seeking reelection have always been good at it, even during periods of high turnover in the 19th century (Kernell 1977). But something happened in the 1960s to ensure even greater success. Although all House members appear to have increased their efforts to woo constituents, newcomers seem to have been particularly adept, giving rise to the well-known "sophomore surge" (Mayhew 1974a). As studies by both Born (1979) and Collie (1981) revealed, pronounced generational effects underlay the growing margins of incumbents. Furthermore, junior members now appear more likely to retain their seats than senior representatives who enjoy large vote totals (Jacobson 1987b;

Hibbing 1988). Somehow, younger legislators have become more skillful or more eager to secure their careers than their senior colleagues who seem more prone to costly mistakes (Bauer and Hibbing 1989). Why this should have come about, and whether it will continue in the future, is not clear.

(2) Personal attributes are as important to the success of challengers as they are for incumbents. According to Jacobson, changes in the percentage of seats won by Democratic candidates are strongly correlated with differences in prior officeholding experience between Democratic and Republican challengers (1989, 777). In addition, previous experience has a strong effect on whether or not challengers are victorious (1989, 782). Finally, Jacobson identifies a strong trend in the postwar years towards personalized elections, especially since 1972. He concludes: "a successful challenge is now far more contingent on local circumstances —on particular candidates and campaigns—than it once was" (1989, 789).

Although challengers rely more on their personal traits and skills to defeat incumbents, they appear less able to mount an effective effort. They typically are underfunded (Jacobson 1980), and in recent years, they have suffered increasing discrimination from PACs (Abramowitz 1989). Not surprisingly, voters have had difficulty recognizing their names and identifying their positive attributes. Lacking visibility and resources, few challengers have been able to offer the electorate a genuine alternative to incumbents (c.f. Hinckley 1980; Jacobson 1987a). This phenomenon, first documented in the 1978 CPS Election Survey, suggests that voters prefer incumbents not only for the service and contact they provide, but also out of ignorance or dislike of their opponents.

Some scholars suggest that challengers are not quite as bad as they appear in public opinion surveys (Eubank and Gow 1983; Gow and Eubank 1984; Eubank 1985).[1] But if voter perceptions, or the way we measure them, are biased toward incumbents, several other patterns suggest that competitive challengers are scarcer than they used to be. In recent years the number of uncontested races (Squire 1989) and lopsided contests (Fowler and Maisel 1991) has risen steadily. As Figure 2.1 illustrates, noncompetitive House races have increased by about 40 percent in the past decade, so that fully three-fifths of the incumbents running in

---

[1]There is a noticeable bias toward incumbents in the opinion surveys from which these findings are derived, because the challengers in the districts surveyed were weaker than the average (Eubank and Gow 1983; Gow and Eubank 1984).

Figure 2.1. *Trends In Noncompetitive House Races Against Incumbents, 1982-1990***

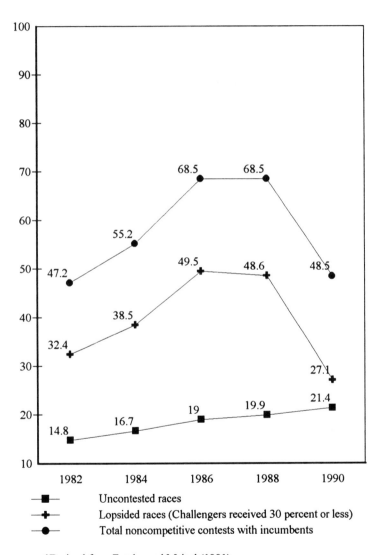

Uncontested races
Lopsided races (Challengers received 30 percent or less)
Total noncompetitive contests with incumbents

*Derived from Fowler and Maisel (1991)

1986 and 1988 attracted little or no opposition. This figure dropped significantly in 1990 due to an anti-incumbent backlash that reduced vote margins, even though it did not lead to significant defeats.

Nor are races dominated by House incumbents the only contests marked by a lack of competition. Throughout the 1980s roughly 40 percent of the open House seats were won by a margin of 2:1 or more (Fowler and Maisel 1991, 31). Even in the high turnover year of 1992, when a record number of retirements created substantial opportunities for candidates, only about a third of the open seat races were rated as a toss-up during the summer before the election (Roll Call 1992, 36-37).

One consequence of personalized campaigns is greater volatility in individual House elections from one cycle to the next. Incumbents enjoy larger margins, but their strong performance in one year is a less reliable predictor of how they will do in the future (Jacobson 1987b; Ansolabe-here, Brady, and Fiorina 1988; Jacobson 1989). Similarly, voters sometimes make radical policy shifts in a relatively short span of time in reaction to the different pairs of candidates on the ballot (Fowler and McClure 1989).

(3) If particular races are less predictable today, House elections in the aggregate appear less susceptible to political change. In recent years, the partisan balance in the House has either been disconnected from national events or has shown modest shifts at times when the presidency and Senate have reflected major swings in public opinion. Although there is a longstanding statistical relationship between economic performance and the two-party division of the vote (Kramer 1971; Tufte 1975), as well as the change in seats (Oppenheimer, Stimson, and Waterman 1986; Marra and Ostrom 1989), some evidence suggests that the connection between local economies and national conditions may be weakening (Owens and Olson 1980; Radcliff 1988). But some politicians still appear to respond to national events that favor their party's fortunes, and this preserves an element of dynamism in an otherwise static situation.

Not long ago, Jacobson and Kernell (1983) attempted to account for a paradox in House elections: that the parties' share of the total vote varied systematically with indicators of economic performance and presidential support even though voters showed little sign of such influences in their choice of candidate. These scholars argued that if politicians and their supporters reacted strategically to national events by offering strong competition when the time was right, then voters collectively would favor one party while making a judgment about the individual merits of the contestants. Political elites acting in an uncoordinated fashion all over the country thus would create a climate in local districts that would add up to a net gain for the party advantaged by national tides.

There have been many efforts to confirm or disconfirm what Jacobson and Kernell term the "strategic politicians hypothesis" with mixed results (Bianco 1984; Abramowitz 1984; Bond, Covington, and Fleisher 1985; Canon 1985; Born 1986; Wilcox 1987; Krasno and Green 1988; Maisel 1987; Ragsdale and Cook 1987). Some analyses support the Jacobson and Kernell argument; others contradict it. Generally, each side's case hinges on questions of measurement—how to estimate the strength of challengers; what economic indicators to use; when to pinpoint the timing of candidates' decisions; how to control for differences from year to year in the number of seats parties have at risk.

Such disagreements are unresolvable at this point because there is simply not enough information about who the prospective candidates are and how they make up their minds, to resolve the dispute over measures. For example, in choosing a date for the decision to run, one could plausibly pick the filing date with the FEC, which occurs in March of an election year for roughly two-thirds of nonincumbent House candidates (Wilcox 1987). On the other hand, a survey conducted in 1978 indicates that at least 40 percent of primary contestants made up their minds to contest a House seat in the year before the election (Maisel 1986). A similar lack of data hinders our understanding of the criteria political elites employ in making resources available. Undoubtedly, officeholding experience is one factor that differentiates strong candidates from weak ones, but there are difficulties with all of the current methods of defining politically relevant experience (Fowler and Maisel 1991). Furthermore, the increasing tendency among Republicans to nominate inexperienced politicians even in open seats suggests that officeholding is valued differently within the parties by people who allocate political resources (Fowler and Maisel 1991). This is particularly true in the South, where the GOP's lack of local offices makes it dependent on candidates without prior officeholding experience (Canon 1990b).

The lively debate over strategic politicians not only highlights the absence of basic information about the way prospective candidates make up their minds, it also exposes the complex interaction between local and national influences and the importance of political elites on the supply of congressional candidates. Canon (1990a) demonstrated, for example, that although experienced candidates are more likely to run when national tides favor their party, amateurs also have a better chance of being elected under favorable national conditions. Why amateurs should do better in contests in which elites are supposedly steering resources toward experienced candidates is not the only puzzle emerging from this literature. An equally curious finding was uncovered by Jacobson when he updated his analysis of strategic politicians: that Democratic candidates timed their candidacies strategically but Republicans did not (1989, 779). In a model that predicted the emergence of experienced challengers, the estimated coefficients for income and presidential approval are significant for the former but not for the latter. Of greater significance, however, was the fact that the most powerful influences governing the emergence of experienced challengers in both parties were variables that controlled for local party strength in the previous election, specifically a shift in control of the seat and the vote total of the challenger's party.

These analyses confirmed the presence of strategic behavior among elites as a determinant of House elections, but they also suggested that scholars needed to consider how local conditions and other types of variables affected candidates' decisions to run. In the wake of the 1990 election, matters took an unexpected turn, as Jacobson (1992) began to argue that elites had become so obsessed with incumbency that they were concentrating resources too heavily on a few marginal and open seat races. According to his analysis, the 1990 challengers were the worst crop of the entire decade, as measured by prior experience and levels of campaign spending, but they did significantly better than any previous group. Thus, Jacobson concluded, parties and PACs missed an important opportunity to capitalize on national tides, and this "strategic misalloca-tion" of resources produced election outcomes that were less competitive than they ought to have been.

There are two important issues regarding the interaction between local and national circumstances in the calculations regarding candidacy. First, how does the local political environment shape the number and type of candidates who will make the strategic calculation about running and not running? Second, what is the relative strength of local conditions *vis-à-vis* national ones, and how does it vary by district, by region, by party, and by year?

In sum, once electoral competition is tied to individuals rather than parties—whether incumbents, challengers, or contestants in open seats—the outcomes only make sense if we understand how one set of alternatives ends up on the ballot instead of another. Matters are somewhat different in the Senate, however.

Senate Elections

Generalizing about the role of candidates in Senate elections is difficult because there has been significantly less research conducted on either voting behavior or candidate activity. Until this situation is partially remedied by the new research made possible by the 1988 NES survey of voting in Senate elections, it seems most useful at this point to highlight a major inconsistency in the literature. On the one hand, members of the Senate seem more subject to political influences beyond their control; on the other hand, individual candidates seem just as prominent in shaping the final results as they are in House elections. Westlye (1992) demonstrated, in fact, that Senate races are highly idiosyncratic both across states in the same election year and within states over time—with both national and local partisan forces seeming to cut in two different directions at once.

Incumbent senators typically have lower reelection rates than House members, and their success at the polls varies considerably by year. In this decade, the percentage of successful incumbents has been as low as 55 percent and as high as 93 percent. Some scholars attribute this greater volatility to the presence of strong challengers (Hinckley 1980; Mann and Wolfinger 1980; Abramowitz 1988). Others demonstrate that Senate races are more susceptible to partisan considerations (Abramowitz 1988), to economic trends (Kuklinski and West 1981; Abramowitz 1988), and to issue voting (Wright and Berkman 1986). Still others speculate that senators are victims of the greater exposure they receive from the news media (Robinson 1975). Indeed, whenever Senate campaigns are intense—and roughly 57 percent of them are (Westlye 1992, 25)—Westlye has argued that the increased salience and information available to voters leads to more competitive outcomes. Complementing these patterns is a long-term shift in party organizational strength, particularly in the South. Where Senate seats were once sinecures for one party or the other, all states now have competitive Senate elections on occasion (Schlesinger 1985).

If political variables matter more than personal characteristics in Senate races, perhaps it is because strong challengers make them visible. The interaction of candidate strength and issue salience was dramatically illustrated over the course of the 1986 California campaign involving Democratic incumbent Alan Cranston and former House member Ed Zschau. In a fascinating case study, Jacobson and Wolfinger (1987) demonstrated how Cranston's lead in the polls responded to developments in Zschau's campaign. Cranston's narrow win is a powerful testament to the importance of individual candidates, even in Senate races. Westlye (1992) reported similar candidate effects in his comparative analysis of hard-fought and low-key campaigns.

Yet one cannot take the emergence of strong challengers for granted in Senate elections. A decade ago, the Senate was awash with amateurs (Canon 1989, 70), and during the 1980s, slightly more than 50 percent of the Senate contests had outcomes in which the margin of victory was more than 2:1 (Ornstein et al. 1987, 60). Nor can one assume that experienced challengers are the strongest Senate candidates. Westlye reported that governors and former senators turned out to be no more successful in beating incumbents than amateurs, and he concluded that overall officeholding experience bore "little relation to whether candidates actually won" (1992, 29). Thus, scholars need to consider what mix of local and national forces affects the supply of prospective senators and why experience appears to be more important for House candidates than for Senate candidates.

As one examines the extensive literature on congressional elections, then, the influence of candidates on individual races as well as the partisan balance in the House and Senate is unmistakable. But many questions about the trends in these relationships and their underlying causes require further investigation.

Recruitment and Representation

There is a long tradition of inquiry among legislative scholars into the backgrounds and social characteristics of the people who serve in Congress (c.f. Matthews 1960). Personal attributes were considered important because of theories of representative government that hold that lawmakers should be like the people they govern. They were also regarded as factors in shaping the roles that legislators would adopt, particularly the classic distinction between trustees and delegates (Davidson 1969; Jewell 1970). In an exhaustive review of the literature that attempted to link individual traits causally to legislative behavior, Matthews concluded: "viewed as independent variables [this approach to recruitment] has been pretty much a wash" (1983, 42). Despite the lack of a direct connection between personal attributes and legislative performance, there is strong evidence that individuals have an impact on the nature of constituency representation practiced in Congress and that recruitment bears some responsibility for the scarcity of female members in the institution.

Personal Styles of Representation

It is hardly coincidental that candidate-centered elections lead to representation based on personal access and style. Researchers using such widely divergent techniques as participant observation and survey data analysis have demonstrated how individual orientations among lawmakers shape constituent expectations, although they have not examined the origins of these relationships.

Richard Fenno's pioneering study of House members in their districts (1978) documented the distinctive home styles lawmakers employ to create trust and empathy with their constituents. Not only were the level of issue responsiveness and the degree of emphasis on personal contact and service to the district dependent upon this approach to representation identified by Fenno, but the constituency itself was interpreted in a highly subjective fashion. Fenno suggested that home style is partly a product of the representative's personality, partly a function of the election coalitions he or she constructs, and partly a reflection of the district's characteristics. But he was unable to confirm this line of argument because his analysis was confined to incumbents rather than prospective House members. Nonetheless, the fact that a highly personal style of representation emerged in a wide variety of districts suggests that scholars might usefully focus on recruitment to explain how home styles emerge.

A variety of studies examining voter reactions to personal contacts with lawmakers, particularly casework, offer further evidence of linkage between the personal attributes of lawmakers and the style of representation they provide to citizens. (See Rivers and Fiorina (1989) for the most recent work on representation and casework.) Yet the widely divergent orientations toward casework among state lawmakers indicate that there is nothing inherent in the American system to produce the emphasis on personal access and service so characteristic of the House and increasingly of the Senate (Jewell 1982). Moreover, the recent tendency among MPs in Britain to rely more heavily on service as a means of securing constituency approval (Cain, Ferejohn, and Fiorina 1987), indicates that even in a highly disciplined party system, changing attitudes among individual lawmakers can lead to different bases for representation. One can make a strong case for lawmakers' desire to insulate themselves from political change by creating a "personal vote" for themselves, but we need to have a better understanding of why recruitment processes favor the emergence of this type of legislator.

Representation of Women

Historically, the Congress has been an assembly of affluent, educated, white, male professionals rather than a cross section of the American public. Indeed, its membership may be more unrepresentative than ever before because of the growing proportion of millionaires in both chambers. Yet the gradual admission of women and members of ethnic minorities has introduced new political points of view to the institution, and that is why the failure of women to make further inroads in the House and Senate is politically significant.

During the past three decades, the number of women in Congress has increased by 150 percent (from 18 to 47), while the number of African Americans has increased by 630 percent (from 3 to 25). The entry of women has not only lagged behind other disadvantaged groups; progress toward equal representation has been much slower in the United States than in most western democracies (Darcy, Welch, and Clark 1987). Projected increases by the year 2000 are as low as one percent (Andersen and Thorson 1984) or as high as three percent (Darcy, Welch, and Clark 1987, 140).

A variety of explanations—male conspiracy, female passivity, voter discrimination—have been offered to account for these disappointing results. Too numerous to review here, these studies all point to recruitment processes in one form or another as the deciding factor in female representation in Congress because voter attitudes do not seem to be the barrier to women that they have been in the past (Darcy and Schramm 1977; Sigelman and Welch 1984).

But however one changes the behavior of parties, campaign contributors, or prospective female candidates to get more women running for Congress, the prospect for significant gains in representation will founder on incumbency. As long as retirement rates among incumbents are low and reelection success is high, the projections noted above are not likely to change. Women will have to contest open seat races if they hope to increase their numbers in Congress, and this will require far higher rates of participation in primary contests than has been the case so far. In 1992, for example, supposedly the "year of the woman" in Congress, only 25 percent of the candidates running for open seats were female, which was why the election outcome turned out to be something less than the revolution heralded by pundits.

It appears that the nature of representation in Congress biases the institution towards particular types of politics and policies in a way that is not typical of most legislatures. We have reason to believe that it makes the institution less accountable (Cain, Ferejohn, and Fiorina 1987) and probably more conservative (Poole and Ziegler 1985). Although such results arise from a combination of weak parties, independent-minded voters, and entrepreneurial candidates, it is probable that explanations extend back into the prenomination processes, which determine the supply of prospective members of Congress.

Recruitment and Lawmaking

Since the 1950s, scholars have viewed Congress as an institution shaped by its individual members, operating in characteristic modes because the representatives and senators want it that way. Explanations of the historical evolution of the contemporary Congress into a professionalized legislature depend upon the simple assumption that senators and representatives developed a strong preference for continuous service in Washington at the turn of the century (Price 1971, 1975; Polsby 1968; Fiorina, Rohde, and Wissel 1975). Similarly, the transformation of the institution into a well-oiled reelection machine has been linked by Mayhew (1974b) and Fiorina (1977) to careerist tendencies among contemporary lawmakers. In recent years, however, the goals of the members seem to be pulling them in different directions: toward greater autonomy and decentralization on the one hand and toward greater partisan discipline on the other. Political recruitment offers some intriguing clues to this apparent contradiction.

Recruitment and Decentralization

Almost a quarter of a century ago, research on congressional candidates revealed a strong connection between recruitment and members' attitudes toward the institution. Fishel found that career expectations among House candidates varied according to whether or not they were self-starters or party-sponsored nominees (1973, 58). Kingdon (1966) and Huckshorn and Spencer (1971) demonstrated that winners were likely to take personal credit for their election success, while losers were likely to blame their party. The independence of lawmakers arriving on Capitol Hill thus seemed to be strongly rooted in the entrepreneurial nature of House campaigns.   Senators' demands for autonomy were also linked to recruitment, albeit for a different reason: their political prestige prior to entering Congress entitled them to it (Matthews 1960).

As the personal and organizational costs of securing seats in the House and Senate have escalated in recent years, it seems plausible to expect that the newest members would want more power in the institution to justify their efforts.   Observers on Capitol Hill have commented routinely on the demands the newest recruits to Congress have made for a greater share of decision-making authority.

Today's lawmakers have been abetted in their desire for autonomy by the increased presence of PACs as contributors to congressional campaigns. Far more funds come from outside the constituency than in the past (Grenzke 1988; Eismeier and Pollock 1988).   In the 1988 congressional elections, for example, PACs contributed one-third of the funds raised by House and Senate candidates (Abramowitz 1989, 23), with roughly 80 percent of this money received by incumbents. But even the relatively small proportion given to nonincumbents represents a significant sum. In 1986, for example, contestants in open House seats received about 14 percent of the total PAC investment in House elections that year, which averaged out to over $200,000 per candidate (calculated from Maisel 1989).   Although it is difficult to assess the impact of outside money on politicians recruited to Congress, some observers believe that it makes the members more receptive to special interests and less amenable to party discipline (Wright 1989), although others dispute this contention (Grenzke 1988). No one can say, however, whether the necessity of going outside the district to raise money influences the type of person who now runs for Congress, although this is just as important a question for scholars to examine as the connection between campaign finance and electoral margins (c.f. Green and Krasno 1988).

The desire for independence shows up in the two key organizational components of Congress—the committee system and the political parties. Committee slots are filled according to self-selection (Shepsle 1978), so that the goals and decision-making rules within particular committees reflect these individual calculations (Fenno 1973; Smith and Deering 1984). Similarly, the limits placed on party leaders in both chambers are a further reflection of how recruitment furthers decentralized lawmaking (Sinclair 1983; Sinclair 1989; Davidson 1989). Indeed, most observers of Congress attribute such developments as the advent of subcommittee government in the House and freelance policymaking in the Senate to the spirit of political entrepreneurship that successful candidates bring with them to Capitol Hill (Deering and Smith 1985).

This drive for autonomy carries over into congressional relationships with the executive branch. The growing separation of the presidential and congressional vote suggests that political elites are less able than in the past to use the recruitment process to link national agendas with local priorities. This not only denies the nation's chief executive partisan majorities in one or both houses, it also ensures the independence of those who share his party label. Many scholars have written about the dangers of divided government (Sundquist 1981; Burnham 1982), but Fiorina states it most succinctly: "No longer expecting to gain much from the president's success or suffer much from his failures, they have little incentive to bear any risk on his behalf" (1984, 218).

Recruitment and Party Discipline

Contrasting with the efforts of members to disperse power in the Congress is a movement to restore some prerogatives to party leaders, especially in the House. The reforms of the 1970s strengthened the Speaker's hand over committee assignments, bill referral and Rules Committee deliberations, and recent developments point to a further consolidation of influence (Dodd and Oppenheimer 1989). Furthermore, party line voting, having hit record lows in the 1970s, became more common in the 1980s. It is hard to reconcile this trend toward increased party discipline with the determined individualism of the members, unless one recognizes the role of political parties in their recruitment to Congress.

The relationship between party organizations and congressional candidates was once characterized as: "separate organizations pursuing separate tasks" (Crotty 1984, 203). Today the situation is sometimes viewed as one of loosely organized "cadres" of party activists who come together to elect particular candidates (Epstein 1986). Yet party organizations in many states and districts have been known to exercise influence over candidate recruitment in the past (Snowiss 1966; Mezey 1970; Polsby 1981; Mayhew 1986), and several recent studies depict parties as playing a far more active role in candidate decision making than many observers have acknowledged (Herrnson 1986, 1988; Gibson et al. 1983, 1985; Haeberle 1985; Kunkel 1988; Sabato 1988; Frendreis et al. 1990; Fowler 1991). Candidates may still make the final decision about running or not running and bear the organizational brunt of organizing their campaigns, but parties play a role in consultation, volunteer mobilization, and fund raising.

The most dramatic example of expanded party activity has been the increase in national party contributions to congressional races. Modest in relative terms, the amounts have been significant nonetheless. The 34 Republican Senate contestants running in 1986, for instance, split a $10 million party war chest among themselves. Some observers believe that the rise in party contributions is directly responsible for the extraordinary cohesiveness of the Republicans during much of the Reagan era (Kayden and Mahe 1985, 194).

Even the primary process, which impinges on party control of nominations, acts in a perverse way to ensure that candidates reflect the ideological differences between Democrats and Republicans. Although primaries for congressional races have not been studied in depth the way they have for presidential contests, there is evidence that partisan differences between Republicans and Democrats are set prior to the campaign and persist until election day despite the strategic pull on candidates to move toward the center. This is true for House candidates (Sullivan and O'Connor 1972) and Senate candidates (Wright and Berkman 1986).

The increased party voting in Congress is linked to recruitment in another way, however. In recent years, Democratic candidates in the South have become increasingly dependent upon and responsive to the large numbers of loyal black voters in their constituencies. Once in Congress, they are less likely to vote with the Conservative Coalition, at least on domestic issues, and party unity scores have risen accordingly (Rohde 1991).

In sum, much of what we know about Congress is linked to what individual members want from a career in the institution and how they go about obtaining it. For this reason, recruitment should be a much more important priority for scholars than it has been in the past. For future inquiries to succeed, however, it will first be necessary to expand and refine the existing theoretical work on ambition.

CONGRESSIONAL RECRUITMENT AND THE THEORY OF AMBITION

From my reading of the literature and my observation of prospective candidates making decisions about their pursuit of a seat in the House, I believe that a theory of recruitment ought to account for two things. It ought to be able to predict which candidates will run for Congress and which will remain on the sidelines. And it ought to be able to explain differences in the composition of the candidate pool—its size and make-up—across states and districts. Existing theoretical work on political ambition accomplishes neither of these objectives, because it is narrowly focused on the probable costs and benefits of winning or losing a particular race.

Typically, scholars treat decisions about running for office as a relatively straightforward calculation of costs and benefits discounted by the perceived probability of winning (Black 1970; Levine and Hyde 1977; Rohde 1979; Banks and Kiewiet 1989). The equation below gives the key elements:

$$U(O) = p(B) + (1-p)C$$

This simple expected utility model predicts that an individual will run if $U(O)$ is positive: an occurrence when the estimated probability of success (p) is high, when the perceived benefits of the office (B) are great, and/or when the costs of losing (C) are low. Alternatively, one can argue that a positive outcome occurs when candidates are tolerant of risk and do not require a "fair" lottery to induce them to run (Fowler 1979). Either way, the logic of the decision is the same.

The methodological individualism underlying this approach makes sense. Congressional candidates are largely self-starting entrepreneurs, and their decision to run or remain on the sidelines ultimately rests on personal considerations (Fowler and McClure 1989). But the cost-benefit model has two drawbacks. First, by taking individual preferences for office as given, it leaves no room for exploring the development of congressional ambition. If the individual ran, we simply must assume that $p(B)$ turned out to be greater than $(1-p)C$. We have no way of explaining why the calculation turned out positive for one individual and negative for another, and this is unsatisfying when many of the prospective candidates who do not run outwardly seem very similar to those who eventually declare themselves.

Second, the cost-benefit model makes no allowance for the fact that individuals make their decisions about running and not running in widely different contexts that may be more or less conducive to congressional ambition. In short, if we accept Fenno's dictum that politicians are both "goal-seeking and situation-interpreting individuals" (1986, 4), then we need to account for systematic influences over the pool of prospective candidates.

At this point, I am not sure that a single theory of ambition can accommodate both the micro-level influences surrounding individual career choices and the macro-level variables that determine who is in a position to think about running. For this reason, I have opted to treat these two questions separately.

Elements of a Micro-Theory of Recruitment

Like any rational choice model, the traditional theory of ambition assumes the desired objective—public office—is a taste whose origins are not relevant. If ambition were randomly distributed throughout the population, or if it were fixed early in life as the product of psychological need or social experience, then we might treat it as a constant in politics. But there are sound reasons to presume that desire for public office varies with changes both in the political environment and the individual's relation to that environment. Individuals learn about their own ambitions and discover how to pursue them through experience: by winning elections for other offices; by comparing themselves with the men and women who have sought the post of senator or representative before them; by hearing the praise and criticism of political activists and party leaders; and by considering how other offices compare with the distinctive careers available in Congress. It is a dynamic process involving the interaction of many different types of individuals and opportunities.

In his seminal work on ambition in American politics, Joseph Schlesinger wrote: " . . . we can develop a theory of ambitions only if we adopt reasonable assumptions about when such ambitions occur. The most reasonable assumption is that ambition for office, like most other ambitions, develops with a specific situation, that it is a response to the possibilities which lie before the politician" (1966, 8). Schlesinger demonstrated that the number of opportunities to run for office and the structure of party competition influenced the level of aspiration among officeholders so that careers among statewide officeholders followed identifiable patterns. Following in Schlesinger's footsteps Mezey (1970) demonstrated that states with strong party organizations tend to produce more experienced candidates for the House, and Rohde (1979) showed how the overlap in constituencies affects the likelihood that House members will run for the Senate.

Analysis of the prior experience of newcomers to the House and Senate reveals a considerable amount of regularity in the starting point politicians choose to launch their careers. Roughly 50 percent of House members have had prior experience as state lawmakers, and many of the former governors in the Senate got their start in state politics as lawmakers. Almost 40 percent of the recently elected senators have served previously in the House.

But the results in Table 2.1 indicate that many lawmakers have chosen other routes to Congress, and a surprisingly high proportion in the House are amateurs (see also Canon 1989, 1990a). Although the data for the earlier Congresses are not strictly comparable to those from later Congresses, nonetheless there seems to be a trend toward more experienced candidates running for the House, a trend that was abruptly reversed, however, in the past three elections (Fowler and Maisel 1991). Moreover, there seems to be a rise in the number of former House members entering the Senate. Such patterns suggest that learning about congressional ambition is a more orderly process for some successful candidates than others, although the reason for these differences is unclear.

One possible influence on the paths prospective candidates chose for pursuing a congressional career is the intervention of political elites. They are the keepers of political reputation and the primary source of intelligence about who could or should run for the media and for outside party and PAC organizations. I have already noted the considerable body of literature on party activity in recruitment. But it is also important to consider how local interest groups and national PACs encourage or discourage individual candidates and how the mass media facilitate or hinder the interaction of activists and prospective candidates.

Perhaps the most puzzling aspect of candidate recruitment, however, is explaining why individuals who could be strong candidates (and are singled out as such by local activists and the press) never think about running for Congress at all. In outward appearances they are as experienced, as involved in public life, and as accomplished as the men and women who actively consider a House or Senate race. Indeed, some may already occupy positions that serve as stepping stones to Congress. Predicting their disinterest in congressional candidacy and preference for other political outlets is perhaps the most difficult challenge to a comprehensive theory of ambition (c.f. Fowler and McClure 1989).

Table 2.1. *Prior Political Experience of Representatives and Senators*

	House		Senate	
	1948-66[a]	1970-84[b]	1947-57[c]	1978-88[d]
No Elected Office				
Party	***	5.1	***	2.7
Congressional Staff	2.5	4.0	***	***
Amateur	35.8	20.5	10.0	9.6
Subtotal	**38.3**	**29.6**	**10.0**	**12.3**
Elective Office				
State Office	36.4	48.2	30.6	32.9
Local Office	17.4	15.8	18.9	11.0
Former House Member	***	3.6	25.0	39.7
Subtotal	**53.8%**	**67.6%**	**74.5%**	**83.6%**
Appointive Office	**3.9%**	**2.7%**	15.6	4.1
Miscellaneous	**4.0%**	***	***	***
Total	**100%**	**100%**	**100%**	**100%**

[a]Adapted from Mezey (1970, 567) for 1948-1966. All members.
[b]Adapted from Banks and Kiewiet (1989, 26) for 1970-1984. Newly elected members only.
[c]Adapted from Matthews (1961, 53-55). All members.
[d]Calculated from Congressional Quarterly Weekly Reports, Profiles of New Members. Newly elected members only.
*** Not applicable or not given in original

The various elements involved in candidates' discovery of their desire for a career in Congress thus include the following: (1) the propensity for political activism that is reinforced by various officeholding or civic responsibilities; (2) the encouragement or rejection of various political elites; and (3) the commitment to the distinctive life of a member of Congress. There are models in the voting behavior literature that employ concepts analogous to these, but what combination provides the best explanations for candidates' eventual decisions to run remains to be seen. Once these factors are ordered to determine whether an individual will consider a race for Congress, it will then be appropriate to estimate the expected benefits and costs of a particular race.

Elements of a Macro-Theory of Recruitment

Determining who is in a position to think about running for Congress is not simply a matter of observing individuals learning from experience. It also depends upon examining whether political rules and institutions create an environment that is generally supportive of congressional candidacy. Given the diversity across states and districts in the way constituency boundaries are drawn, campaigns are financed, public service is compensated, and so forth, it is inevitable that communities will vary in both the number and kind of candidates who aspire to Congress. Thus we need to develop a theory of recruitment that will explain systematic differences in the supply of candidates. Such knowledge is an especially important complement to the work noted earlier on strategic politicians: strong contenders are more likely to emerge in response to national tides where the candidate pool is well-developed Stewart (1989).

There is not very much information about the composition of the candidate pool, aside from a small number of case studies of particular localities (Snowiss 1966; Seligman 1961; Kazee 1983; Fowler and McClure 1989). I have derived a list of structural variables from my observations of candidate decision making in New York's 30th District (Fowler and McClure 1989), some of which may also define the reservoir of prospective senators.

Political Geography

The boundaries and physical characteristics of states and districts determine whether it will be more or less difficult to run for Congress from a particular locality. The nature of area media markets, the cohesiveness of communities, the proximity to Washington, D.C., the degree of overlap between constituencies for lesser offices and those for the House and Senate all affect how individuals perceive the organizational costs of running. The congruence between a district's media markets and its boundaries, for example, aids challengers because it enhances name recognition (Campbell et al. 1984; Niemi, Powell, and Bicknell 1986; Stewart and Reynolds 1990). Such variation is particularly difficult to pin down in House districts, however, that cut across political jurisdictions in often idiosyncratic ways—ways that change every decade.

Economic Opportunities

In some communities public service is far more attractive economically than in others. Where private sector salaries are low, ambitious individuals may be more attracted to federal office. Where state and local government compensation is high, politicians may find the relatively low salaries paid to members of Congress and the high cost of living in Washington a disincentive for considering a congressional career.

Professionalism of State Government

In states with highly professionalized bureaucracies, legislatures, and judicial systems, many people will develop the skills and credentials to be strong congressional candidates. On the other hand, these same institutions offer many opportunities for the exercise of political power and make attractive alternatives to careers on Capitol Hill.

Rules of the Game

There are a variety of formal and informal rules that govern electoral competition and hence facilitate the development of a candidate pool for Congress. Among the more important are: regulations governing parties and party nominations; procedures influencing turnout and primary voting; restrictions on campaign finance practices; and regulation of interest groups and lobbyists.

As an example of how contextual influences structure who can think about running for Congress, consider the case of women, who hold a bare five percent of the seats in the nation's legislature—just 10 more than served during the Eisenhower administration. Some scholars attribute this pattern to the fact that the pool of eligible women with prior political experience is still too small to support significant efforts by women to contest House seats (Darcy, Welch, and Clark 1987); and they contend that the figures will change as the number of women in local offices increases. But this argument fails to take account of the highly skewed distributions of female officeholders and winnable congressional races.

If female representation in Congress were directly related to the size of the pool of eligible women, then we could predict that the probability of a female state legislator being elected to Congress in 1990 would be .05. (This figure is derived from the fact that women comprised roughly 17 percent of state lawmakers in 1988 and that approximately one-third of newly elected lawmakers served previously in the state legislature, e.g., (.16)(.33) = .05.) Such a forecast is misleading, however, because the great majority of female lawmakers are found in states with small congressional delegations and part-time legislatures. Very few seats will be competitive in the sense of being open or held by a marginal incumbent; and the supply of state lawmakers per district will be relatively plentiful and inexperienced compared to other types of officeholders in the community, such as mayors or statewide officials. Indeed, the top 10 states in terms of proportion of female state legislators account for 38 percent of all women in this position but contain just nine percent of the House seats in the nation. Conversely, large states have more opportunities for open and marginal seats, but they tend to have relatively few women in their highly professional and stable legislatures.

In the Appendix, I compare the probability of a female state lawmaker being elected to Congress from New Hampshire and New York: in the former state it is .00013 and in the latter it is .0003. The odds are so low in both states because the numerous women in the New Hampshire legislature have relatively few competitive races open to them and almost no likelihood of winning regardless of their gender. State legislators simply do not win congressional seats in the Granite State. Similarly, there are relatively few female lawmakers in New York to take advantage of the favorable opportunities available to state legislators in the Empire State.

Once we recognize the dynamic elements of personal ambition for Congress and the structural influences that constrain how many and what types of individuals will develop it, then the limitations of the cost-benefit approach toward recruitment become apparent. It not only begs the most interesting questions about the ebb and flow of candidate aspirations for higher office, it also treats the differences in the decision-making context as a purely subjective phenomenon subsumed within each prospective candidate's subjective probability estimate. Richer formulations at both the micro and macro level of theory are needed.

RECRUITMENT AND PROBLEMS OF RESEARCH DESIGN

Recruitment to Congress involves both individual motivations and social and political processes. The complex interactions among individuals, groups, and institutional arrangements are not always accessible to political observers, however, and some are more amenable than others to systematic analysis. These problems raise issues regarding research design, which scholars interested in the study of recruitment will have to address.

Declared vs. Undeclared Candidates

Most of what we know about candidate decision making has been gleaned from surveys and interviews with declared candidates. These studies are typically conducted during or after the campaign when the participants have every reason to justify their behavior to themselves and to the researcher. Inflated expectations and emphasis on the "thrill of the game" emerge as consistent themes among the losers (Huckshorn and Spencer 1971; Fowler 1979; Kazee 1980; Maisel 1986). Self-congratulation and underestimation of the role of parties and external events are typical among the winners (Kingdon 1966; Leuthold 1971; Fishel 1973; Goldenberg and Traugott 1984). Not surprisingly, the most significant variables that emerge from this body of literature are the probability of winning and the benefits of running.

But there is another way to assess ambition for Congress, and that is by examining the calculations of individuals who could have run but chose to remain on the sidelines. Like Sherlock Holmes, who based his deduction about a murder on the fact that the dog didn't bark, we can make inferences about ambition by studying politicians who have the attributes of prospective congressional candidates but decline to pursue the offices for which they outwardly seem well-suited. Fowler and McClure (1989) studied these "unseen" candidates in an upstate New York open seat race. Kazee (1983) investigated the deterrent affect of popular incumbents on would-be challengers in three southern districts, and Rohde (1979) endeavored to predict which House members would attempt to run for the Senate.

One immediate payoff from this approach is the discovery of powerful disincentives to the pursuit of congressional office. The costs of running and winning are thrown into relief, and the merits of alternative careers become evident. Equally important, structural and environmental constraints over which potential candidates have no control emerge as powerful barriers to congressional office seeking.

If a full understanding of ambition for Congress requires an explanation of the decision not to run, then scholars will need to give serious consideration to the problems of defining the pool of would-be contestants. There are state, partisan, and perhaps gender differences to examine in determining who is in a position to run. The earlier comparison between New Hampshire and New York, for example, suggests that eligible politicians in one state may be very different from those in another. Moreover, there is a good deal of historical evidence showing that Republicans are more likely than Democrats to run for office without prior service in public office (Schlesinger 1966; Mezey 1970; Fowler and Maisel 1989; Canon 1990b). Finally, there is some recent data pertaining to local officeholders indicating that women assign more weight to contextual factors than men (Bledsoe and Munro 1988).

Such differences are not easily controlled for unless we have a better idea of what they are and where they are most prevalent. Thus, two research strategies seem in order. The first would be an application of the snowball interviewing technique in a representative set of states and districts in order to identify common traits among potential candidates. Such a strategy is presently being pursued by a group of political scientists organized by Thomas Kazee. The second tactic would be to study politicians who share similar backgrounds, such as House members (Rohde 1979) or state legislators (Robeck 1982; Fowler, Jones, Maisel, and Stone 1988) and determine what characteristics of the state and district—such as institutional settings and campaign finance laws—are associated with the propensity to run for Congress.

Candidate Characteristics

The interaction among individuals and groups that eventually lures some into the electoral arena may be highly subjective in terms of how prospective candidates perceive the elite discourse and political events taking place around them. We need a good deal more information about how this interpretation takes place. As Richard Fenno has observed: "we can gain valuable knowledge of [politicians] actions, perceptions and interpretations by trying to see their world as they see it" (1986, 4).

Yet many attributes of candidates that shape their decision to run are readily observed and counted from afar. First is the definition of candidate quality. There is a lively debate among congressional scholars about just who should be judged a strong candidate and who a weak one, and it is an important dispute both for assessing the competitiveness of individual races and for evaluating the impact of national trends on the partisan makeup of the Congress.   Elsewhere, Maisel and I have summarized the main points of the argument and pointed out the drawbacks of the existing measures, including our own (1991).   An important dimension missing from this discussion, moreover, is the fact that a candidate who is "strong" for one type of community may not be so strong in another.   A black clergyman running in New York City or Atlanta, for example, would be ranked among the community's most experienced politicians, while lacking the credential of prior officehold-ing.   Thus systematic comparisons are needed regarding the relative performance of various measures of candidate quality and some means must be found for assessing local idiosyncrasies.

It is also important to consider how important judges of candidate quality—voters and political activists—perceive them. There has been some interesting work on presidential elections comparing the different criteria the two groups use in judging who is a good candidate. It is also important to track how these perceptions develop among both the mass and elite publics. How do candidates' reputations evolve? How are they transmitted? And ultimately, how do those who determine nominations in primaries and participate in campaigns as volunteers and contributors ultimately decide whom to back? Equally important is an examination of how social background characteristics affect voters' perceptions of candidates. In the past there was so little variation among members of Congress that background variables explained nothing about candidate success. But today, as women woo voters on the basis of their status as outsiders and African Americans attempt to broaden their appeal outside their traditional urban communities, race and gender may have strategic consequences that scholars have yet to examine.

Controlling for Historical Trends

As noted earlier, there seems to be a decrease in competitive candidates in both houses, as well as a change in their level of experience and their dependence on outsiders for support. Some of these patterns seem to be related to party differences, some are connected to the power of incumbency and some may be rooted in institutional rules and structures within the states.   Whatever their causes, they complicate analysis of congressional elections. More work is needed, therefore, in defining long-term trends among those who run for Congress and in controlling for the distorting effects of such patterns.

Model Specification

If contextual factors affect the composition of the candidate pool, as I have argued, then their omission reduces the explanatory power of statistical models to predict candidates' entry into a race. A good example of this problem occurs in Jacobson's (1989) reformulation of the strategic politicians hypothesis. In demonstrating the presence of local influences in the decision of experienced candidates to run, he has shown how important it is to include such variables in models of recruitment. The fact that incumbents' electoral margins are less effective predictors of future success than they used to be suggests that more effort needs to be made in developing indicators of local political conditions.

As more scholars undertake research on candidate decision making, other issues and challenges will emerge. But for now, it is important to recognize how our current understanding of recruitment is colored by whom we choose to study and what variables we select or omit in assessing candidates' entry into the electoral arena.

SUMMARY AND CONCLUSIONS

In any election year many people could run for Congress, but very few actually become candidates. Their decisions to compete or to remain on the sidelines have profound implications; for in the candidate-centered contests so typical of American elections, who wins often depends upon who runs. By determining the number and type of nominees on the ballot, these individuals shape the competitiveness of local contests and influence the overall make-up of the national legislature. Ultimately, the choices made by prospective candidates many months before election day influence both representation at home and policymaking in Washington. I have argued that further research into the "undertilled field" of congressional recruitment would yield significant benefits in terms of improved understanding of congressional politics. But some areas of inquiry seem more pressing at this point than others.

At the top of the list is a definition of the pool of prospective candidates for Congress. Who is eligible to run and who thinks about running are important questions that underpin many of the issues raised throughout this essay. We simply need to know whom to study before we can make progress in explaining why some individuals run and others remain on the sidelines. Similarly, we need to recognize the array of possibilities from which political elites choose before we can predict whom they will winnow out.

Second, we need to pursue the interaction of local contexts and national events in shaping the strategic calculations of potential members of Congress and their likely supporters. A precondition for this type of research, however, is the identification and systematic comparison of the structural variables that define the local decision-making environment for candidates. Another necessary foundation for such inquiries is the analysis of trends in the pool of prospective candidates to pinpoint the regional and partisan changes that produce them. Some work has been done in this area, but a good deal more is required.

Third, we need to focus on predicting opportunities for candidates to run in open seats and to challenge incumbents. Studies that forecast retirements among incumbents and research that develops more consistent indicators of incumbent vulnerability than prior electoral margins would be valuable additions to the literature.

Finally, we should look for the presence of systematic influences on the recruitment of women to Congress, in particular the incentives and disincentives keeping them from open seat primaries.

In pursuing these topics, different research methods will be appropriate—participant observation to see how candidates define their decision-making environment; formal theories to predict individual choices and the supply of prospective candidates; statistical analyses of contextual factors and institutional arrangements; surveys of potential candidates and various types of local and national elites. It is a rich field of study, offering research opportunities for many different types of scholars.

REFERENCES

Abramowitz, Alan I. 1984. "National Issues, Strategic Politicians, and Voting Behavior in the 1980 and 1982 Congressional Elections." *American Journal of Political Science* 28:710-721.
_____. 1988. "Explaining Senate Election Outcomes." *American Political Science Review* 82:385-403.
Andersen, Kristi, and Stuart S. Thorson. 1984. "Congressional Turnover and the Election of Women." *Western Political Quarterly* 37:143-56.
Ansolabehere, Stephen, David Brady, and Morris Fiorina. 1988. "The Marginals Never Vanished?" Working Paper P-88-1. Hoover Institution, Stanford University.
Arnold, R. Douglas. 1982. "Overtilled and Undertilled Fields in American Politics." *Political Science Quarterly* 97:91-103.
Auden, W. H., and L. Kronenberger. 1962 *The Viking Book of Aphorisms.* Dorset Press.
Banks, Jeffrey S., and D. Roderick Kiewiet. 1989. "Explaining Patterns of Candidate Competition in Congressional Elections." *American Journal of Political Science* 33:997-1015.
Bauer, Monica, and John R. Hibbing. 1989. "Which Incumbents Lose in House Elections: A Response to Jacobson's 'The Marginals Never Vanished.'" *American Journal of Political Science* 33:262-71.
Bianco, William T. 1984. "Strategic Decisions on Candidacy in U.S. Congressional Districts." *Legislative Studies Quarterly* 9:351-64.
Black, Gordon S. 1972. "A Theory of Political Ambition: Career Choices and the Role of Structural Incentives." *American Political Science Review* 66:144-59.
Bledsoe, Timothy, and Mary Herring Munro. 1988. "Victims of Circumstances: Women in Pursuit of Political Office in America." Presented at the annual meeting of the American Political Science Association, Washington, D.C.
Bond, Jon R., Cary Covington, and Richard Fleisher. 1985. "Explaining Challenger Quality in Congressional Elections." *Journal of Politics* 47:510-29.
Born, Richard. 1979. "Generational Replacement and the Growth of Incumbent Reelection Margins in the U.S. House." *American Political Science Review* 73:811-17.
_____. 1986. "Strategic Politicians and Unresponsive Voters." *American Political Science Review* 80:599-612.

Broder, David S. 1989. "Plain Old Ambition." *Washington Post.* April 16:B7.

Burnham, Walter Dean. 1982. *The Current Crisis in American Politics.* New York: Oxford University Press.

Cain, Bruce, Morris P. Fiorina, and John Ferejohn. 1987. *The Personal Vote.* Cambridge: Harvard University Press.

Campbell, James E., et al. 1984. "Television Markets and Congressional Elections." *Legislative Studies Quarterly* 9:665-78.

Canon, David T. 1985. "Political Conditions and Experienced Challengers in Congressional Elections, 1972-1984." Presented to the annual meeting of the American Political Science Association, New Orleans.

_____. 1989a. "Contesting Primaries in Congressional Elections." Presented to the annual meeting of the Midwest Political Science Association, Chicago.

_____. 1989b. "Political Amateurism in the United States Congress." In *Congress Reconsidered,* 4th ed., ed. Lawrence C. Dodd and Bruce I. Oppenheimer, Washington, D.C.: Congressional Quarterly Press, 65-90.

_____. 1990a. *Actors, Athletes, and Astronauts: Political Amateurs in the United States Congress.* Chicago: University of Chicago Press.

_____. 1990b. "Political Ambition, Political Opportunity, and the Emergence of the Republican Party in the South, 1964-1988." Paper presented at the conference "Back to the Future: The U.S. Congress in the Twenty-first Century." The Carl Albert Center, University of Oklahoma, Norman, April 11-13.

Carroll, Susan J. 1985. *Women as Candidates in American Politics.* Bloomington, Ind.: Indiana University Press.

Collie, Melissa P. 1981. "Incumbency, Electoral Safety, and Turnover in the House of Representatives, 1952-1976." *American Political Science Review* 75:119-31.

Cotter, Cornelius P., et al. 1984. *Party Organizations in American Politics.* New York: Praeger.

Crotty, William. 1984. *American Parties in Decline,* 2d ed. Boston: Little, Brown.

Deering, Christopher S., and Steven S. Smith. 1985. "Subcommittees in Congress." In *Congress Reconsidered,* 3d ed., ed. Lawrence C. Dodd and Bruce I. Oppenheimer, Washington, D.C.: Congressional Quarterly Press, 189-210.

Eismeier, Theodore, and Philip H. Pollock III. 1988. "The Political Geography of Political Action Committees: National Cash and the Local Connection in Congressional Elections." Presented at the annual meeting of the American Political Science Association, Washington, D.C.

Epstein, Leon D. 1986. *Political Parties in the American Mold.* Madison: University of Wisconsin Press.

Eubank, Robert B., and David John Gow. 1983. "The Pro-Incumbent Bias in the 1978 and 1980 National Election Studies." *American Journal of Political Science* 27:122-39.

_____. 1985. "Incumbent Effects on Individual-Level Voting Behavior in Congressional Elections: A Decade of Exaggeration." *Journal of Politics* 47:958-67.

Fenno, Richard F., Jr. 1973. *Congressmen in Committees.* Boston: Little, Brown.

_____. 1978. *Home Style: House Members in Their Districts.* Boston: Little, Brown.

_____. 1986. "Observation, Context, and Sequence in the Study of Politics." *American Political Science Review* 80:1-15.

Fiorina, Morris P. 1977. *Congress: Keystone of the Washington Establishment.* New Haven: Yale University Press.

_____. 1984. "The Presidency and the Contemporary Electoral System." In *The Presidency and the Political System,* ed. Michael Nelson, Washington, D.C.: Congressional Quarterly Press.

_____, David W. Rohde, and Peter Wissel. 1976. "Historical Change in House Turnover." In *Congress in Change,* ed. Norman J. Ornstein, New York: Praeger, 24-57.

Fishel, Jeff. 1973. *Party and Opposition: Congressional Challengers in American Politics.* New York: David McKay, Inc.

Fowler, Linda L. 1979. "The Electoral Lottery: Decisions to Run for Congress." *Public Choice* 34:399-418.

_____. 1989. "Local Influences on Congressional Recruitment." Presented to the annual meeting of the Midwest Political Science Association, Chicago.

_____, and Robert D. McClure. 1989. *Political Ambition: Who Decides to Run for Congress.* New Haven: Yale University Press.

_____, and L. Sandy Maisel. 1991. "The Changing Supply of Competitive Candidates in House Election, 1982-1988." Revised version of a paper presented at the annual meeting of the American Political Science Association, Atlanta.

_____. 1991. "The Partisan Context of Congressional Recruitment." In *Political Parties and Elections in the United States: An Encyclopedia,* ed. L. Sandy Maisel, New York: Garland Publishing.

Frendreis, John P., James L. Gibson, and Laura L. Vertz. 1990. "The Electoral Relevance of Local Party Organizations." *American Political Science Review* 84:225-36.

Gibson, James L., et al. 1983. "Assessing Party Organizational Strength." *American Journal of Political Science* 27:193-222.

_____. 1985. "Whither the Local Parties?: A Cross-Sectional and Longitudinal Analysis of the Strength of Party Organizations." *American Journal of Political Science* 29:139-60.

Goldenberg, Edie N., Michael W. Traugott, and Frank Baumgartner. 1986. "Preemptive and Reactive Spending in U. S. House Races." *Political Behavior* 8:3-20.

Gow, David John, and Robert B. Eubank. 1984. "The Pro-Incumbent Bias in the 1982 National Election Study." *American Journal of Political Science* 28:224-30.

Green, Donald Philip, and Jonathan S. Krasno. 1988. "Salvation for the Spendthrift Incumbent: Reestimating the Effects of Campaign Spending in House Elections." *American Journal of Political Science* 32:884-907.

_____. 1988b. "PACs and the Congressional Supermarket: The Currency is Complex." *American Journal of Political Science* 33:1-24.

Grenzke, Janet M. 1988. "Comparing Contributions to U.S. House Members from Outside their Districts." *Legislative Studies Quarterly* 13:83-103.

Haeberle, Steven H. 1985. "Closed Primaries and Party Support in Congress." *American Politics Quarterly* 13:341-52.

Herrnson, Paul S. 1986. "Do Parties Make a Difference?: The Role of Party Organizations in Congressional Elections." *Journal of Politics* 48:589-615.

_____. 1988. *Party Campaigning in the 1980s.* Cambridge: Harvard University Press.

_____. 1989. "Campaign Professionalism and Fundraising in Congressional Elections." Manuscript.

Hibbing, John R. 1988. "Changing Electoral Careers in the Modern House of Representatives." Presented at the annual meeting of the Midwest Political Science Association, Chicago.

Hinckley, Barbara. 1980. "House Reelections and Senate Defeats: The Role of the Challenger." *British Journal of Political Science* 10:441-60.

Huckshorn, Robert J., and Robert C. Spencer. 1971. *The Politics of Defeat: Campaigning for Congress.* Amherst: University of Massachusetts Press.

Jacobson, Gary C. 1987a. *The Politics of Congressional Elections,* 2d ed. Boston: Little, Brown.

_____. 1987b. "The Marginals Never Vanished: Incumbency and Competition in Elections to the U.S. House of Representatives." *American Journal of Political Science* 31:126-41.

_____. 1989. "Strategic Politicians and the Dynamics of U.S. House Elections, 1946-1986." *American Political Science Review* 83:773-93.

_____. 1992. "When Opportunity Knocks, No One's Home: The Misallocation of Resources in House Campaigns." Paper presented at the annual meeting of the Midwestern Political Science Association, Chicago, April 9-11.

_____, and Samuel Kernell. 1981. *Strategy and Choice in Congressional Elections.* New Haven: Yale University Press.

_____, and Raymond E. Wolfinger. 1989. "Information and Voting in California Senate Elections." *Legislative Studies Quarterly* 14:509-29.

Jewell, Malcolm E. 1982. *Representation in State Legislatures.* Lexington: University Press of Kentucky.

Jones, Charles O. 1981. "New Directions in Congressional Research: A Review Article." *Legislative Studies Quarterly* 6:455-68.

Kayden, Xandra, and Eddie Mahe, Jr. 1985. *The Party Goes On: The Persistence of the Two-Party System in the United States.* New York: Basic Books.

Kazee, Thomas A. 1980. "The Decision to Run for the U.S. Congress." *Legislative Studies Quarterly* 5:79-100.

_____. 1983. "The Deterrent Effect of Incumbency on Recruiting Challengers in U.S. House Elections." *Legislative Studies Quarterly* 8:469-80.

Kernell, Samuel. 1977. "Toward Understanding 19th Century Congressional Careers: Ambition, Competition and Rotation." *American Journal of Political Science* 13:369-93.

Kingdon, John W. 1968. *Candidates for Office: Beliefs and Strategies.* New York: Random House.

Kramer, Gerald H. 1971. "Short-Term Fluctuations in U.S. Voting Behavior, 1896-1964." *American Political Science Review* 65:131-43.

Krasno, Jonathan S., and Donald Philip Green. 1988. "Preempting Quality Challengers in House Elections." *Journal of Politics* 50:920-36.

Kuklinski, James H., and Darrell M. West. 1981. "Economic Expectations and Voting Behavior in United States House and Senate Elections." *American Political Science Review* 74:436-47.

Kunkel, Joseph A., III. 1988. "Party Endorsement and Incumbency in Minnesota Legislative Nominations." *Legislative Studies Quarterly* 13:211-23.

Leuthold, David. 1968. *Electioneering in a Democracy: Campaigning for Congress.* New York: Random House.

Levine, Martin D., and Mark S. Hyde. 1977. "Incumbency and the Theory of Political Ambition: A Rational Choice Model." *Journal of Politics* 39:959-83.

Lipset, Seymour Martin. 1983. "The Congressional Candidate." *Journal of Contemporary Studies* 6:87-105.

Maisel, L. Sandy. 1986. *From Obscurity to Oblivion: Running in the Congressional Primary,* 2d ed. Knoxville: University of Tennessee Press.

_____. 1987. "Candidates and Non-Candidates in the 1986 Congressional Elections." Paper presented to the annual meeting of the Midwest Political Science Association, Chicago.

_____. 1989. "Candidate Quality in the 1988 Congressional Election." Paper presented at the annual meeting of the Midwest Political Science Association, Chicago.

_____, and Joseph Cooper. 1981. *Congressional Elections.* Beverly Hills: Sage Publications.

Mann, Thomas E. 1978. *Unsafe at Any Margin.* Washington, D.C.: American Enterprise Institute.

_____, and Raymond E. Wolfinger. 1980. "Candidates and Parties in Congressional Elections." *American Political Science Review* 74:617-32.

Marra, Robin F., and Charles W. Ostrom, Jr. 1989. "Explaining Seat Change in the U.S. House of Representatives, 1950-1986." *American Journal of Political Science* 33:541-69.

Matthews, Donald R. 1960. *U.S. Senators and Their World.* Chapel Hill: University of North Carolina Press.

_____. 1983. "Legislative Recruitment and Legislative Careers." In *Handbook of Legislative Research,* ed. Gerhard Loewenberg,

Samuel C. Patterson, and Malcolm E. Jewell, Cambridge: Harvard University Press.

Mayhew, David. R. 1974a. *Congress: The Electoral Connection.* New Haven: Yale University Press.

_____. 1974b. "Congressional Elections: The Case of the Vanishing Marginals." *Polity* 6:295-317.

Mezey, Michael L. 1970. "Ambition Theory and the Office of Congressmen." *Journal of Politics* 32:563.

Oppenheimer, Bruce I., James A. Stimson, and Richard W. Waterman. 1986. "Interpreting U.S. Congressional Elections: The Exposure Thesis." *Legislative Studies Quarterly* 11:227-47.

Ornstein, Norman J., et al. 1987. *Vital Statistics on Congress 1987-1988.* Washington, D.C.: American Enterprise Institute.

Owens, John R., and Edward C. Olson. 1980. "Economic Fluctuations and Congressional Elections." *American Journal of Political Science* 24:469-93.

Polsby, Nelson W. 1968. "The Institutionalization of the U.S. House of Representatives." *American Political Science Review* 62:144-68.

_____. 1981. "Coalition and Faction in American Politics: An Institutional View." In *Party Coalitions in the 1980s,* ed. S. M. Lipset, San Francisco: Institute for Contemporary Studies, 153-78.

Prewitt, Kenneth. 1974. "Political Ambition, Volunteerism and Electoral Accountability." In *Public Opinion and Political Attitudes,* ed. Allen Wilcox, New York: John Wiley.

Price, David. 1989. "From Outsider to Insider." In *Congress Reconsidered,* 4th ed., ed. Lawrence D. Dodd and Bruce I. Oppenheimer, Washington, D.C.: Congressional Quarterly Press.

Price, H. Douglas. 1971. "The Congressional Career: Then and Now." In *Congressional Behavior,* ed. Nelson W. Polsby, New York: Random House, 14-27.

_____. 1975. "Historical Change in House Turnover." In *Congress in Change,* ed. Norman J. Ornstein, New York: Praeger, 2-23.

Radcliff, Benjamin. 1988. "Solving a Puzzle: Aggregate Analysis and Economic Voting Revisited." *Journal of Politics* 50:440-45.

Ragsdale, Lyn, and Timothy E. Cook. 1987. "Representatives' Actions and Challengers' Reactions: Limits to Candidate Connections in the House." *American Journal of Political Science* 31:45-81.

Rivers, Douglas, and Morris P. Fiorina. 1989. "Constituency Service, Reputation, and the Incumbency Advantage." In *Home Style and*

Washington Work, ed. Morris P. Fiorina and David W. Rohde, Ann Arbor: University of Michigan Press.

Robek, Bruce. 1982. "State Legislator Candidacies for the U.S. House: Prospects for Success." *Legislative Studies Quarterly* 7:507-14.

Robinson, Michael J. 1975. "A Twentieth-Century Medium in a Nineteenth-Century Legislature: The Effects of Television on the American Congress." In *Congress in Change,* ed. Norman J. Ornstein, New York: Praeger, 240-61.

Rohde, David W. 1979. "Risk-Bearing and Progressive Ambition: The Case of Members of the United States House of Representatives." *American Journal of Political Science* 23:1-26.

_____. 1991. *Parties and Leaders in the Postreform House.* Chicago: University of Chicago Press.

Roll Call, June 22, 1992:36-37.

Sabato, Larry J. 1988. *The Party's Just Begun: Shaping Political Parties for America's Future.* Boston: Little, Brown.

Schlesinger, Joseph A. 1966. *Ambition and Politics: Political Careers in the United States.* Chicago: Rand McNally and Co.

_____. 1985. "The New American Political Party." *American Political Science Review* 79:1152-69.

Seligman, Lester G. 1961. "Political Recruitment and Party Structure: A Case Study." *American Political Science Review* 55:77-86.

Shepsle, Kenneth A. *The Giant Jigsaw Puzzle: Democratic Committee Assignments in the Modern House.* Chicago: University of Chicago Press.

Sigelman, Lee, and Susan Welch. 1984. "Race, Gender and Opinion toward Black and Female Presidential Candidates." *Public Opinion Quarterly* 48:472.

Smith, Steven S., and Christopher J. Deering. 1984. *Committees in Congress.* Washington, D.C.: Congressional Quarterly Press.

Snowiss, Leo M. 1966. "Congressional Recruitment and Representation." *American Political Science Review* 60:627-39

Squire, Peverill. 1989. "Competition and Uncontested Seats in U.S. House Elections." *Legislative Studies Quarterly* 14:281-95.

Stewart, Charles, III. 1989. "A Sequential Model of U.S. Senate Elections." *Legislative Studies Quarterly* 14:567-601.

_____, and Mark Reynolds. 1990. "Television Markets and U.S. Senate Elections." *Legislative Studies Quarterly* 15: 495-523.

Sullivan, John L., and Robert E. O'Connor. 1972. "Electoral Choice and Popular Control of Public Policy: The Case of the 1966 House Elections." *American Political Science Review* 57:1256-68.

Sundquist, James L. 1981. *The Decline and Resurgence of Congress.* Washington, D.C.: Brookings Institution.

Tobin, Richard J., and Edward Keynes. 1975. "Institutional Differences in the Recruitment Process: A Four State Study." *American Journal of Political Science* 19:667-82.

Tufte, Edward. R. 1975. "Determinants of Outcomes of Midterm Congressional Elections." *American Political Science Review* 69:812-26.

Westlye, Mark C. 1992. *Senate Elections and Campaign Intensity.* Johns Hopkins University Press.

Wilcox, Clyde. 1987. "The Timing of Strategic Decisions: Candidacy Decisions in 1982 and 1984." *Legislative Studies Quarterly* 12:565-72.

Wright, Gerald C., Jr., and Michael B. Berkman. 1986. "Candidates and Policy in United States Senate Elections." *American Political Science Review* 80:667.

Wright, John R. 1989. "Contributions, Lobbying and Committee Voting in the U.S. House of Representatives." Manuscript.

APPENDIX

The Probability of a Female State Legislator
Securing a House Seat in New Hampshire or New York*

	NEW HAMPSHIRE	NEW YORK
Ratio of women in legislature	138/424	22/211
National rank based on percent women in legislature	1	34
Probability of female legislator	.33	.10
Probability of open/marginal seat (average over 1982-1988)	.125	.16
Probability of female legislator in open/marginal seat	.04	.016
Probability state legislator runs in open/marginal seat	.01	.50
Probability state legislator wins if runs in open/marginal seat	.001	.33
Probability of female state legislator entering House	.00013	.0003

*Data from Center for the American Woman and Politics, "Fact Sheet: Women in State Legislatures 1988," Eagleton Institute of Politics, Rutgers University. Also Barone et al., *Almanac of American Politics*, 1984-1988 editions (Washington: National Journal).

Chapter 3

The Career Paths of Members of Congress

John R. Hibbing
University of Nebraska-Lincoln

Most analyses of congressional careers deal with the extent to which service in Congress is in fact a career. Typically asked questions include the following. What paths do people take to get to Congress? Once there, how long do they stay? Are they staying longer than they used to? Why do they leave, and where do they go upon departure? And why do some try to move up and others try to move out? Research on these questions is undeniably important. Much good work has already been done in this area, and it needs to continue.

At the same time, by focusing on congressional comings and goings, a major aspect of career paths is missed. Setting 1992 aside, in recent congresses particularly, the number of representatives entering and leaving is paltry. While it is important to understand why legislators arrive and depart, the fact is that, at any given time in the modern Congress, most of them stay—and these are the individuals about whom we need to know more. They are following career paths, too. Just because these paths do not cross institutional lines does not mean they should be disowned by those who study elected politicians. We know too little about the evolution of legislators while they are in Congress.

This chapter consists of two main parts. The first will be a summary and synthesis of existing literature on what might be called the external career. Here Congress is seen as merely one stop on a longer political career, and the primary concerns involve entry to and exit from Congress. The literature on these matters is what is usually thought of as the literature on congressional careers. The second part addresses what might be called the internal career, since with this approach the center of attention is career moves within the House of Representatives. In this section, from where the representative came before entering and to where the representative goes upon leaving are largely irrelevant. Instead, concerns revolve around the acquisition of party and/or committee leadership positions as careers progress.

After these two sections, I conclude with an overview of what we know about career paths in Congress and with some recommendations for where future research would, in my opinion, most profitably be directed. Throughout this chapter, emphasis will be placed on the House of Representatives since this is where previous research has concentrated. On occasion, reference will be made to the Senate, but for the most part we know much less about senatorial careers. This in itself is an important and unnecessary deficiency in the study of congressional careers.

THE EXTERNAL CONGRESSIONAL CAREER

The basic questions relevant to the external congressional career are: (1) where do representatives come from, and why do they run for Congress, and (2) where do representatives go, and why do they leave? Linda Fowler's paper in this volume deals with the first set of questions, freeing me to focus on the latter.

Organizing answers to these questions is facilitated by Joseph Schlesinger's (1966) threefold categorization of political ambition: progressive, static, and discrete. In the case of United States representatives, those with progressive ambition wish to move up the ladder, probably to a Senate seat, but perhaps to a governor's mansion or to the White House. Those with static ambition desire to remain right where they are, firmly ensconced in the House of Representatives. Finally, those with discrete ambition wish to run for an office lower on the political ladder (perhaps state legislator) or, more likely, to leave the world of elective office altogether.

Departure from the House of Representatives can occur in all three ambition categories: the progressively ambitious leave because they are seeking higher office; those with static ambition by definition run for re-election, so the only way they can depart is via electoral defeat (i.e., the unsuccessful attempt to secure reelection to the House); and those with discrete ambition leave not to seek higher office but to seek lower office or to retire from elective office altogether.

In the 1980s, aggregate departures from the House of Representatives were at an all-time low. Indeed, low turnover rates became an issue in the popular press, no doubt partially because members of Congress increasingly defined turnover in partisan terms. Republicans indignantly pointed to the microscopic entering classes of 1986 (49), 1988 (33), and 1990 (44). In 1988, for the first time in the history of the Republic, over 400 representatives were reelected to the House of Representatives. Democrats (see A. Swift 1989) attempted to counter this fact by noting that in the five 1980s elections, approximately 56 percent of the House membership was replaced (244 of 435)—and, of course, turnover levels in 1992 were unusually high.

Figure 3.1 displays congressional departures by year and by source (deaths and resignations excluded). Relatively high total turnover occurred in 1964 and 1974, volatile electoral years thanks to the LBJ landslide and the Watergate fallout, respectively. The figure also indicates that very few recent departures have been caused by electoral defeat, as the number of electoral casualties has dropped sharply. Voluntary retirements from politics were high from 1972 till 1980 but much lower from 1982 through 1990. And the number of representatives leaving to seek higher office has remained reasonably constant through the years, although there were highs in 1976 and 1986 and lows in 1966 and 1980.

In 1986, 1988, and 1990, very few representatives lost, and the numbers attempting to move up or out were not high either. The result is that total turnover was lower than it had ever been, down nearly 22 percent from the 1970s and averaging a little less than 10 percent of the body every two years. The level of membership turnover in 1992, however, was markedly higher than it was in the 1980s. Fifty-three members of the House "voluntarily" retired, another 13 sought higher office, 19 lost in primaries, and 24 lost in the general elections. Since one incumbent died in office, a total of 110 new faces are present in the 103rd Congress. Still, 1992 notwithstanding (redistricting, the House Bank scandal, and FEC regulations on converting campaign cash to personal property conspired to make 1992 something of a special case), the modern House is characterized by low turnover and by long careers. To emphasize this point, in January of 1992 Jamie Whitten (D-MS) broke the record of Carl Vinson (D-GA) and "Manny" Celler (D-NY) as the longest serving representative in history. What turnover there is comes predominantly from voluntary (that is, leaving due to something other than electoral defeat) rather than involuntary departures.

With this general information on congressional turnover as background, I now focus on the correlates of decisions to run for higher office and the correlates of decisions to leave electoral politics altogether

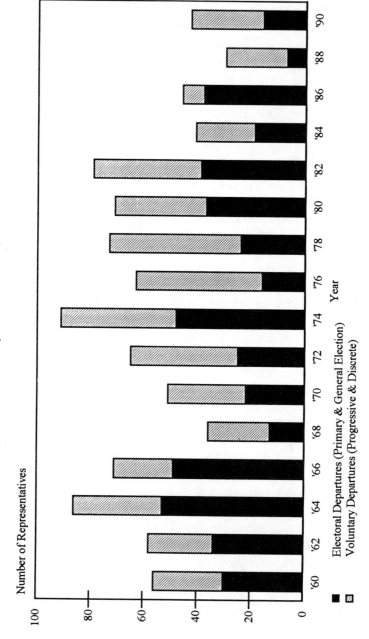

Figure 3.1. *Sources of House Turnover, 1960-90*

(on the correlates of electoral defeat in the modern Congress, see Bauer and Hibbing 1989).

Departures Caused By Progressive Ambition

What is presently known about the decision to leave the House in order to run for higher office? Quite a bit, actually. Studies by Schlesinger (1966), Rohde (1979), Brace (1984), and Copeland (1989) have provided a reasonably thorough and consistent description of the situations under which representatives are most likely to attempt to move up.

The Senate is the most frequently pursued office, but even so, taking a shot at the Senate is not a common practice for representatives. Rohde's data cover the years of 1954-1974, and he finds that approximately 5.8 percent of all those representatives who had an opportunity to run for a Senate seat in any given year actually did so. (Copeland's data on the 1980s indicate that this percentage may have declined just a little, to around 4 percent.) Approximately 1.6 percent of those representatives with an opportunity to run for governor actually did so. Beyond this, a scattering of individual representatives have run for such positions as president and vice president of the United States, lieutenant governor, and state attorney general, but their numbers are so small that further discussions will pertain only to bids at becoming a governor or a senator.

Obviously, running for higher office is not something representatives do casually, but bearing this in mind, is it possible to determine the kind of representative most likely to go against the trend by seeking a position in the Senate or in a governor's mansion? By combining the results of Rohde, Brace, and Copeland it is possible to produce a prototypical higher-office-seeking situation. I will divide the relevant factors into those that are personal and those that are contextual.

First, a higher-office-seeking representative is probably between the ages of 40 and 48. Representatives who are younger or, especially, older than this, are more likely to stand pat with their House seat. Brace calculates that from 1952 to 1976 the mean age for higher-office-seekers was 43. Probabilities of leaving the House to run for senator or governor drop off rapidly over this age and gradually under this age. Somewhat relatedly, House leaders are much less likely to run for higher office than are non-House leaders (see especially Copeland 1989, Tables 1 and 2).

There is a slight indication that, compared to their colleagues, representatives who run for higher office are safer electorally, as measured by previous margin of victory (see Copeland) as well as by increase in previous margin of victory compared to four years previously (see Payne 1982), although the coefficients are usually not significant. Nonetheless, it does not appear to be the case that representatives in electoral difficulty frequently adopt a "what have I got to lose" attitude and take a chance at higher office. Brace does detect an exception to this statement, however, in that those representatives who have been adversely redistricted seem more likely to take a flyer on higher office.

Republicans, frequently referred to as members of the permanent minority party in the House of Representatives, are slightly more likely to run for the Senate than comparable Democrats, although it is interesting to note that this tendency diminished rather than increased during the time (1980-1986) when the Republicans were in the majority in the Senate (see Copeland 1989).

Finally, both Rohde and Brace note a tendency for "risk-takers" to be more likely to leave the House with the intention of running for higher office. According to Rohde, a politician is a risk-taker if he/she took a risk in order to get into the House in the first place (or at some earlier career stage). Thus, we can conclude that if someone has taken a risk before, they are more likely to do so again by running for senator or governor.

In addition to the representative's age, party affiliation, House position, and risk-taking proclivities, several contextual variables also influence the decision to seek higher office. The nature of the higher office itself obviously matters. Rohde demonstrates convincingly that when the governor serves only a two-year term (as is the case in a small number of states), representatives are much less likely to run than when the governor serves a four-year term and, as has already been mentioned, regardless of term length, representatives are less likely to seek a governorship than a Senate seat.

Many of the contextual factors have to do with the chances of winning the Senate seat. For example, if the Senate seat is open (no incumbent), the chances of representatives running for it increase dramatically. Further, if there is an incumbent senator, the margin of that senator's most recent victory seems to make some difference. On average, incumbent senators opposed by representatives are in a slightly more precarious electoral situation than senators who are not; moreover, incumbent senators challenged by representatives tend to be more junior than senators who are not challenged, although both the marginality and seniority relationships are weak (see Brace 1984).

A clearer and more consistent relationship appears between running for higher office and hailing from a lightly populated state. The chances of representatives running for higher office are much lower in heavily populated states such as California, New York, Texas, Pennsylvania, Florida, and Illinois, than they are in lightly populated states such as Alaska, Wyoming, the Dakotas, New Hampshire, and Delaware. Two explanations for this relationship immediately suggest themselves. First, representatives in lightly populated states have already represented all or nearly all of the state, thereby making easier the transition to a campaign for senator or governor. Second, the pool of highly qualified competitors is diminished in lightly populated states, largely because the number of representatives is much reduced.

In addition, chances of running for higher office are decreased if the incumbent in the higher office is of the same party as the representative and if the incumbent has a substantial amount of cash on hand (see Copeland 1989). But the effects of the overall level of statewide partisan competitiveness are uncertain (see Brace 1984).

So the composite picture is not too surprising. Those representatives most likely to leave the House in order to seek higher office are those who have a reasonable chance of winning the seat, perhaps because it is open or perhaps because the incumbent has shown signs of vulnerability by running poorly the last time or by failing to raise a massive war chest this time; those representatives who are not giving up a party or committee leadership position by leaving the House; those who are not green but are still young enough to anticipate potentially long service in the higher office; those who tend to be risk-takers and good fund-raisers; those who are in lightly populated states; those who are members of the minority party in the House, and those presented with the opportunity to run for an attractive higher office (such as the Senate or perhaps a four-year governorship).[1] The decision to run for higher office can be seen as a function of the desirability of the presently held office, the desirability of the higher office in question, the odds of successfully capturing the higher office, and the personal style of the representative contemplating the situation.

---

[1]How frequently are representatives successful when they run for the Senate? Copeland reports that the success rate is usually around 50 percent, although in 1982 only one of 13 won.

Departures Caused By Discrete Ambition

In the last 20 years, most turnover has been caused not by electoral defeat, nor by the desire to seek higher office, but by the desire to leave the world of elective office altogether. As was the case with progressive ambition, several studies have dealt with the causes of discrete ambition among the members of the U.S. House of Representatives (see, for example, Frantzich 1978a, 1978b; Cover 1981; Cooper and West 1981a, 1981b; Hibbing 1982a, 1982b; and Brace 1985).

Much of this attention was generated by the sizeable increase in the number of voluntary retirements from about 80 in the 1960s to nearly 150 in the 1970s. What made this increase even more remarkable was that it reversed a century-long trend toward fewer and fewer voluntary departures. Many scholars were anxious to learn why presumably ambitious politicians were suddenly turning their backs on additional congressional service at the same time as reelection to the House for those who did run was becoming more assured (see Erikson 1971).

The explanation favored by most researchers was that the demands of congressional service had become too great. Several observers believed that representatives were leaving because, to use the popular expression, "it was no longer any fun to serve in Congress." This sentiment was particularly evident in the work of Cooper and West as well as that of Frantzich. After testing for traditional explanations of voluntary retirement—advanced years, electoral vulnerability, and general infirmity—and finding them wanting, Cooper and West concluded that the "key causal factor is . . . the growing dissatisfaction with service in the House" (1981a, 86).

Just what is so distasteful about service in the modern House? If given the chance, members rattle off a litany of horror stories. Frequently voiced complaints include the intense and demanding lifestyle, scrutiny from an aggressive press, familial sacrifices, public cynicism, insufficient remuneration, ethics requirements, and the unremitting need to raise campaign funds, to perform constituency service, and to endure a byzantine and balkanized legislative process with poorly scheduled committee meetings, trivial roll call votes, and acerbic new participants (see Cooper and West 1981a; Hibbing 1982a).

The demands on modern members of Congress are undeniably intense and probably lead to the premature burnout of some. Even so, not all congressional scholars were willing to embrace the "serving in Congress is no longer fun" explanation. Albert Cover (1981) stressed the sheer demographics of the 1970s surge in involuntary retirements. He noted that most members of the large entering classes shortly after World War II were, by the early 1970s, well on in years and that this fact, in combination with the small retirement classes of the 1960s, produced a bulge of elderly members that was naturally relieved by the 1970s increase in retirements.

Moreover, the "no longer fun" argument has major holes. For one thing, the average age of retirees was not down in the 1970s. This suggests that, despite the publicity surrounding the retirements of young, rising stars like Barbara Jordan (D-TX), John Cavanaugh (D-NE), and Gary Myers (R-PA), most retirees in the 1970s were really quite senior. In fact, although voluntary retirements were up in virtually all categories in the 1970s, the biggest increase came among senior Democrats.

How is this occurrence explained? In addition to Cover's point, congressional reforms, notably the weakening of the seniority norm, must be brought into the discussion. Many senior Democrats watched in disbelief as their hard-earned seniority currency was devalued before their eyes, starting in 1969 with the decision to revitalize the Democratic Caucus, continuing in 1971 and 1973 when large numbers of negative votes were cast against several senior chairs including John McMillan, W. R. Poage, Chet Holifield, and Wright Patman, and culminating in 1975 when Poage, Patman, and F. Edward Hebert were unceremoniously dumped. Is it any wonder that all three were out of the House within two years, along with many of their suddenly nervous contemporaries? The seniority ranks of retiring Democratic representatives in 1968 were 7, 10, 18, 22, 24, 32, 33, 51, and 67. But in 1978 the seniority ranks of retiring Democrats were 1, 2, 4, 6, 7, 8, 10, 12, 14, 15, and 18.

In other words, seven of the 10 most senior majority party members retired in a single year. In the early 1980s, I had a chance to visit with 26 recently retired members of the House, and every senior retiree with whom I spoke expressed bitterness over the seniority reforms. One said, "Some of the actions of the reformers were clearly out of line, and I am thinking especially of what they did to Bob Poage. They were just out for blood, and Bob was handy. Men who voted against him were ashamed of it later because Bob was a perfect gentleman and an outstanding chairman."

There were many perfectly understandable reasons for the increase in voluntary retirements quite apart from the demands of congressional service. Most of the retiring representatives were old, the seniority changes made their status within the institution somewhat uncertain, their friends were leaving, and the pension system was more lucrative than ever (congressional pension is a function of the highest three salaried years; a large salary increase took place in 1969; the big jump in retirements came—not coincidentally—in 1972, the first year maximum benefit from the salary increase could be derived). Though they would deny this, most representatives are hard-drivers who thrive on a demanding schedule (see Loomis 1988), so the "no fun" argument just does not ring true in most instances.[2]

The events of the 1980s seem strongly supportive of this conclusion. The rate of voluntary retirement in the 1980s dropped sharply to a level even lower than that existing in the 1960s. In an average election during the last decade only about 15 members of the House have voluntarily left with no intention of running for other office. Most, though certainly not all, were elderly. Is it suddenly fun again to serve in Congress? I have heard no one—neither academic nor member—claim that it is. The truth of the matter is that most members retire for very understandable reasons: because of financial considerations, because they are of retirement age, or because of their concern for their status within the institution.[3]

This style of argument is supported by the tentative but intriguing findings of Steve Jardine (undated) who concludes that those representatives who are blocked from serving as a committee chair by the presence of a younger but more senior committee member (of the same party) are more likely to retire voluntarily than those who are not blocked. This is additional evidence that retirements are usually more the products of rational calculations concerning, among other things, career possibilities, than of vague judgments regarding job satisfaction.

Gary Jacobson and Samuel Kernell, in their influential book on strategic choice in Congress (1983), devote a chapter to voluntary retirements. They conclude that retirements usually increase *for a particular party* when it appears that that party is going to have a

---

[2]Of course it would be possible to view such variables as electoral marginality and seniority reform as contributing to a diminution in job satisfaction. However, because these factors cause dissatisfaction among a subset of members, it is best to disassociate them from the concept of job satisfaction, which has usually been employed to refer to a general unhappiness with the pace, demands, and lifestyle of congressional existence.

[3]A larger point is that voluntary retirement rates are inadequate indications of the enjoyment members derive from congressional service. Even during the 1970s, at least 400 of the 435 members sought reelection.

difficult electoral year. For example, this argument anticipates disproportionate Republican retirements in 1964 and 1974 and disproportionate Democratic retirements in 1978 and 1984. These predictions are generally accurate, and the logic has certain appeal. Jacobson and Kernell are definitely on target when, after noting that no retiree willingly admits to electoral concerns, they impishly ask what it was "about 1974 [that] made family men out of a disproportionate number of Republican congressmen" (1983, 50).

At the same time, the Jacobson and Kernell argument is less compelling now that the concept of good and bad electoral years for particular parties in Congress is fading away. We no longer have massive partisan electoral swings. Shifts of 116 seats (to the Republicans in 1894), 75 seats (to the Democrats in 1922), and 71 seats (to the Republicans in 1938) have been replaced by shifts of 15 seats (to the Republicans in 1978), 26 seats (to the Democrats in 1982), and 5 seats (to the Democrats in 1986). The absence of coattails and midterm disasters in modern American politics lessens the motivation for retirements to occur because of expectations that one's party will do poorly in the upcoming election. Besides, there is longitudinal evidence (see Hibbing 1982c) that a substantial amount of the variance in the number of voluntary retirements (during the twentieth century at least) can be explained by salary increases, redistricting, pension improvements, allegiance to the seniority norm, and a counter variable (the latter simply records the passage of the years in an effort to capture the decreasing turnover accompanying the House's institutionalization).[4]

This line of thought receives a substantial boost from the events of 1992. Voluntary retirements were up 400 percent from 1990 not because the nature of the job changed dramatically in the course of 24 months, but because many members were scared by redistricting, a close call in the previous election, bounced checks, or, worse yet, some combination of the above. Several other retirees were in a position to convert hundreds of thousands of dollars in campaign contributions to personal financial windfalls, though most made knowingly unverifiable protestations that they would not do so.

---

[4]Some of the historical work on congressional career moves has been concerned with the status of the House *vis-à-vis* the Senate. Do representatives leave to run for the Senate or do senators leave to run for the House (see E. Swift 1989)?

So, with regard to voluntary departures from elective office, the key conclusion seems to be that decisions are motivated by the same things that motivate most people: financial considerations, concern for insuring comfortable retirement years, the desire to avoid losing face, and by calculations concerning the opportunities for career advancement.

THE INTERNAL CONGRESSIONAL CAREER

Increasingly through the years, extended portions of the entire careers of some elected officials have taken place within the House. Numerous modern representatives have served 20-, 30-, and 40-year stints in the House. The study of congressional careers needs to reflect this fact. It is not enough to document that careers are longer than they used to be. It is not enough to know why members arrive and why they depart. What we need to know more about is how representatives evolve over the course of what are now frequently lengthy careers. At what rate do representatives acquire formal House positions? Do they pay less attention to constituents as they stay in the House (see Fenno 1978)? Do they become more active? More legislatively effective? More legislatively specialized? Do they alter their roll call behavior? Do they become more electorally savvy and successful?

In a recent manuscript (Hibbing 1991), I analyze the longitudinal patterns of many components of congressional life, including the electoral career, the roll call career, the legislative activity career (see also Canon 1990, 147-54), the constituency activity career, and the formal position career. Given space constraints, I will concentrate on the formal position careers of representatives (i.e., on what we know about the tendency of members of the House to move in to and out of formal committee or party positions), but it is important to note that our understanding of a wide variety of congressional behaviors would be significantly enhanced by the adoption of an individual-level, longitudinal perspective.

Generalizing about career paths within Congress is a hazardous endeavor. There are about as many "paths" as there are representatives (see Loomis 1988). Some members display formal position careers that are extraordinarily stable. James Delaney (D-NY) entered the House in 1949 and immediately went on the Rules Committee. He spent the next 28 years there, casting several monumental votes along the way. For 26 of those years, Delaney's formal responsibilities within the House changed not at all—no party leadership positions and no subcommittee chairs. After 26 years, Delaney finally became Chair of the Rules

Committee; a position he held for only one term before he promptly retired from public service. Similarly, Edward Patten (D-NJ), after first being elected to the House in 1962, spent a single term on the Science and Technology Committee before jumping to Appropriations where he remained—without getting a subcommittee chair or seeking any party posts—for the next 16 years.

Other members display formal position careers that are incredibly unstable. Consider the House career of Olin Teague (D-TX). Teague was first elected in 1946, in a House class that included John F. Kennedy, Richard Nixon, and Carl Albert, and immediately took a seat on the Veterans Affairs Committee. By 1955 he had worked his way up to Committee Chair, but he had also taken a spot on the District of Columbia Committee—in fact, he had a subcommittee chair on the latter. In addition, Teague was a charter member of the Science and Aeronautics Committee, and he subsequently chaired the Manned Space Flight Subcommittee. In 1971, the personally popular Teague capitalized on his racquetball connections and good-old-boy style to swipe the chairmanship of the Democratic Caucus from a startled Dan Rostenkowski, who forgot to look over his shoulder while eyeing the position of Majority Leader. Two years later, Teague traded his Veteran's Affairs Chair (while retaining the number two ranking) for the top position on Science and Aeronautics, and two years after that, "Tiger" Teague, as he was commonly called, rotated out of the Caucus Chair as is required by caucus rules. Before retiring in 1978, he also added several terms of service on the Ethics Committee to his continuing positions on Science and Aeronautics and Veterans Affairs.

Teague's Texas colleague, Omar Burleson, was a rarity in that he gave up a full committee chairmanship in 1971 to transfer to the bottom of the seniority ladder on another committee. Such an action is easier to understand when it is noted that he moved to the Ways and Means Committee from the pre-Wayne Hays Administration Committee (though Burleson also was forced to give up the chairmanship of a powerful Foreign Affairs subcommittee). Still, the norm is for this kind of move to be made before the member becomes chair of a committee. In Burleson's case, he was strongly encouraged to move by the powerful Texas delegation and by the oil industry, both of which wanted a forceful and sympathetic voice in Ways and Means' discussions of the oil depletion allowance and related matters. The tremendously disparate nature of these few House careers demonstrates the need for statements about "typical" careers to be interpreted with considerable caution.

Party Positions

What do we know about the correlates of acquiring House positions? With respect to positions of party leadership, we know, for example, that ideological moderates are most likely to obtain party positions in Congress, although there is some controversy here as to whether the moderation is a precondition or a result of being a party leader (see Truman 1959; Hinckley 1970; Sullivan 1975; Loomis 1984). We know that in the House, more so than in the Senate, there is a leadership ladder such that it is common for the Whip to move up to Party Leader and for the Party Leader to move up to Speaker, although Republicans are less likely than Democrats to abide by this type of practice (see Peabody 1976; Nelson 1977; and Canon 1989, for a summary of much of this literature). We know that those embarking on a party leadership track usually have a safe seat (see Peabody 1976, 471), and, relatedly, a fair bit of seniority, although the moderately precarious electoral situation of Robert Michel's Peoria district and the rapid ascension of junior members such as Tony Coelho (before his even more rapid descent) and Newt Gingrich suggest all this may be changing in the House (and as the cases of Lyndon Johnson and Howard Baker testify, seniority appears never to have been a requirement for party leadership in the Senate). We know that the parties now feel some pressure to make sure blacks, hispanics, and women are represented in the expanded party organization (see Loomis 1984, 187). And we know some of the correlates of being appointed to Speaker's Task Forces (see Sinclair 1981; Garand 1990).

Thus, with regard to party positions, we know a little about patterns of ascension once a member is on the leadership ladder, but outside of a few anecdotes and some hypotheses about the effects of ideology and seniority/electoral safety (for which empirical testing has produced inconclusive results), we are not in a position to understand let alone to predict who will want to dabble in the leadership and who will not. As one member told Loomis, "you've got to ask yourself, 'Do you want to sit on the heating and ventilating subcommittee or do you want to become a whip?'" (1984, 194). In the end we do not know much about why some members choose to become a whip and others do not.

Committee Positions

Committee position options are structured quite differently from those involving party positions. Since everyone has committee assignments and since the seniority norm is relevant, the issue is not who comes on board and who does not; and the issue is not who moves up and who does not. The issue is why some committee careers are characterized by stable progression while others are distinguished by fits and starts, reversals and alterations. What is known about committee position paths?

The major contributors to our understanding of the committee assignment process are Charles Bullock (see, for example, 1972, 1973, and 1976) and Kenneth Shepsle (1978). The initial committee assignments given to newly elected members are obviously important. Research indicates that freshmen are usually given their requests, since these preferences probably reflect the issues that are relevant to the district, the member's previous occupation, and strategic considerations such as whether or not it is realistic to expect to acquire a seat on a highly valued committee. Why are some new members more likely than others to have their requests honored? In addition to political reasons (being from a large state and knowing the correct people), conventional wisdom (see Masters 1961) is that electorally marginal members will be more likely to get their wish, but empirical support has never been marshalled to support this wisdom (see Bullock 1972). Other research has explored why some new members list second and third committee choices while others mention only one and has attempted to determine the success rate of the different strategies (see Shepsle 1978).

Some scholars have investigated why certain nonfreshman members attempt to transfer to a new committee. Unfortunately, the usual purpose is to establish the pecking order of committees. Other than this, the major findings have been the unsurprising ones that poor initial assignments encourage requests for transfer at a later time, just as seniority discourages transfer requests (there is more to give up by transferring).

So committee assignments have received some attention (see Eulau 1984 for a good summary), but the requests of freshmen and the responses of the committee on committees to these requests have attracted the largest amount of scholarly work to date. Committee transfers deserve more research. They can do more than reveal which committees are desirable and which are undesirable. They can tell us about career progressions. It would be helpful to know, for example, once seniority and the desirability of initial assignment are controlled, who moves and who does not. Are the correlates related to the correlates *office*-seeking behavior? What about the contextual effects on transferring? Did the amount of transferring change with the devaluation of seniority in the 1970s (Copeland's research [1987] suggests it did not)?

The lack of much information on mid-career committee transfers is indicative of a larger tendency to avoid looking at position careers over time. Scholars do not frequently trace individual careers from year to year, and they should. In other words, too much of the previous research is cross-sectional when it should be longitudinal. When it is longitudinal, an undue emphasis is often placed on a small number of classes (or even a single class). Other problems also exist with most research on internal career moves. Individual positions are usually treated separately from each other so that conclusions obtained for, say, subcommittee chairs are not necessarily valid for members of the Steering and Policy Committee. Finally, attempts to understand internal position advancement generally fail to control for the overall contextual increase from the 1950s to the 1980s in the total number of positions available.

Combining Party and Committee Positions

To avoid some of these problems, I asked journalists, top-level congressional staffers, and political scientists to rate positions in the House on a scale of 1 to 100. Utilizing the resultant mean ratings (presented in Table 3.1), I was then able to compile each representative's position(s) onto a common metric, thus avoiding separate conclusions for separate positions. Further, this calculation was performed for all Democratic members of all congresses from 1955 till 1986. This permits analysis of more than just selected classes, and, most important, it allows for standardization across congresses (to control for the growing number of positions in the House). The restriction to Democrats is necessary since many of the relevant positions are only available to members of the majority party, which was the Democratic party for this entire period. A more complete description of these procedures is available in Hibbing 1991, Chapter 3.

To illustrate the advantages of these procedures, consider the many unresolved questions concerning the changing rate at which members acquire quality House positions. Conventional wisdom holds that members of the House are now able to advance to positions of authority much more quickly than was the case years ago when a rigid seniority norm made progression painstakingly slow. Somewhat surprisingly, empirical support for this widespread belief has been mixed, or worse. The most careful work on the topic is that done by Charles Bullock and

Table 3.1.   *Rating of Selected House Positions in the Modern Era*
Rating of Position

Position	Rating of Position
Party Leadership	
Speaker	100
Majority Leader	80
Majority Whip	59
Deputy Whip	34
Caucus Chair	39
Member of the Steering and Policy Committee	30
Committee Leadership	
Chair of Prestige Committee	72
Chair of a Policy/ Constituency Committee	59
Chair of a Less Desirable Committee	34
Subcommittee Leadership	
Chair of An Appropriations Subcommittee	56
Chair of a Subcommittee of a Policy Constituency Committee	40
Chair of a Subcommittee of a Less Desirable Committee	17
Committee Membership	
Member of a Prestige Committee	34
Member of a Policy/Constituency Committee	17
Member of Less Desirable Committee	1

Burdett Loomis (1985; see also, Loomis 1984). The major interpretation from their tables is that on occasion conventional wisdom is supported, but on many other occasions career progression in recent years is as slow as it was years ago. For example, after one portion of their analysis, Bullock and Loomis conclude that there is "no clear trend for legislators to become their party's most senior member [chair or ranking minority member] on a committee earlier in their careers" (1985, 75). Elsewhere they note that "the survivors of earlier classes were more likely to be senior members of subcommittees after five terms than were the representatives elected in 1979 (1985, 76). To be sure, at some junctures they detect evidence of the expected contour change, but the key point here is that support for conventional wisdom is anything but pristine. As a result, previous research makes it impossible to say for sure whether or not recent careers are characterized by a more rapid acquisition of formal positions.

The procedures described earlier make it possible to explore the rate of position acquisition. To begin, the mean class position rankings are presented in Figure 3.2. Despite the fact that all classes from 1955 to 1985 are available, I present just four sample classes for inspection. Placing any more than four classes on a single graph makes it difficult to read. As can be seen from the figure, members of all classes acquired better positions later in their careers. No one doubted that this was the case. What we want to know is whether or not there was a change in the rate at which these better positions are acquired. Unfortunately, the rapidly changing context of the House renders it difficult to make this determination. More specifically, the main change from class to class in Figure 3.2 is that the intercept is constantly moving up. The class of 1957 in its first term averages 15.9 points, less on average than the equivalent of a single membership on a policy or constituency committee. Contrast this with the Class of 1975, which in its first term compiled an average formal position rating of over 30, nearly the equivalent of a chairmanship of a policy or constituency committee subcommittee.

These results are not unexpected given the tremendous increases taking place between 1957 and 1975 in the number of quality positions available. During this time, "lesser" party positions such as Whip, Deputy Whip, Caucus Chair, Caucus Secretary, Campaign Committee Chair, and Steering and Policy Committee member were either created or expanded. Exerting even greater influence on the intercepts in Figure 3.2 is the fact that the number of committees grew by two during this time period while the number of subcommittees grew at a very rapid rate, from 83 in the 84th Congress to 140 in the 96th. Moreover, existing committees (especially Ways and Means and later Rules) were allowed to grow in size, and the committee ratios of Democrats to Republicans was made more favorable to Democrats on several key committees. All these factors contributed to the growing number of positions available to House Democrats (see also Smith and Deering 1984, 51).

This contextual change must be controlled before we can say more about the true changes in the contours of the position career in the House. Such a control is introduced in Figure 3.3. Here, the positions of each representative are standardized for the changing number and quality of

Figure 3.2. *Mean Position Rating for Four House Classes*

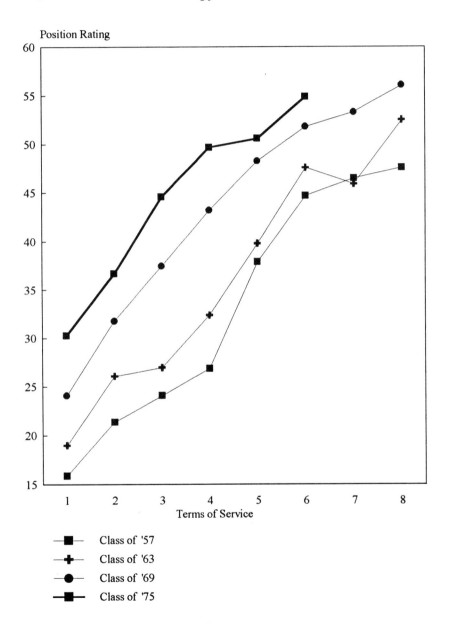

Position Rating

Terms of Service

- ■ Class of '57
- + Class of '63
- ● Class of '69
- ■ Class of '75

**Figure 3.3.   *Mean Position Rating for Four House Classes, Relative to
the Existence of Positions in Each Congress***

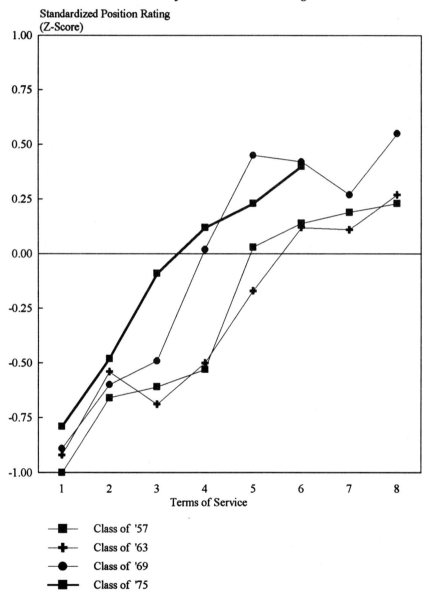

Standardized Position Rating
(Z-Score)

Terms of Service

———■——— Class of '57
———+——— Class of '63
———●——— Class of '69
———■——— Class of '75

positions available to Democrats in that congress. Any value below a z-score of 0 means formal positions less than the mean in the pertinent congress. A value over 0 represents formal positions greater than the mean.

Figure 3.3 makes it clear that conventional wisdom is accurate in anticipating that formal positions are acquired more quickly than used to be the case, although some qualifications deserve to be appended. The four classes all increase by about the same amount from their first to their second terms, but after this, the similarity ends. From their second to third terms, the Class of 1957 improves ever so slightly, the Class of 1963 actually sees its positions-held situation decline relative to other Democrats in the 90th Congress, and the Class of 1969 improves only modestly. The Class of 1975, however, improves markedly from .48 standard deviations below the mean to very nearly the mean (-.09). As we move from the third to the fourth terms, the Class of 1969 makes up a lot of ground on the Class of 1975, but the two earlier classes lag far behind, even though the scores have been standardized. At the fourth term of their respective careers, the mean position score for the earlier classes of 1957 and 1963 are -.53 and -.50 respectively while the later classes of 1969 and 1975 have already surpassed the average score for all Democrats in the corresponding congresses (z-scores of .02 and .12 respectively). However, by the seventh term, the earlier classes have nearly caught up.

Thus, significant movements come early for recent classes; later for earlier classes. While conventional wisdom is largely accurate, it turns out that the distinction between recent and earlier careers is much more ephemeral than had been thought. Class differences are generally insignificant except for those members in their third, fourth, fifth, and sixth terms who now are likely to have a greater share of the internal House positions than their counterparts 30 years ago. So there has been a shift in the contours of careers, and this shift is not simply a function of more positions being available today than yesterday. The new career contour is one that shows earlier gains but little difference in status by the later stages of the career (it is even possible that this pattern may have been a factor in some voluntary retirement decisions, consistent with our earlier discussion of changes in the seniority system).

RECOMMENDATIONS FOR FURTHER RESEARCH

In addition to the lack of attention to the Senate,[5] and the absence of truly longitudinal research on individual representatives, three big problems exist in the study of congressional careers. For the most part, these problems can be placed at the doorstep of inadequate theory. We supposedly have a theoretical undergirding for the study of external careers. It is called ambition theory, and it is almost invariably traced to the important 1966 work of Joseph Schlesinger, *Ambition and Politics*. Studies by Prewitt and Nowlin (1969), Prewitt (1970), Mezey (1970), Fishel (1971), Black (1972), Hain (1974), Rohde (1979), Hibbing (1982b), Brace (1985), and Canon (1990) all pay homage to the ambition theory of Joseph Schlesinger. It has become the obligatory cite. But the truth of the matter is that we currently have no theory of ambition available and the mistaken notion that we do has become a major hindrance to the study of congressional careers and perhaps political careers more broadly.

Schlesinger's imaginative and deservedly influential book makes many contributions, but it does not provide a theory of ambition. As stated by Schlesinger, "the central assumption of ambition theory is that a politician's behavior is a response to his office goals" (1966, 6). So far, so good. But problems arise when office goals are equated with office-seeking behavior, when offices are employed where positions should have been, and when this "central assumption" goes untested.

Schlesinger and many of those following in his wake proceed as if office goals can be inferred from office-seeking behavior. In this scheme, if a representative runs for the Senate, he/she has progressive ambition; if the representative runs for reelection in the House, he/she has static ambition; and if the representative retires voluntarily from public service, he/she has discrete ambition. These assumptions are unwarranted. Many of those running for reelection to the House would give their eye-teeth for a Senate seat but recognize that they would lose. Some representatives who are retiring from public service have not lost all ambition but simply understand that their electoral situations have become untenable.

The larger point is that we probably cannot measure ambition (office goal) since it is a psychological predisposition. I appreciate the desire to assume behavior can be employed as a surrogate for this predisposition

----

[5]On progressive ambition in the Senate, see Abramson, Aldrich, Rohde 1987.

(Schlesinger) as well as the desire to assume all politicians have progressive ambition (Rohde), but in the end both of these assumptions are flawed. We can measure opportunity. This is why we are able to discover that representatives will be more likely to run for a Senate seat if it is open. But we cannot currently determine the effects of ambition once opportunity is controlled.[6] Research in this area should not pretend that it is about ambition when it is not. Schlesinger's work serves much better as a basis for "opportunity" theory than for ambition theory. Indeed, the chapter titles and text itself are dominated by the word opportunity.[7]

The second problem focuses specifically upon those representatives running for reelection to the House. Schlesinger's approach should stress *position*-seeking rather than *office*-seeking. By not doing so, he misses the fact that the numerous committee and party positions in the House make it possible for the entire gamut of position-seeking behavior to be demonstrated by those very people Schlesinger classifies as having static ambition. Progressive behavior can just as easily be displayed by running for Party Whip as by running for the Senate.

Recognizing this, research should be redirected toward the key question of why some members vent progressive ambitions by employing the many ladders *within* the House, while others do so by attempting to jump to a different institution with a different set of ladders, such as the Senate. Why do some members attempt to move up internally while others pursue external routes? We should not pretend that progressive ambition is only evident among those leaving the House to pursue political opportunities outside it. More work needs to be done on internal career moves.

Concentrating on the ladders within the House itself opens up an entire world of intricate and fascinating career moves and strategies. The internal opportunity structure is constantly evolving. Positions and bases of power change continuously and often at a break-neck pace. Electoral defeat suddenly ends the career of a well-placed member; scandal brings down two Democratic party leaders within a few weeks; a plane crash claims the life of a central figure; the seniority system is revamped; the Rules Committee is brought to heel; a new subcommittee is created; a

---

[6]Unless there is a desire to attempt to ascertain ambition by constructing elaborate psychological profiles (see Barber 1972; Laswell 1948) or by hooking representatives to machines.

[7]See, for example, 1966, 8, 11-12.

committee chair's frailty finally becomes too much; redistricting shuffles the deck. As a result, internal goals and opportunities are probably more fluid than external goals and opportunities. Research on internal careers may be correspondingly more difficult, but it would also be more rewarding.

The final problem with extant knowledge of congressional careers involves testing the central tenet of so-called ambition theory. Although I do not believe we can accurately measure them, I heartily agree with the contention that office goals affect behavior. Unfortunately, this central tenet of ambition theory is not tested by Schlesinger. Very little of *Ambition and Politics* addresses the actions politicians take in order to put themselves in a position to acquire another office. Schlesinger believes that "our ambitious politician must act today in terms of the electorate of the office he hopes to win tomorrow" (1966, 6). But he does not test the veracity of this belief and few have since.[8]

Schlesinger's observations need to be tempered with realism about our inability to measure ambition and our resultant need to rely upon surrogates such as office-seeking behavior—surrogates that are obviously contaminated by the divergent opportunities that present themselves to politicians.

Schlesinger's observations need to be broadened. Representative Phil Landrum was ambitious for a seat on the Ways and Means Committee, but he knew his conservative voting record would prohibit him from acquiring one. He promptly became much more liberal and after a few years was rewarded with a Ways and Means slot at which time he became conservative again (see Shepsle 1978). He was acting today in terms of the position (not office) he hoped to win tomorrow, and his actions were directed at the Committee on Committees (not an "electorate") but the principle is the same.

---

[8]For exceptions, see Hibbing (1986), and Herrick and Moore (1990). In both of these instances, however, it is instructive to note that office-seeking behavior (leaving the House to run for the Senate) was used as a measure of office goals. Herrick and Moore explicitly note (p. 5) that there were undoubtedly other House members who wanted to run for the Senate and therefore behaved in the House in such a way as to facilitate a run for the Senate but who demurred from ever making the run, not for want of ambition but for want of opportunity. In fact, they conclude their paper with a call for "a more sophisticated indicator of ambition" (p. 11).

Most significantly, Schlesinger's observations need to be tested systematically. What behaviors are undertaken as a result of an elected politician's attempts to secure a different (or the same) position? Only by knowing the answer to this question will we begin to appreciate the consequences and anticipated consequences of career-path decisions. If Schlesinger is correct when he writes that "in politics the relation between motive and action is more obvious than in any other social endeavor" (1966, 1), political scientists have done a very poor job of elucidating the obvious.

REFERENCES

Abramson, Paul R., John H. Aldrich, and David W. Rohde. 1987. "Progressive Ambition among United States Senators: 1972-1988." *Journal of Politics* 49:3-35.

Barber, James D. 1972. *The Presidential Character*. Englewood Cliffs, N. J.: Prentice Hall.

Bauer, Monica, and John R. Hibbing. 1989. "Which Incumbents Lose in House Elections." *American Journal of Political Science* 33: 262-71.

Black, Gordon. 1972. "A Theory of Political Ambition." *American Political Science Review* 66:144-59.

Brace, Paul. 1984. "Progressive Ambition in the House." *Journal of Politics* 46:556-71.

_____. 1985. "A Probabilistic Approach to Retirement from the U.S. Congress." *Legislative Studies Quarterly* 10:107-24.

Bullock, Charles S., III. 1972. "Freshman Committee Assignments and Reelection in the United States House of Representatives." *American Political Science Review* 66:996-1007.

_____. 1973. "Committee Transfers in the United States House of Representatives." *Journal of Politics* 35:85-120.

_____. 1976. "Motivations for U.S. Congressional Committee Preferences." *Legislative Studies Quarterly* 1:201-12.

_____, and Burdett Loomis. 1985. "The Changing Congressional Career." In *Congress Reconsidered Third Edition*, ed. Lawrence C. Dodd and Bruce I. Oppenheimer, Washington D.C.: Congressional Quarterly Press.

Canon, David T. 1989. "Institutionalization of Leadership in the U.S. Congress." *Legislative Studies Quarterly* 14:415-43.

_____. 1990. *Actors, Athletes, and Astronauts*. Chicago: Chicago University Press.

Cooper, Joseph, and William West. 1981a. "The Congressional Career in the 1970s." In *Congress Reconsidered Second Edition*, ed. Lawrence C. Dodd and Bruce I. Oppenheimer, Washington D.C.: Congressional Quarterly Press.

_____. 1981b. "Voluntary Retirement, Incumbency, and the Modern House." *Political Science Quarterly* 96:279-300.

Copeland, Gary W. 1987. "Seniority and Committee Transfers: Career Planning in the Contemporary House of Representatives." *Journal of Politics* 49:553-64.

_____. 1989. "Choosing to Run: Why House Members Seek Election to the Senate." *Legislative Studies Quarterly* 14:549-66.

Cover, Albert. 1981. "The Greening of Congress: Patterns of Voluntary Retirement." Paper presented at the annual meeting of the Midwest Political Science Association, Cincinnati, Ohio.

Erikson, Robert S. 1971. "The Advantage of Incumbency in Congressional Elections." *Polity* 8:623-32.

Eulau, Heinz. 1984. "Legislative Committee Assignments." *Legislative Studies Quarterly* 9:587-634 .

Fenno, Richard F., Jr. 1978. *Home Style: House Members in Their Districts.* Boston: Little Brown.

Fishel, Jeff. 1971. "Ambition and the Political Vocation." *Journal of Politics* 33:25-56.

Frantzich, Stephen E. 1978a. "De-Recruitment: The Other Side of the Congressional Equation." *Western Political Quarterly* 31:105-26.

_____. 1978b. "Opting Out: Retirement from the House of Representatives." *American Politics Quarterly* 6:251-73.

Garand, James. 1990. "Membership of Speaker's Task Forces." *American Politics Quarterly* 18:81-102.

Hain, Paul. 1974. "Age, Ambition, and Political Careers." *Western Political Quarterly* 27:265-74.

Herrick, Rebekah, and Michael K. Moore. 1990. "Ambition's Influence on Behavior: An Analysis of Congressional Careers." Paper presented at the annual meeting of the American Political Science Association, San Francisco, September 1990.

Hibbing, John R. 1982a. "Voluntary Retirement from the U.S. House: The Costs of Congressional Service." *Legislative Studies Quarterly* 7:57-74.

_____. 1982b. "Voluntary Retirement from the U.S. House of Representatives: Who Quits?" *American Journal of Political Science* 26:467-84.

_____. 1982c. "Voluntary Retirements from the House in the Twentieth Century." *Journal of Politics* 44:1020-34.

_____. 1986. "Ambition in the House: Behavioral Consequences of Higher Office Goals Among U.S. Representatives." *American Journal of Political Science* 30:651-65.

_____. 1991. *Congressional Careers: Contours of Life in the U.S. House of Representatives.* Chapel Hill, N.C.: University of North Carolina Press.

Hinckley, Barbara. 1970. "Congressional Leadership Selection and Support: A Comparative Analysis." *Journal of Politics* 32:268-87.

Jacobson, Gary C., and Samuel Kernell. 1983. *Strategy and Choice in Congressional Elections.* New Haven, Conn.: Yale University Press.

Jardine, Stephen. Undated. "Career Obstacles and the Retirement of Middle Age Members of Congress." Unpublished paper. University of Oklahoma.

Lasswell, Harold. 1948. *Power and Personality.* Stanford, Calif.: Stanford University Press.

Loomis, Burdett A. 1984. "Congressional Careers and Party Leadership in the Contemporary House of Representatives." *American Journal of Political Science* 28:180-202.

_____. 1988. *The New American Politician.* New York: Basic Books.

Masters, Nicholas A. 1961. "Committee Assignments." *American Political Science Review* 55:345-57.

Mezey, Michael. 1970. "Ambition Theory." *Journal of Politics* 32: 563-79.

Nelson, Garrison. 1977. "Partisan Patterns of House Leadership Change, 1789-1977." *American Political Science Review* 71:918-39.

Payne, James L. 1982. "Career Intentions and the Performance of Members of the U.S. House." *Legislative Studies Quarterly* 7:93-100.

Peabody, Robert L. 1976. *Leadership in Congress.* Boston: Little Brown.

Prewitt, Kenneth. 1970. "Political Ambitions, Volunteerism, and Electoral Accountability." *American Political Science Review* 64:5-17.

_____, and William Nowlin. 1969. "Political Ambitions and the Behavior of Incumbent Politicians." *Western Political Quarterly* 22:298-308.

Rohde, David W. 1979. "Risk-Bearing and Progressive Ambition: The Case of the United States House of Representatives." *American Journal of Political Science* 23:1-26.

Schlesinger, Joseph A. 1966. *Ambition and Politics.* Chicago: Rand McNally .

Shepsle, Kenneth A. 1978. *The Giant Jigsaw Puzzle.* Chicago: University of Chicago Press.

Sinclair, Barbara. 1981. "The Speaker's Task Force in the Post-Reform House of Representatives." *American Political Science Review* 75: 397-410.

Smith, Steven S., and Christopher J. Deering. 1984. *Committees in Congress.* Washington, D.C.: Congressional Quarterly Press.

Sullivan, William E. 1975. "Criteria for Selecting Party Leadership in Congress." *American Politics Quarterly* 3:25-44.

Swift, Al. 1989. "The Permanent Congress is a Myth." *Washington Post Weekly* 6 (June 26-July 2):29.

Swift, Elaine K. 1989. "Reconstitutive Change in the U.S. Congress." *Legislative Studies Quarterly* 14:175-204.

Truman, David. 1959. *The Congressional Party.* New York: John Wiley.

Careers of Legislators
in Subnational Governments

Introduction

Edward L. Lascher, Jr.
Harvard University

Throughout this volume we have argued that the political careers of elected officials, both within and between institutions, are ripe for further study. This is particularly true with respect to research on lawmakers in American subnational governments. Despite the fact that most of the approximately one half million elected officials in this country (McLeod 1989) are subnational legislators of some type (state lawmakers, county supervisors or commissioners, city council members, etc.), relatively little research has been conducted on their careers, especially in comparison to the attention given to members of Congress.

The limited attention accorded to state and local lawmakers is especially unfortunate given political scientists' emphasis on the structure of opportunities. While the opportunities available to members of Congress may vary significantly, such differences pale in comparison to those facing different subnational legislators. Some state and local lawmakers are virtual shoo-ins if they decide to seek reelection, while others commonly face stiff opposition (for example, incumbent California state legislators are significantly more electorally secure than incumbent California county supervisors; see Lascher 1989). Some subnational legislators represent tiny populations and hence have meager political bases for seeking higher office, while others number their constituents in the tens or even hundreds of thousands. Some state and local lawmaking positions have historically been used as political springboards, while others have not. As Peverill Squire emphasizes in his chapter, the 99 state legislatures "vary on almost every characteristic thought to matter in the study of legislatures: membership size, district size and type, partisanship, level of professionalization, cost of campaigning, etc." This conclusion about institutional differences would only be reinforced by extending Squire's observation to local lawmaking bodies.

In our contributions to this section, Squire and I aim to use research on state and local lawmakers to augment what has been learned through the dominant ambition theory approach to political careers. Our orientations differ significantly, however. Focusing on state legislators, Squire emphasizes the importance of structural factors that have not been adequately explored in previous research. Drawing from research on local lawmakers in California, I stress the significance of personal evaluations of previous elective positions, independent of the structure of opportunities.

More specifically, Squire argues that the career choice of an individual state legislator is a function of the interaction between the prospects for advancement to higher office and the level of compensation provided state lawmakers. While the former is commonly emphasized by ambition theorists, Squire's research is unique in stressing the latter. After summarizing key trends with regard to state lawmakers, such as the increasing portion of legislators who devote themselves full time to their positions, Squire offers a system for classifying legislatures in terms of the career opportunities available to incumbents and prospective members. He finds significant differences in office tenure across these different types of legislatures, and explains these differences in terms of the varying incentives lawmakers face.

Beginning with Joseph Schlesinger (1966), ambition theorists commonly have hypothesized that differences in career plans affect officeholders' behavior but, with a few exceptions, have been less effective at providing evidence to support this claim (see Hibbing, this volume). Furthermore, they have concentrated almost entirely on advancement *between* institutions, not *within* them. Squire's own research and his review of other work support the notion that differing career orientations matter to the way legislatures operate. He also points to studies showing that the willingness of members to serve a greater number of terms is associated with longer apprenticeship for legislative leaders.

While Squire indicates that an increasingly sophisticated view of incentives facing state legislators can shed significant light on career decisions, he emphasizes that much remains to be learned. He finds that more systematic information is needed about how career patterns affect the influence exercised by external actors such as bureaucrats and lobbyists. We have not yet reached the point where we can "feel confident that we understand legislative careers," he writes.

In my chapter I stress the need to move beyond structural incentives and to consider how legislators are influenced by their experiences in elective office. I reject the notion that lawmakers are equally ambitious given the same set of opportunities (see for example Rohde 1979), arguing instead that individual differences in enthusiasm for political careers are very significant. In particular I emphasize the potential influence of job satisfaction on lawmakers' career decisions. I summarize key work satisfaction findings from industrial and organizational psychology, and suggest these may be applicable to legislators.

Because job satisfaction is rarely addressed by political scientists (for an important exception, although one that places greater emphasis on individual personality theory, see Barber 1965), I draw upon my own study of California county supervisors. I find that a high degree of work satisfaction is associated with ambitions beyond the county supervisorial level, while dissatisfaction is associated with the desire to leave the electoral politics arena altogether. Moreover, the impact of job satisfaction operates independently from a major structural factor influencing plans to seek higher office: the size of the constituency that a county supervisor represents. In making decisions about higher positions lawmakers look to experiences in past elective office for clues as to how happy they will be. My study suggests that future research should include efforts to use job satisfaction as a dependent variable.

REFERENCES

Barber, James D. 1965. *The Lawmakers: Recruitment and Adaptation to Legislative Life.* New Haven and London: Yale University Press.

Lascher, Edward L., Jr. 1989. "Must One Be Crazy to Do This Job? Causes and Consequences of Job Satisfaction Among Local Legislators." Unpublished ph.d. dissertation.

McLeod, Ramon G. 1989. "504,404 Politicians in U.S." *San Francisco Chronicle*, January 25, 1+.

Rohde, David. 1979. "Risk-Bearing and Progressive Ambition: The Case of Members of the United States House of Representatives." *American Journal of Political Science* 23:1-26.

Schlesinger, Joseph A. 1966. *Ambition and Politics: Political Careers in the United States.* Chicago: Rand McNally.

Chapter 4

State Legislative Careers

Peverill Squire
University of Iowa

Over the last three decades state legislatures have changed dramatically. Member salaries have increased markedly, sessions have grown longer, and facilities have been greatly improved (Rosenthal 1989). As a general result of this professionalization, state legislative careers have been changed, with significant implications for members and institutions (Moncrief and Thompson 1992). In particular, membership stability has increased, and state legislatures have, by and large, increased both their influence in the political process and stature relative to the governor.

Although state legislatures have changed, very little research on who serves in these bodies and why has been conducted (see, for instance, Jewell 1981; Matthews 1985). In this chapter I survey the literature on state legislative careers. I begin by discussing why state legislators are important to study and look at the sorts of people who serve as legislators. I then turn to an examination of legislative turnover and member career ambitions. I argue that the political and structural environments in which members serve determine the sorts of career ambitions they can reasonably pursue. These career orientations influence the internal organization of legislatures. There is an interactive relationship: members mold bodies to serve their career needs, and potential members are differentially attracted by a given structure. That is, members can change the rules determining how power within the body is allocated to better serve their goals. For example, a seniority system might be instituted when most members hold a long-term orientation to service. Such a system might, in turn, appeal to prospective members who would like to make service in that legislative body a career. In addition, the relationship between legislative careers and member performance, leadership tenures, and advancement opportunities are examined. Finally, I offer suggestions for future research directions.

STATE LEGISLATORS AS A SUBJECT OF STUDY

State legislators and their careers are worthy of extensive examination for at least three reasons. First, over the last decade the role of state legislatures in making public policy has become increasingly important. This has happened, in large part, because Reagan's New Federalism shifted much of the authority for making policy decisions and the burden for funding them away from the national government and to the states (Van Horn 1989; Nathan 1989). Simply stated, state legislatures are once again charged with making important decisions. Second, as Polsby (1975, 267-68) observes, most legislatures act as talent pools from which candidates for other governmental positions are drawn. State legislatures perform such a function in the American political system (Schlesinger 1966). In 1987, for example, 50 percent of all U.S. representatives had previously served in a state legislature, as had 38 percent of senators and 60 percent of governors. In addition, one recent president (Jimmy Carter), a Supreme Court justice (Sandra Day O'Connor) and several cabinet secretaries (e.g., Weinberger, Derwinski, Martin, Madigan) had been state legislators.

The third reason is methodological. Over 7,400 people serve in state legislatures. The 99 bodies in which they serve vary on almost every characteristic thought to matter in the study of legislatures: membership size, district size and type, partisanship, level of professionalization, cost of campaigning, etc. Despite this great variation, state legislatures are inherently comparable. Problems produced by differences in political cultures and traditions among the states pale in comparison to those faced in comparative analyses of national legislatures (Loewenberg 1972, 14). The benefit of this to students of legislatures is that, as Price (1975, 20) observed, "One does not need to go, like Darwin, to the Galapagos Islands to rediscover long missing species of legislative operation."

BACKGROUNDS

During the first half of this century, state legislatures were dispropor-tionately populated by lawyers and farmers: each group represented over 20 percent. Other occupations were usually represented as well (Hyneman 1940; Zeller 1954, 71; Key 1956, 258-63). Recent data (Bazar 1987) show a significant decline in the number of attorneys serving in state legislatures, to 16 percent in 1986. Indeed, in the state of Delaware, not a single lawyer serves in the General Assembly. The percentage of farmers holding legislative office also has declined, to 10 percent. This is not surprising given their decrease as a percentage of the nation's population. Most farmer-legislators are found in Iowa, Kansas, Nebraska, and the Dakotas.

The number of members claiming full-time legislator as their occupation has increased substantially. Forty years ago, very few, if any, legislators made such a claim. Now, 11 percent do. As Table 4.1 shows, the percentage of full-time legislators is strongly related to the professionalization level of the legislature (Squire 1992a, 1988a; Rosenthal 1989). Moreover, these numbers probably underestimate the number of full-time legislators in the more professionalized bodies (Rosenthal 1989, 99; Stavisky 1981, 708) In Michigan, for example, observers believe that two-thirds of the members are full-time legislators (Rosenthal 1989, 72), but none of the members will publicly admit it because they fear negative electoral repercussions (Bazar 1987, 4). Those who admit to being full-time legislators are concentrated in the most professionalized legislatures, such as California and New York. In a majority of states, however, very few members claim to make their living from public office.

A wide variety of other occupations are represented in current legislatures. Most prominent among these are educator (8 percent), business owner (14 percent), and business employee (11 percent). The number of homemakers, students, and retirees combined is just 9 percent. They are concentrated in the highly unprofessionalized New Hampshire and Vermont legislatures, constituting 48 percent and 25 percent of the membership respectively.

The number of women and minorities serving at the state level has increased over the last few decades. In 1986 women held 15 percent of all state legislative seats, blacks 5 percent, and Hispanics 2 percent (Stanley and Niemi 1988, 333-34.) As we would expect, blacks are elected to legislatures in states where they represent a substantial percentage of the population. What may be unexpected is that the percentage of blacks in a legislature is positively related to the body's level of professionalization (Squire 1992a). The percentage of women serving in state legislatures is negatively related to level of professionalization (Squire 1992a, but see Nechemias 1987). Certainly, women who are homemakers, students, or retired serve in large numbers in more amateur legislatures, but those working in the professions or business world also are less likely to be elected to seats in more professionalized bodies.

Table 4.1. *Prior Political Experience of Representatives and*
                Senators

State	Profession-alization	Percent Legislator	State	Profession-alization	Percent Legislator
NY	.659[a]	60[b]	LA	.185	3
MI	.653	0	OR	.183	7
CA	.625	36	SC	.178	4
MA	.614	55	VA	.170	1
PA	.336	65	ME	.161	7
OH	.329	33	MS	.160	0
AK	.311	0	NV	.160	0
IL	.302	47	AL	.158	1
CO	.300	9	KS	.152	0
MO	.287	18	RI	.148	0
HA	.276	14	VT	.145	0
WI	.270	42	IN	.139	1
FL	.225	13	TN	.135	0
NJ	.255	13	GA	.133	4
AZ	.250	13	WV	.125	1
OK	.250	1	ID	.119	0
CT	.233	20	MT	.110	0
WA	.230	0	AR	.105	0
LA	.225	9	KY	.101	0
TX	.210	3	NM	.098	0
MD	.204	1	SD	.083	0
NC	.203	1	UT	.082	0
MN	.199	6	ND	.075	1
DL	.192	0	WY	.056	0
NE	.186	8	NH	.042	1

[a]The number is taken from Squire (1992A) and represents how closely the state legislature approximates the salary, time demands, and staff resources of congressional service in 1986-1987, with 1 representing equality.

[b]This number is taken from Bazar (1987) for the year 1986.

MEMBERSHIP STABILITY

It is difficult for any organization to function with a sizable proportion of its membership being replaced every two years, as has been the
case in many state legislatures during this century. Beginning with
Hyneman's (1938) initial study of the problem, most political scientists
have expounded the idea that more stable memberships are necessary to
produce less amateur legislatures and, consequently, better public policy
(e.g., Keefe 1966; Lockard 1966; Herzberg and Rosenthal 1971).
Generally this belief anticipates that state legislatures will follow the
pattern of institutionalization of the United States House of Representatives, with longer member service and less turnover as legislators begin
to see service in the body as an attractive career (Polsby 1968, 1975,
297).

Although several variables can be hypothesized to have an effect on
membership stability, I have demonstrated (Squire 1988a) that it is a
function of external advancement prospects and financial incentives. The
time demands a legislature places on its members, the level of staff
support and facilities provided to legislators, and the number of leadership positions available within the body do not matter. Whether stability
is measured as turnover, or mean years of member service, it is increased
by higher pay and decreased by high external advancement opportunities.

The opportunity for advancement beyond the lower house in different
states, as I measure it (Squire 1988a), depends primarily on the number
of seats in the upper house of that state and the size of its delegation in
the United States House of Representatives. Obviously other higher
elective offices are available: United States senator, governor, statewide
constitutional offices, and other idiosyncratic major offices like mayoralties and county executives. Because the most prominent of these
offices—U.S. senator and governor—do not vary in frequency across
states, the number of upper state house and congressional seats captures
most of the differences in advancement opportunities among states.[1]
Other things being equal—vacancies and party competition in particular—advancement opportunities should be greater the higher the ratio of

---

[1]There is also the possibility of using state legislative service as a springboard to nonelective political office. Addition of such opportunities might refine
the relationships described here.

the sum of seats in the upper house and the U.S. House to the number of seats in the lower house.[2]

Candidates for higher office, however, can come from outside the legislature as well as from within it. Thus, the extent to which prospects for advancement are good depends not only on the ratio of higher positions to lower seats, but also on the success previous members have had in advancing. Consequently, the measure I formulated for advancement prospects is the interaction of these variables—the ratio of higher elective positions to seats in the lower house and the percentage of those higher positions held by former members of the lower house.[3]

There is virtually no correlation between these two variables. That is, there is no linear relationship between the number of opportunities for advancement and the percentage of those spots filled by ex-lower house members. California, for instance, has favorable numbers on both variables; 1.04 higher positions to every seat in the lower house, with 50 percent of those spots filled by ex-members. Other states have either poor opportunity ratios (e.g., Vermont, .21:1), or no history of lower house members attaining those offices (e.g., Pennsylvania, .20; Rhode Island, .18). Thus, service in some legislatures offers great prospects for upward political mobility. In legislatures where prospects are dim other routes (e.g., positions in local government or with community groups) are pursued.

Finding that the level of pay determines whether a legislator can consider legislative service as a full-time career option is not surprising. Many studies have found financial problems to be a major reason state legislators leave office (e.g., Hyneman 1938; Wahlke et al. 1962, 127-28; Rosenthal 1974; Smith and Miller 1977; Francis and Baker 1986). Even

---

[2]On one level, being one of 1 million people in New Hampshire means one would have a better chance of becoming governor or senator than if one were a resident of California with 27 million people—although the odds in either state are extremely long. What I am arguing here is that the 120 state legislators in California have a better chance of becoming senator or governor than their 424 counterparts in New Hampshire because there are fewer of them to compete for the offices.

[3]Thus, if a legislative body had a ratio of 60 higher positions to 100 seats in the lower house, and 50 percent of the higher positions were held by former lower house members then the advancement prospect for that body would be .30. For a different measure of advancement prospects that produces similar results, see Rosenthal (1974, 612-13).

Blair and Henry (1981), who argue, based on their research in Arkansas, that family considerations are more important than financial considerations, still conclude that the latter are significant. Keep in mind that the level of compensation varies greatly across states. A few states, such as New Hampshire and Rhode Island, pay very little: in 1989, $200 and $300 respectively. Legislators in California, New York, and Michigan make more than $40,000 annually.

Almost all turnover in state legislatures is voluntary, not due to electoral defeat. Jewell and Breaux's (1988) analysis of 1968 to 1986 election results in 14 states shows that state legislative incumbents win reelection at rates similar to members of the U.S. House, and by even larger average margins (see also Calvert 1979; Ray and Havick 1981; Squire 1988b). Moreover, legislators are highly unlikely to be unseated by a primary loss (Grau 1981; Jewell 1982). State legislators leave on their own initiative.

Finally, the cost of campaigns is usually low and does not account for turnover. Comparative state legislative campaign spending data are rare (e.g., Sorauf 1988; Rosenthal 1981; Jones 1984). A few states, such as California, have expensive state legislative races, but most do not. In general, expenses increase with the population size of the legislative district (Rosenthal 1981). In most states, legislative elections are like congressional campaigns in that incumbents get most of the contributions, and challengers, who need the funds to be competitive, get very little (e.g., Sorauf 1988).

AMBITIONS AND CAREER OPPORTUNITIES

Many state legislators harbor progressive political ambitions (Rosenthal 1981, 54; Wahlke et al. 1962, 129; Francis and Baker 1986), particularly those who are under 45 years of age (Hain 1974, see also Squire 1988a, 76). But state legislators do not have equal probabilities of achieving their ambitions. As I have argued, the prospects for some are brighter than for others not just because of personal characteristics and abilities, but as a result of the structure of political opportunities in which they operate (Squire 1988a).

I assume that most potential candidates think strategically about public offices and the career possibilities they offer (Schlesinger 1966, 4; Jacobson and Kernell 1981, 22-23). For example, Rosenthal (1981, 50) observes:

Not many legislators in Arkansas . . . have any hope of higher office. In the past decade or so those who have run for higher office have been unsuccessful. No governor in memory came out of the legislature. Indeed, if an individual were interested in higher office, he or she would probably not have run for the legislature in the first place.

While individuals in any legislature may have a variety of career objectives, it is probable that structural factors will determine the utility of any given office in fulfilling certain career objectives (Schlesinger 1966, 10-11; Wahlke et al. 1962). It is likely that a majority of any legislature's membership have the same basic career aim. As Price (1975, 3) observes, "in general, any legislature will have some mixture of career types, but one type may be numerically predominant."

There is evidence to support this assertion. The Oklahoma House of Representatives, for example, is a body where members have poor prospects for political advancement. According to a survey of its members (Kirkpatrick 1978, 82), 48 percent have never considered seeking election or appointment to some other full-time political office. Another 8 percent have only thought a little about such a move. Just 18 percent of the representatives have thought a great deal about moving up.

This evidence supports the idea that legislatures offer a particular opportunity for a political career to their members and that individuals are differentially attracted to service. Divergent opportunities for political careers attract people with different ambitions as members. As a result, differences in opportunities for political careers account for observed contrasts in member turnover rates among legislatures.

Pay and advancement opportunities can be used to classify state legislatures in terms of the career opportunities they afford incumbent and prospective members (Squire 1988a). A *career legislature* offers sufficient financial incentives so that most members can make service within that body a career. It also usually requires members to devote a significant portion of their time to legislative duties, although this does not have to be the case. Most members enter the body with the expectation of long service. The obvious example of such a legislature is the modern United States House of Representatives.

A second type of body offers great opportunities for political advancement beyond it, and as such can be considered a *springboard legislature*. In Kansas, for example, Harder and Davis (1979, 151) report, "Members of the state House of Representatives regularly retire to run for the state Senate, and members of both houses use their positions to run for statewide or congressional office." A springboard legislature can have career characteristics in terms of compensation levels, but its utility to members as a stepping stone to better political positions makes it different. Describing New York state legislators between 1930 and 1960, Ruchelman (1970, 100) observed:

> For many of them, legislative office is but a way-station where they can establish eligibility for more desirable positions on the political career ladder. The act of departure, in such cases, is probably planned and anticipated from the moment of first arrival in the legislature.

Such behavior can be expected in legislative bodies located in political structures that have enough political offices that are attractive in terms of pay, prestige, or both, to make advancement to them desirable, as well as a history that suggests that members can attain them.

Not all legislatures are like the two described above. A third type can be considered a *dead end* because it gives its members so few prospects for advancement beyond it or incentives to stay within it.[4] As Keefe (1966, 68) notes of such situations, "simple arithmetic tells the member that the state legislature may be a dead end in politics. The governor's office, the governor's cabinet, the court, Congress—there are not enough good jobs to go around. . . . " Moreover, the lack of adequate financial incentives makes it difficult for members who are not independently wealthy to survive financially. As noted above, financial and family pressures can force a member to leave; such reasons are cited by many legislators who do not seek reelection. The plight of one Texas legislator evidences these problems (Flocke 1983, 11):

> After a week of meetings, hearings, sessions and appointments with lobbyists, reporters, and constituents, Billy Clemons loads his pick-up once more for the [200 mile] drive home. On Thursday nights . . . he'll work in the family restaurant. . . . The next two days he spends handling train orders for Southern Pacific. Sunday he works the restaurant again.

Thus, dead-end legislatures suffer great membership instability, because members have no incentive to stay. And, as suggested in the Arkansas example above, ambitious politicians in states with dead-end legislatures

---

[4]The concepts of career, springboard, and dead-end legislatures mirror Schlesinger's (1966, 10) individual level typology of static, progressive, and discrete political ambitions.

find alternative routes, such as district attorney or county supervisor, to Congress or other higher offices.

Using pay and advancement prospects I have classified the career type of 25 lower houses (Squire 1988a). I consider legislatures with high advancement prospects, *regardless* of financial incentives, as "springboard legislatures." Thus, a well-paying body like California is grouped with Alaska, New Jersey, South Carolina, and Washington, all of which are low-paying legislatures. "Career" legislatures are bodies that offer high pay but have low or moderate advancement prospects, such as New York and Pennsylvania. "Dead-end" legislatures, such as Connecticut, South Dakota, and West Virginia, are those with poor advancement prospects and no financial incentives to stay.

This typology is useful because legislatures with these different characteristics have contrasting patterns of membership stability (Squire 1988a). High-paying legislatures generally have longer tenure levels than low-paying legislatures. High-paying legislatures with good advancement opportunities have lower mean years of service than bodies with the same financial incentives but with more limited advancement prospects. Among high-incentive legislatures, the lowest tenure level is found in the one springboard body, California. California's figure is lower than the mean for all 25 legislatures studied. Among both high- and low-paying legislatures, mean years of service increase as advancement prospects decrease.

Mean tenure in low-paying legislatures is generally low. Legislatures with poor advancement prospects and low pay offer an interesting paradox. It is plausible to expect high turnover in such bodies because their members have no career reasons to stay. This seems to be the case in Connecticut, South Dakota, and West Virginia. Members might, however, remain in such legislatures because the demand on their time is low, and they may find their service rewarding in other, nonfinancial ways. Both Oklahoma and Virginia, which have high years of service figures, may exemplify this. Several of the dead-end legislatures have higher service averages than does California. This confirms the proposition that provision of adequate career incentives alone will not produce a career body because other factors, specifically advancement prospects, influence the ability of a legislature to retain its members.

Overall, career legislatures have the highest average years of service. The mean tenure in career bodies is over five years. Dead-end legislatures average just over four years of service, while springboard legislatures are less than four years. This last figure is lower than we might expect because several springboard bodies have many of the characteristics that might qualify them to be career legislatures. Yet they have the lowest tenure levels. Their only distinguishing feature is their ample advancement prospects.

The identification of springboard legislatures resolves an anomaly of legislative research. Patterson (1983, 156), for example, has puzzled about why the California Assembly's high member pay and excellent staff and facilities have not resulted in a more stable body. The answer is that the Assembly offers its members a successful route to other, higher political offices. Even with incentives that make long service within it attractive, a springboard legislature like the Assembly will suffer losses as members leave for higher posts. Thus the lower houses in California and New York, for example, have different levels of membership stability despite similar professionalization ratings.

THE EFFECTS OF DIFFERING CAREER OPPORTUNITIES

Internal Organization

The system by which positions of power, such as the speakership or committee chairs, are distributed in a legislature has been shown to be consistent with the career aspirations of the majority of members (Squire 1988b). In the New York Assembly, where members are well paid but have limited prospects for advancement, members adopt a long-term perspective toward their service. Although no explicit seniority rule exists, members gain power the longer they serve. Senior members dominate the leadership and get most of the positions on the important committees. Junior members serve on less important committees and have very limited opportunities to author legislation. Overall, service in this career body is very reminiscent of that in the U.S. House.

Like their New York counterparts, Connecticut representatives do not have good advancement prospects. But the Connecticut House fails to encourage members to pursue a career within it because it offers relatively low pay. Consequently, few representatives serve for very long. Organizationally, power is concentrated in the hands of the leadership. Seniority means little because few serve long enough to gain it. As a result of short tenures, most members have little opportunity to acquire expertise about government programs, or sufficient institutional knowledge to challenge the leadership. Thus most representatives have very little influence on policy decisions. Instead, on major issues they give their support to their party leaders and in return they get assistance in getting district bills passed.

Members of the California Assembly operate in a legislature where pay is good, and advancement opportunities are impressive. Basing legislative power on seniority makes little sense from the perspective of individual members. Most of them intend to jump at their first chance to move on to higher office. What they want is a system that allows them to gain power early in their careers. In the California Assembly members can hold leadership posts and positions on powerful committees without first accruing seniority. First-term members are able to author important legislation. Ex-Assembly members serving in the U.S. House have expressed a preference for the former's encouragement of more active legislative roles for junior members (BeVier 1979, 223; Bell and Price 1975, 169). (In addition, the compatibility of the California Assembly's internal organization with the career goals of its membership has significant implications for Polsby's (1968) concept of institutionalization. Although the California Assembly has developed like the House in many important respects, it has not adopted a seniority system. The concept of institutionalization needs to be expanded in order to allow for consideration of nonseniority-based power distribution systems (Squire 1992c.)

Differences in Legislative Performance

One of the tenets of legislative professionalization is that longer tenures will produce better, more informed legislators. Evidence to support this is sketchy. According to Bell and Price's (1975) study of members of the California Assembly, most legislators take two years to gain a working understanding of the legislative process. Studies by Francis (1962), Meyer (1980), and Weissert (1988) found that influence in the legislature was positively related to length of service. Along these same lines, Thompson and Moncrief (1988) found that more senior North Carolina legislators were better able to deliver pork barrel projects to their districts. But a study of Ohio state legislators found little difference between junior and senior members in their orientation toward reelection and constituency service as goals (Goodman et al. 1986).

Ambition has also been linked to behavior. Barber (1965) found that his "lawmakers"—those members who were ambitious for more power within the Connecticut legislature—were the most active policymakers. Soule (1969) determined that Michigan legislators with progressive career ambitions were more apt to make decisions not based on constituent concerns and to take state interest rather than local interests into account. There is some evidence that ambitious legislators at other governmental levels also adopt broader constituencies (e.g., Prewitt and Nowlin 1969; Black 1970; Hibbing 1986).

The effect of state legislative experience on performance in higher legislative office is not clear. Asher (1973) reports that first-year members of the U.S. House with state legislative experience did not have opinions on apprenticeship much different from their colleagues who had different political backgrounds. But Canon's (1989) discussion of amateurs in Congress reveals that more senior members of Congress think that former state legislators are more likely to have productive early careers.

Leadership Tenures

In the past, most state legislative leaders served only one or two terms. Indeed, in many states, by tradition leadership positions were regularly rotated. For example, Campbell (1980, 43), in a study of the lower houses in Illinois, Iowa, and Wisconsin during the late 1800s, found that 13 speakers served during the 15 legislative sessions he examined. This rotation system continues in many states: according to a 1980 leadership survey (Jewell 1980) 13 lower houses had a new speaker every term or two and another eight only had a single leader in a 33-year period who broke that mold. The only lower houses where one leader served six or more terms were in one-party states—Georgia, Mississippi, South Carolina, and Virginia.

Longer leadership tenures are important because they increase the power wielded by leaders, especially relative to the executive (Jewell and Patterson 1986, 119). Chaffey and Jewell (1972) examined leadership posts in eight lower state houses from 1945 to 1970 to link the process by which they were filled to the legislature's level of professionalization. They concluded that leaders in more professionalized bodies tended to have longer apprenticeships before achieving those positions and longer tenures once in them. They also suggested that clear patterns of succession were found in more professionalized legislatures. More recent studies tend to confirm these relationships (Squire 1992d).

State Legislative Service as a Springboard to Other Office

I have argued that the utility of state legislative service as a spring-board to higher office is determined by a state's political career structure and history (Squire 1988a). For the overwhelming majority of state legislators, legislative service is the apex of their political career. Although many may express progressive ambitions, only a few act on that desire (e.g., Hain 1976). A small number of state legislators do move up to other offices, often to the U.S. House. Robeck (1982) found that only about 1 percent of state legislators run for the House in any particular year and that most of these candidates are legislators serving in less professionalized bodies. (But Robeck does not tell us how likely legislators in a given state legislature are to run for the House.) Legislators in more professionalized bodies may not challenge an incumbent because they calculate that their prospects for winning the race are too low to risk losing their current position (e.g., Fowler and McClure 1989, 74-100). They are more apt to run when a seat is open (Robeck 1982; Squire and Wright 1990).

State legislators are more likely to win a House race than are those not holding that position (Squire and Wright 1990). Among state legislators, the prospects for winning a House seat increase with the size of the state legislative district represented. Those from large state districts, particularly in California, have had to raise large sums of money to contest those seats (Rosenthal 1981; Sorauf 1988) and are able to transfer that skill to congressional races and, thereby, get more votes (Squire and Wright 1990). It also is likely that legislators with district staff and greater resources to provide constituent services are advantaged when trying to move up the electoral ladder. But, while state legislators may move directly to the House, in recent years they have lost every attempt for the U.S. Senate (Squire 1989) and enjoyed very little success in winning the governorship (Squire 1992b).

State legislative leaders are not immune from progressive career ambitions. Simon's (1987, 250) examination of the career paths of the 99 state legislative presiding officers serving in 1981 reveals that 20 had sought higher office within six years, although only 10 were successful. These data suggest more than that a substantial number of leaders will seek other offices; they also demonstrate that leaders are not necessarily able to exploit their position to advance their political careers. This latter finding has been confirmed by an examination of the careers of legislative leaders in California, Iowa, and New York (Squire 1992d) and by a study of gubernatorial elections from 1977 to 1989 (Squire 1992b).

One affliction shared by all state legislators is a lack of media attention. State politics usually gets very little coverage and even legislative leaders are generally ignored (Squire 1992d; Stavisky 1981, 703). Individual legislators, particularly in rural districts, may get some attention from local media (Jewell 1982, 64). But, overall, current and potential constituents do not have much opportunity to learn about their state representatives. Not surprisingly, constituents know little if anything about their state legislators, including their names (e.g., Patterson, Hedlund, and Boynton 1975, 79; Jewell 1982, 177-79). These conditions magnify legislators' needs for campaign money, particularly to run for higher office.

DIRECTIONS FOR FUTURE RESEARCH

Certainly there is a great deal left to learn about state legislative careers. Most of what we know about the recruitment process is based on studies of state legislatures before the full effects of the professionalization revolution were realized (e.g., Key 1956; Sorauf 1963; Patterson and Boynton 1969; Seligman et al. 1974; Tobin and Keynes 1975). I would anticipate that recruitment patterns have changed as the value of state legislative office to the holder and others has increased.

Increased member careerism needs to be the focus of future state legislative research. On the individual level, we need to better understand how an individual approaches legislative service, to learn about his or her orientation towards a career in the organization. We need to determine how a long-term career orientation influences a legislator's behavior, compared to that adopted by a short-termer who intends to leave politics, or to move to higher office (e.g., Dodd and Kelly 1989). At the organizational level, legislatures filled with full-time legislators ought to assert their independence from other political entities, especially the executive. The relative influence in the legislative process exercised by different external entities—the executive, bureaucrats, lobbyists, party officials—may well be related to career orientation of the majority of a body's membership. One study (Squire 1986), based on nonsystematic data, finds support for this hypothesis. In California, for example, the strong influence of interest groups in the state legislature may be explained by the legislators' reliance on special interest campaign contributions to further their political careers. In New York, where legislators are more focused on continued service, reelection funds are funnelled through the party leadership in each house. As a result, the leadership exercises considerable influence over the legislative behavior of the members. In both legislatures power gravitates towards those who greatly assist legislators in achieving their career goals. Obviously, much more research, particularly of a comparative nature, is needed before students of state legislatures can begin to feel confident that we understand legislative careers and their effects on legislative organization and public policy.

REFERENCES

Asher, Herbert B. 1973. "The Learning of Legislative Norms." *American Political Science Review* 67:499-513.

Barber, James D. 1965. *The Lawmakers.* New Haven: Yale University Press.

Bazar, Beth. 1987. *State Legislators' Occupations: A Decade of Change.* Denver: National Conference of State Legislatures.

Bell, Charles G., and Charles M. Price. 1975. *The First Term.* Beverly Hills, Calif.: Sage Publications.

BeVier, Michael. 1979. *Politics Backstage.* Philadelphia: Temple University Press.

Black, Gordon. 1970. "A Theory of Professionalization in Politics." *American Political Science Review* 64:865-78.

Blair, Diane Kincaid, and Ann R. Henry. 1981. "The Family Factor in State Legislative Turnover." *Legislative Studies Quarterly* 6:55-68.

Calvert, Jerry. 1979. "Revolving Doors: Volunteerism in State Legislatures." *State Government* 52:174-81.

Campbell, Ballard C. 1980. *Representative Democracy.* Cambridge: Harvard University Press.

Canon, David T. 1989. "Political Amateurism in the United States Congress." In *Congress Reconsidered*, 4th ed., ed. Lawrence C. Dodd and Bruce I. Oppenheimer, Washington, D.C.: Congressional Quarterly Press.

Chaffey, Douglas C., and Malcolm E. Jewell. 1972. "Selection and Tenure of State Legislative Party Leaders: A Comparative Analysis." *Journal of Politics* 34:1278-86.

Dodd, Lawrence C., and Sean Q. Kelly. 1989. "Legislators' Home Style in Traditional and Modern Systems: The Case of Presentational Style." Presented at the annual meeting of the Midwest Political Science Association, Chicago.

Flocke, Lynne. 1983. "A Not-So-Common Working Man." *Southern Pacific Bulletin* 67(March-April): 10-11.

Fowler, Linda L., and Robert D. McClure. 1989. *Political Ambition: Who Decides to Run for Congress.* New Haven: Yale University Press.

Francis, Wayne L. 1962. "Influence and Interaction in a State Legislative Body." *American Political Science Review* 56:953-60.

_____, and John R. Baker. 1986. "Why Do U.S. State Legislators Vacate Their Seats?" *Legislative Studies Quarterly* 11:119-26.

Goodman, Marshall R., Debra S. Gross, Thomas A. Boyd, and Herbert F. Weisberg. 1986. "State Legislator Goal Orientations: An Examination." *Polity* 18:707-19.

Grau, Craig. 1981. "Competition in State Legislative Primaries." *Legislative Studies Quarterly* 6:35-54.

Hain, Paul L. 1974. "Age, Ambitions and Political Careers: The Middle Age Crisis." *Western Political Quarterly* 27:265-74.

_____. 1976. "Constituency Characteristics, Political Ambition and Advancement." *American Politics Quarterly* 4:47-85.

Harder, Marvin A., and Raymond G. Davis. 1979. *The Legislature as an Organization.* Lawrence, Kan.: The Regents Press of Kansas.

Herzberg, Donald G., and Alan Rosenthal. 1971. *Strengthening the States: Essays on Legislative Reform.* Garden City, N.Y.: Doubleday.

Hibbing, John R. 1986. "Ambition in the House: Behavioral Consequences of Higher Office Goals Among U.S. Representatives." *American Journal of Political Science* 30:651-65.

Hyneman, Charles S. 1938. "Tenure and Turnover of Legislative Personnel." *Annals of the American Academy of Political and Social Science* 23:21-31.

_____. 1940. "Who Makes Our Laws." *Political Science Quarterly* 55:556-81.

Jacobson, Gary C., and Samuel Kernell. 1981. *Strategy and Choice in Congressional Elections.* New Haven: Yale University Press.

Jewell, Malcolm E. 1980. "Survey on Selection of State Legislative Leaders." *Comparative State Politics Newsletter* 1(4):7-21.

_____. 1981. "Editor's Introduction: The State of U.S. State Legislative Research." *Legislative Studies Quarterly* 6:1-25.

_____. 1982. *Representation in State Legislatures.* Lexington, Ky.: University of Kentucky Press.

_____, and David Breaux. 1988. "The Effect of Incumbency on State Legislative Elections." *Legislative Studies Quarterly* 13:495-514.

_____, and Samuel C. Patterson. 1986. *The Legislative Process in the United States,* 4th ed. New York: Random House.

Jones, Ruth S. 1984. "Financing State Elections." In *Money and Politics in the United States,* ed. Michael J. Malbin, Chatham, N.J.: Chatham House.

Keefe, William J. 1966. "The Functions of the State Legislature." In *State Legislatures in American Politics,* ed. Alexander Heard, Englewood Cliffs, N.J.: Prentice-Hall Inc.

Key, V. O., Jr. 1956. *American State Politics.* New York: Knopf.

Kirkpatrick, Samuel A. 1978. *The Legislative Process in Oklahoma.* Norman, Okla.: University of Oklahoma Press.

Lockard, Duane. 1966. "The State Legislator." In *State Legislatures in American Politics,* ed. Alexander Heard, Englewood Cliffs, N.J.: Prentice-Hall Inc.

Loewenberg, Gerhard. 1972. "Comparative Legislative Research." In *Comparative Legislative Behavior: Frontiers of Research,* ed. Samuel C. Patterson and John C. Wahlke, New York: Wiley.

Matthews, Donald R. 1985. "Legislative Recruitment and Legislative Careers." In *Handbook of Legislative Research,* ed. Gerhard Loewenberg, Samuel C. Patterson, and Malcolm E. Jewell, Cambridge: Harvard University Press.

Meyer, Katherine. 1980. "Legislative Influence: Toward Theory Development Through Causal Analysis." *Legislative Studies Quarterly* 5:563-85.

Moncrief, Gary F., and Joel A. Thompson, eds. 1992. *Changing Patterns in State Legislative Careers.* Ann Arbor: University of Michigan Press.

Nathan, Richard P. 1989. "The Role of the States in American Federalism." In *The State of the States,* ed. Carl E. Van Horn, Washington, D.C.: Congressional Quarterly Press.

Nechemias, Carol. 1987. "Changes in the Election of Women to U.S. State Legislative Seats." *Legislative Studies Quarterly* 12:125-42.

Niemi, Richard G., and Laura R. Winsky. 1987. "Membership Turnover in U.S. State Legislatures: Trends and Effects of Districting." *Legislative Studies Quarterly* 12:115-23.

Patterson, Samuel C. 1983. "Legislators and Legislatures in the American States." In *Politics in the American States,* ed. Virginia Gray, Herbert Jacob, and Kenneth N. Vines, Boston: Little, Brown and Co.

_____, and G. R. Boynton. 1969. "Legislative Recruitment in a Civic Culture." *Social Science Quarterly* 50:243-63.

_____, Ronald D. Hedlund, and G. R. Boynton. 1975. *Representatives and the Represented.* New York: Wiley.

Polsby, Nelson W. 1968. "The Institutionalization of the U.S. House of Representatives." *American Political Science Review* 62:144-268.

_____. 1974. "Legislatures." In *The Handbook of Political Science,* vol 5: *Governmental Institutions and Processes,* ed. Fred

I. Greenstein and Nelson W. Polsby, Reading, Mass.: Addison-Wesley.

Prewitt, Kenneth, and William Nowlin. 1969. "Political Ambitions and the Behavior of Incumbent Politicians." *Western Political Quarterly* 22:298-308.

Price, H. Douglas. 1975. "Congress and the Evolution of Legislative 'Professionalism.'" In *Congress in Change*, ed. Norman J. Ornstein, New York: Praeger.

Ray, David, and John Havick. 1981. "A Longitudinal Analysis of Party Competition in State Legislative Elections." *American Journal of Political Science* 25:119-28.

Robeck, Bruce W. 1982. "State Legislator Candidacies for the U.S. House: Prospects for Success." *Legislative Studies Quarterly* 7:507-14.

Rosenthal, Alan. 1974. "Turnover in State Legislatures." *American Journal of Political Science* 18:609-16.

_____. 1981. *Legislative Life*. New York: Harper & Row.

_____. 1989. "The Legislative Institution: Transformed and at Risk." In *The State of the States*, ed. Carl E. Van Horn, Washington, D.C.: Congressional Quarterly Press.

Ruchelman, Leonard. 1970. *Political Careers*. Rutherford, N.J.: Fairleigh Dickinson University Press.

Schlesinger, Joseph A. 1966. *Ambition and Politics*. Chicago: Rand McNally and Co.

Seligman, Lester G., Michael King, Chong Lim Kim, and Roland Smith. 1974. *Patterns of Recruitment: A State Chooses its Lawmakers*. Chicago: Rand McNally.

Shin, Kwang S., and John S. Jackson III. 1979. "Membership Turnover in U.S. State Legislatures: 1931-1976." *Legislative Studies Quarterly* 4:95-114.

Simon, Lucinda. 1987. "The Climb to Leadership: Career Paths and Personal Choices." *The Journal of State Government* 60:245-51.

Smith, Roland E., and Lawrence W. Miller. 1977. "Leaving the Legislature: Why Do They Go?" *Public Service* 4:6-8.

Sorauf, Frank J. 1963. *Party and Representation*. New York: Atherton.

_____. 1988. *Money in American Elections*. Glenview, Ill.: Scott, Foresman.

Soule, John W. 1969. "Future Political Ambitions and the Behavior of Incumbent State Legislators." *Midwest Journal of Political Science* 13:439-54.

Squire, Peverill. 1986. "Career Opportunity Structures and the Organization and Behavior of Legislatures." Ph.D. dissertation. University of California, Berkeley.

_____. 1988a. "Career Opportunities and Membership Stability in Legislatures." *Legislative Studies Quarterly* 13:65-82.

_____. 1988b. "Member Career Opportunities and the Internal Organization of Legislatures." *Journal of Politics* 50:726-44.

_____. 1989. "Challengers in U.S. Senate Elections." *Legislative Studies Quarterly* 14:531-47.

_____. 1992a. "Legislative Professionalization and Membership Diversity." *Legislative Studies Quarterly* 17:69-79.

_____. 1992b. "Challenger Profile and Gubernatorial Elections." *Western Political Quarterly* 45:125-42.

_____. 1992c. "The Theory of Legislative Institutionalization and the California Assembly." *Journal of Politics* 54:1026-54

_____. 1992d. "Changing State Legislative Leadership Careers." In *Changing Patterns in State Legislative Careers*, ed. Gary F. Moncrief and Joel A. Thompson, Ann Arbor: University of Michigan Press.

Squire, Peverill, and John R. Wright. 1990. "Fundraising by Nonincumbent Candidates for the U.S. House of Representatives." *Legislative Studies Quarterly* 15:89-98.

Stanley, Harold W., and Richard G. Niemi. 1988. *Vital Statistics on American Politics.* Washington, D.C.: Congressional Quarterly Press.

Stavisky, Leonard P. 1981. "State Legislatures and the New Federalism." *Public Administration Review* 41:701-10.

Thompson, Joel A., and Gary F. Moncrief. 1988. "Pursuing the Pork in a State Legislature: A Research Note." *Legislative Studies Quarterly* 13:393-401.

Tobin, Richard J., and Edward Keynes. 1975. "Institutional Differences in the Recruitment Process: A Four State Study." *American Journal of Political Science* 19:667-82.

Van Horn, Carl E. 1989. "The Quiet Revolution." In *The State of the States*, ed. Carl E. Van Horn, Washington, D.C.: Congressional Quarterly Press.

Wahlke, John C., Heinz Eulau, William Buchanan, and LeRoy C. Ferguson. 1962. *The Legislative System.* New York: John Wiley and Sons.

Weissert, Carol S. 1988. "Changing Determinants of Influence in the North Carolina State Legislature 1977-1987." Presented at the annual meeting of the American Political Science Association, Washington D.C..

Zeller, Belle, ed. 1954. *American State Legislatures.* New York: Thomas Y. Crowell.

Chapter 5

The Impact of Job Satisfaction on the Career Decisions of Local Lawmakers

Edward L. Lascher, Jr.
Harvard University

Studies of political careers generally ignore the manner in which politicians evaluate their past experiences in elective office. Politicians commonly are seen as looking to the future and the possibilities it holds, rather than to the past and what it has brought for them. Yet there is good reason to believe that such an outlook neglects important considerations affecting decisions to seek reelection or run for higher office. In particular, satisfaction with prior elective positions may affect political career choices.

This article will stress the importance of work satisfaction for legislators' career decisions, based on an analysis of a particular group of local elected lawmakers: California county supervisors. An emphasis on legislators' evaluations of their work requires modifications in the prevailing model of political career choices, which focuses on the structure of opportunities available to elected officials as the key determinant. The significance of job satisfaction also suggests future research that may provide a more complete understanding of politicians' career paths.

THE PREVAILING MODEL OF POLITICAL CAREER CHOICES

Political scientists have used many different approaches to study recruitment to political office and career choices once in office (Levine and Hyde 1977; Matthews 1984; see also the Prinz chapter in this volume). However, a single approach to the study of political careers has come to dominate the political science literature over the past 25 years. This school of thought, commonly known as ambition theory, traces its roots to Joseph Schlesinger's seminal 1966 work, *Ambition and Politics: Political Careers in the United States.* Ambition theory views politicians as rational goal seekers and emphasizes the structure of incentives and opportunities facing potential candidates for office. It is assumed that politicians' behavior is to a significant extent a response to their aspirations and that these aspirations are in turn influenced by the potential for advancement in the offices they hold. People who hold offices that commonly lead to other positions are more likely to develop upward ambitions than people who hold offices that generally lead nowhere. Politicians are also cognizant of the risks they face in seeking another office (e.g., whether they will have to relinquish their present positions if they fail in this quest).

Schlesinger acknowledged that politicians were not all alike in terms of political ambition, leading him to develop his now-famous categories of "discrete," "static," and "progressive" ambition. However, the moving force in ambition theory is the structure of opportunities facing office-holders, and not differences between individuals (see Black 1972). Indeed John Hibbing argues in a previous chapter that the term "ambition theory" is a misnomer, because Schlesinger and his followers actually provide a theory of political opportunity rather than a theory of politicians' office-seeking goals. Therefore it is only a small step for some of Schlesinger's followers to drop the notion of inherent differences in aspirations among politicians. Thus David Rohde (1979) assumed that all politicians were progressively ambitious in the sense that they would take a higher position if one were offered to them without cost or risk.

The various selections in this volume indicate that ambition theory has a number of advantages as an explanation of career choices among politicians. Compared to many other approaches to this topic, particularly studies emphasizing the social background of officeholders, ambition theory is relatively parsimonious, relatively explicit with regard to its propositions about individual behavior, and relatively conducive to mathematical formalization. Furthermore, ambition theory is grounded in the rational choice perspective that has emerged as a major analytical approach in political science (for a critical analysis of the dominance of rational choice models in political science, see Kelman 1988). Additionally, ambition theory focuses on the characteristics of political institutions, rather than a particular set of political actors. Thus propositions derived from this theory may have relevance in a wide variety of settings (see Black 1972; Squire, this volume).

Most importantly, ambition theory has explained successfully a variety of real world political phenomena (Matthews 1984; Prinz, this volume). For instance, David Rohde (1979) showed that, as hypothesized, members of the U.S. House of Representatives from small states are more likely to seek a position in the U.S Senate than are large state House members, and that House members with insecure seats are relatively less likely to seek reelection. Both of these hypotheses were derived from analysis of the opportunity structure facing House members. Similarly John Hibbing, in his chapter for this volume, demonstrates the importance of both the intra-House and external opportunity structure for House member career decisions. And in the previous chapter Peverill Squire explains much of the variance in advancements from the state legislature to federal office through analysis of the opportunity structure facing state lawmakers.

Nevertheless, there are several reasons to believe that ambition theory offers an incomplete explanation of political career choices. Most importantly, ambition theory ignores substantial variation in the career aspirations of politicians. There is strong evidence that individuals in the same political circumstances differ significantly with regard to career desires, and that, in contrast to Rohde's assumption, many are not politically ambitious. This point was emphasized by Kenneth Prewitt and William Nowlin on the basis of their study of San Francisco Bay Area city council members:

> In *The Great Game of Politics* Frank Kent instructs those of us who, in his view, are "in a state of ignorance about politics" that every man "who has held office wants to keep it or get a better one." Our evidence suggests that Kent, insider though he was, is wrong. At all levels of politics a sizable portion of elected officials will be content with their present post, [and] will harbor no ambitions for higher office (Prewitt and Nowlin 1969, 308).

Studies of small town elected officials particularly have emphasized the general absence of political ambition among these politicians and the wide variety of motives that underlie their involvement in local politics (Sokolow 1987, 1989). Recent evidence suggests that the assumption that progressive ambitions are universal may be problematic even with respect to members of Congress (Herrick and Moore 1990).

In analyzing differences in career aspirations of politicians, it seems both feasible and desirable to assess how politicians evaluate any past experiences in elective office. The rationale for using this information is the assumption that politicians look to past experiences in elective office for clues about how they will enjoy another position. Such behavior may be quite rational, given that political office is quite different from other occupations, and the pluses and minuses of particular positions are likely to be uncertain.

The approach recommended here harks back to the important work of David Barber, who argued that the behavior of politicians can be explained in part through use of a simple psychological classification system. One of the two principal components of this system is how well politicians enjoy their jobs (Barber 1965, 1985). Barber, however, grounded his analysis in a more elaborate theory of individual personality. The approach recommended here is less oriented toward depth psychology and more oriented toward examining the proximate attitudes about work. These attitudes, according to industrial and organizational psychologists, are affected by both work values and work rewards. That is, although there are regularities in how people weigh the characteristics of their jobs, different people hold different values as to the importance of high pay, meaningful work, good social contacts, and the like. Individuals also have divergent perceptions as to the level of such benefits they actually obtain from their jobs. The interaction between values and perceptions determines overall satisfaction (see Mottaz and Potts 1986). The literature on job satisfaction is enormous; Edwin Locke (1976, 1984) and Michael Gruneberg (1979) provide useful summaries.

A Job Satisfaction Approach to the Study of Legislators' Political Careers

The work satisfaction approach to the study of lawmakers' political careers rests on two simple assumptions and one simple expectation. The first assumption is that it is reasonable to regard modern legislative positions in the United States as jobs. If legislative positions were mere sidelines to incumbent officeholders' main occupations, it might not make sense to apply concepts and terminology derived from the study of regular workers. However, a strong trend at all levels of government is toward requiring a regular work week from lawmakers, and a weaker trend is toward offering lawmakers a level of compensation commensurate with their responsibilities as full-time public employees. The long-term trend toward professionalism in Congress and among state legislatures has been remarked on by a number of scholars (see for example

Polsby 1975; Rosenthal 1981; Matthews 1984; Squire, this volume; Ehrenhalt 1991). Local legislative bodies, such as city councils, are sometimes considered the last bastion of volunteerism among lawmakers (e.g., Prewitt 1970). Yet even here there is considerable evidence of increased professionalism (Marando and Thomas 1977; Ehrenhalt 1987, 1988, 1991). A second and related assumption is that attitudes toward work among legislators are similarly structured to attitudes toward work among people in other occupations. Job satisfaction studies have showed that people have overall attitudes about their work and that these broad views are affected by evaluations of specific dimensions of work life. A number of dimensions have emerged consistently from past research, including an "intrinsic rewards" dimension, relating to the attitude of workers toward the content of their jobs (e.g., feelings of accomplishment); an "instrumental rewards" dimension, pertaining to judgments about the benefits that workers obtain as a consequence of holding a job (e.g., a sense that they are well paid or poorly paid); a "social rewards" dimension, relating to attitudes about interaction with colleagues; and a "supervisorial" dimension, pertaining to judgments about the quality of contacts with supervisors (Smith, Kendall, and Hulin 1969; Locke 1976; Gruneberg 1979; Mottaz 1985). To the extent that legislators' attitudes are structured in this manner, it should be possible to tap their sentiments, using questions about overall job satisfaction and components of job satisfaction.

Most importantly, previous research on people in other occupations suggests that the degree of work satisfaction among lawmakers affects their decisions to seek reelection or to run for other offices. The industrial and organizational psychology literature indicates that the effects of work satisfaction, while complicated and dependent on circumstances, are of major potential significance for individuals and organizations (see especially Henne and Locke 1985). There is strong evidence that job evaluations have significant effects on career choices. Research consistently has shown that dissatisfaction with work is associated with voluntary exit. Indeed, work satisfaction's relationship with long-term choices such as leaving one's job is much more well established than its association with short-term, on-the-job behavior such as productivity, which is influenced also by a multitude of other factors (Smith et al. 1969; Locke 1976; Gruneberg 1979; Thierry and Koopman-Iwema 1984; Henne and Locke 1985).

THE CALIFORNIA COUNTY SUPERVISORIAL STUDY

The political opportunity structure can be investigated without directly assessing the attitudes and values of politicians; many scholars (e.g., Rohde, Squire) have made important contributions drawing solely from published information. An assessment of the impact of job satisfaction, however, requires direct contact with politicians, through such mechanisms as interviews and surveys. This creates difficulties for someone interested in the effect of work evaluations, because research that includes direct assessment of politicians' attitudes and values rarely touches upon issues pertaining to job satisfaction. For this reason the remainder of this chapter will concentrate on a study of California county supervisors I conducted that specifically focused on work evaluations.

The choice of California county supervisors as the subjects of this research is likely to prompt a number of questions. Who are these people, and what are their responsibilities? How typical are they of other lawmakers? To what extent can their positions be considered full-time jobs as opposed to sidelines to other careers? To what extent is analysis of political career choices relevant to these people? In short, why is it useful to concentrate upon a set of political actors who generally have been ignored by political scientists? (On the lack of attention given to county elected officials, see Marando and Thomas 1977.)

It is appropriate to begin the response to these questions with a brief description of county supervisorial duties and characteristics. Each of California's 58 counties is governed by an elected board of supervisors. Boards are the principal policymaking units within county government (Koehler 1983) and have both administrative (e.g., contract approval) and legislative (e.g., development of local ordinances) responsibilities. All boards meet regularly in public session to act on policy issues appearing on the agenda. County supervisorial races are nonpartisan, and board members serve four-year terms. With a single exception, county boards all have five members.[1] The large majority of supervisors are elected on a district rather than an at-large basis.

There are four reasons for believing that a study of job satisfaction among county supervisors can produce results that are more broadly relevant to lawmakers generally. First, along with notable differences,

---

[1]San Francisco, which is the state's only combined city and county, has an 11-member board of supervisors and a separately elected mayor.

there are significant similarities between county and state or federal lawmakers in terms of responsibility and authority. All have independent authority to enact laws. All control the purse strings for their level of government (although county supervisors' fiscal decisions are sharply constrained by mandates from higher level governments). All provide a significant amount of oversight over administrative agencies. And all can act as political entrepreneurs, bringing items to the agenda for the entire body to consider.

Second, county supervisorial offices are typical of late-20th century positions in American legislatures that have become significantly professionalized, particularly with respect to the amount of work required. The study I conducted indicates that the average supervisor devotes about 52 hours a week to his or her position and does not have an outside job. This finding is consistent with other research (Koehler 1983; Sokolow 1987).

Third, political career considerations are relevant to county supervisors, because many use their position as springboards to other offices. It has been estimated that between 15 percent and 20 percent of California state legislators are former supervisors (Koehler 1983), as are four members of the current California delegation in the U.S. House of Representatives. Some board members are explicit with regard to their desire to obtain higher office, as was one former supervisor during a personal interview.

> I had grown up in Seaside County . . . left for college and law school . . . came back with the intention of getting elected to office. . . . I felt that elective politics was a viable forum for [effecting social change], so I came back to where I had a base, a home base. I had decided originally to run for Congress. . . . After looking over the situation, I felt that a race for Congress was not practical. There was a strong incumbent, a Republican, who had been there for 18 or 20 years. I felt that I would run for supervisor, for Gary Christianson's vacant seat, learn something about politics, establish a reputation.[2]

Fourth, analysis of county supervisors is conducive to the study of political ambition because the opportunity structure facing board members differs substantially from county to county. Thus it may be possible to

---

[2]In drawing upon personal interviews, names and other identifying information have been changed to preserve confidentiality.

assess how much of the variance in ambition is attributable to the opportunity structure and how much to other factors. In particular, counties differ with regard to the size of the political base they provide for board members. Some counties are very small (the smallest, Alpine, has just a little over 1,000 people), and supervisorial districts in these jurisdictions are a tiny fraction of state legislative and congressional districts. Other counties are large and would seem more conducive to serving as springboards. At the extreme, supervisors in gigantic Los Angeles County, with a population of about 8.3 million in 1987, have more constituents than do several state governors (on the importance of Los Angeles supervisorial positions, see Guerra, this volume).

The main source of data for this study of job satisfaction and career choices among county supervisors is a statewide mail survey of current county supervisors I conducted in the spring of 1988. Among the topics covered are job attitudes (with many of the questions drawn from prior job satisfaction studies) and future political plans. All board members in the state were sent questionnaires, except those from four counties in which personal interviews were conducted. Responses were received from 201 supervisors, or 73 percent of those to whom they were mailed. This is an excellent response rate for a survey of this type. Respondents were also geographically representative of the total population of supervisors. The median population size for the counties from which survey respondents hailed is about 133,000, whereas the median population size for the 54 counties in which supervisors were mailed surveys is about 126,000. Responses were received from at least one board member in all 54 counties that were included in the survey.[3] Other data sources also have been used. The second most important source was a set of open-ended interviews with 17 current supervisors and 10 former supervisors in four counties. Additionally, the results of a mail survey of former supervisors complemented the data gathered from current board members. A total of 131 former supervisors responded to my questionnaire.

---

[3]Unfortunately demographic data for the entire supervisorial population is unavailable, making it impossible to assess the representativeness of the sample with respect to such characteristics as age and gender.

· **FINDINGS**

A good place to begin the analysis of the impact of job satisfaction on career choices is with an examination of reelection intentions. If work satisfaction does indeed influence career choices, it would be expected that more satisfied county supervisors would be significantly more likely to plan to run again than less satisfied board members. If no such relationship existed, the importance of work evaluations might be questioned.

To evaluate this topic, responses to four survey questions were examined. The first three pertained to overall job satisfaction, and were based on questions commonly asked in other work satisfaction studies. A job satisfaction scale was developed that combined responses to all three questions. The fourth question pertained to intentions to run again at the next election (see Appendix for job satisfaction questions used in this study).

The data presented in Table 5.1 strikingly reveal the importance of work satisfaction for the intention to seek reelection. Board members who evaluated their work most positively were much more inclined to say they wanted to run again. Thus 83 percent of highly satisfied county supervisors reported they would run again, while only 14 percent of unsatisfied board members indicated they would seek reelection.

A skeptic might question whether job satisfaction, broadly defined, affects reelection plans, arguing instead that what matters is the relative abundance or scarcity of instrumental rewards such as compensation. Highly paid supervisors might seek reelection, while poorly paid board members might not. To test for this possibility, the relationship between job satisfaction and reelection plans was re-examined, controlling first for salary and then for satisfaction with salary and benefits. The skeptical view is not upheld. Overall job satisfaction has a strong impact on intentions to seek reelection even with these controls applied (see Table 5.2). The effect of general work satisfaction appears to be more than the effect of its component parts.

A skeptic might also wonder if the apparent connection between satisfaction and seeking reelection is an artifact of supervisorial concerns about reelection. Ambition theory suggests that decisions to seek reelection are heavily influenced by the probability of winning. Unfortunately objective data to test this proposition (e.g., margin of supervisorial victory in the last election) is lacking. Nevertheless, there is no evidence that subjective evaluations of reelection electoral danger lie behind the

Table 5.1.   *Relationship Between Work Satisfaction and Supervisors'
Intent to Seek Reelection (N=186)*

	Overall Satisfaction			
Intent to Seek Reelection	High	High-Medium	Low-Medium	Low
Intending to Run Again	83%	73	48	14
Not Intending to Run Again*	17	27	52	86
	(64)	(90)	(25)	(7)

Pearson X^2 = 22, p < .01   Gamma = .502

*Includes both respondents who indicated they definitely were not running again, and
those who indicated they were unsure about whether they would run again.
Source: California County Supervisors Survey, 1988

apparent effect of work satisfaction; adding a control variable relating to
supervisorial reelection concerns does not diminish the relationship
between satisfaction and desire to run again.

These findings do not reveal anything about supervisors' intentions
beyond their board positions. One of the strongest aspects of ambition
theory is that it addresses questions about long-term political career plans.
If job satisfaction analysis is to supplement ambition theory, it should
shed light on what happens to county supervisors after they leave office.

Three hypotheses about the effects of job satisfaction on long-term
political career plans need to be examined. The null hypothesis is that
there is no relationship between these two variables. A second hypothesis is that dissatisfied supervisors will be especially likely to seek higher
office. This hypothesis is based on the idea that people who desire
elective positions are "hooked on politics," (for an example of this type
of argument, see Payne, Veblen, Coogan, and Bigler 1984). The only
question for these people is which office they will pursue. Those
politicians who dislike their present positions might be particularly
inclined to believe that a change in office would bring them the satisfac-

Table 5.2. *Job Satisfaction and Reelection Intentions, Controlling for Supervisors' Salary*

I. Supervisors Paid Less than $20,000 Annually (N=66)

	Overall Satisfaction			
	High	High-Medium	Low-Medium	Low
Intending to	83%	61	50	0
Run Again	(18)	(33)	(12)	(3)

Pearson X^2 = 9, p <.05   Gamma = .502

II. Supervisors Paid $20,000 to $39,999 Annually (N=90)

	Overall Satisfaction			
	High	High-Medium	Low-Medium	Low
Intending to	81%	80	40	33
Run Again	(31)	(46)	(10)	(3)

Pearson X^2 = 10, p < .05   Gamma = .413

III. Supervisors Paid $40,000 or More Annually (N=30)

	Overall Satisfaction			
	High	High-Medium	Low-Medium	Low
Intending to	87%	82	67	0
Run Again	(15)	(11)	(3)	(1)

Pearson X^2 = 5, not significant   Gamma = .469

Source: California County Supervisors Survey, 1988

tion they desire. A third hypothesis is that supervisors generalize from their prior experiences to political positions more universally. Those who are especially satisfied with previous elective office would be inclined toward greater political ambition.

My research lends credence to the third hypothesis. High levels of satisfaction are associated with greater political ambition. A variety of data supports this conclusion. The first are the results of the survey of current county supervisors. Respondents with varying degrees of work satisfaction differed markedly in terms of their political ambitions, and the patterns were consistent with the third hypothesis (see Table 5.3). This was made apparent by dividing the sample into four categories on the basis of how positively supervisors evaluated their jobs, and classifying board members in terms of Schlesinger's categories of discrete, static, and progressive ambitions. Highly satisfied supervisors were most likely to have progressive ambitions and least likely to have discrete ambitions. Dissatisfied board members, on the other hand, were most likely to have discrete ambitions and least likely to have progressive ambitions.

Furthermore, the relationship between work satisfaction and ambition is even stronger for supervisors who are of primary age to consider a long-term career in politics. Research has consistently shown that increased age has a dampening effect on progressive ambitions (see for example Schlesinger 1966; Prewitt and Nowlin 1969). This finding was duplicated in my survey; 61 percent of board members under the age of 50 have progressive ambitions, as opposed to only 20 percent of supervisors aged 50 or more. Yet as shown in the second part of Table 5.3, among younger supervisors those who evaluated their jobs most positively were especially likely to have progressive ambitions, while those who evaluated their work more negatively were especially likely to have discrete ambitions. For instance, three quarters of the supervisors under the age of 50 who expressed greatest work satisfaction were classified as having progressive ambitions, while the two younger supervisors who fell into the lowest category of satisfaction were classified as having discrete ambitions.

Additionally, there appears to be a positive relationship between high satisfaction and actually running for another office while serving on the board, although the small number of respondents who had sought another office suggests that this finding should be interpreted with caution (only 14 supervisors indicated they had run for another office while serving on the board). Thirteen percent of highly satisfied supervisors had run

Table 5.3. *Relationship of Job Satisfaction and Political Ambition Among County Supervisors*

I. All County Supervisors (N=180)

Type of Ambition*	Overall Work Satisfaction			
	High	High-Medium	Low-Medium	Low
Progressive	42%	40	35	14
Static	50	44	26	0
Discrete	8	16	39	86

Pearson X^2 = 33, p < .001   Gamma = .279

II. Supervisors Under the Age of 50 (N=84)

Type of Ambition*	Overall Satisfaction			
	High	High-Medium	Low-Medium	Low
Progressive	75%	51	67	0
Static	25	32	0	0
Discrete	0	17	33	100

Pearson X^2 = 24, p < .001   Gamma = .446

* Supervisors with *progressive ambitions* are defined as those who indicated they were "very likely" or "somewhat likely" to seek another office. Board members with *static ambitions* are those who were "not very likely" or "very unlikely" to run for another office, *and* indicated they intended to run for reelection. Supervisors with *discrete ambitions* are those who were "not very likely" or "very unlikely" to seek another office, and indicated they did not intend to run for reelection or were unsure of their intentions.
Source: California County Supervisors Survey, 1988

for higher office while serving on the board, in contrast to 5 percent of supervisors who were not highly satisfied (see Table 5.4).[4] It is also interesting, and consistent with other findings, that all supervisors who made unsuccessful efforts to obtain another position intended to seek reelection to the county board, as opposed to only 69 percent of supervisors who had not run for another office.

Data from the survey of former supervisors also tend to support the idea that more satisfied board members are more ambitious. The results of this survey are only suggestive, because the sample is not representative of ex-supervisors as a group. Yet the consistency of this information with that obtained from interviewing current supervisors is striking. Former supervisors who had left office to seek another elective position tended to be more satisfied with their jobs than ex-board members who had left for other reasons, such as retirement from politics.

Finally, scattered information from interviews with county supervisors tends to support the judgment derived from review of survey data. A great many county supervisors previously had served on city councils, boards of education, or other local offices. In larger counties, these positions can themselves require full-time or nearly full-time work weeks. Some supervisors in larger counties indicated that their satisfaction with these positions convinced them that they would be most happy to remain in politics and encouraged them to consider running for the board. One supervisor, while emphasizing that the timing was right to seek an open board seat, explained her decision to seek higher office in clear job satisfaction terms.

> The Anacapa City Council has a two-term limit. And I was coming to the end of my second term. I had to make a decision about what I was going to do: whether I was going to run for another office, or go back to my original educational experience, which was social services. The thing that was most appealing to me was to stay in government. . . . After spending time in social services I realized I really didn't want to do that. I really enjoyed my job [as a council member].

---

[4]A Pearson X^2 goodness of fit test indicates that the null hypothesis of no relationship between actual office seeking and job satisfaction cannot be rejected using standard statistical tests. However, the remainder of the survey data lend credence to the conclusion that such a relationship exists.

Table 5.4. *Job Satisfaction and Actual Pursuit of Higher Office By County Supervisors (N=186)*

	Overall Work Satisfaction	
Had Sought Another Office While Serving As Supervisors?	High	Medium/Low
Yes	13%	5
No	87	95
	(64)	(122)
Pearson X^2 = 3, not significant	Gamma = .468	

Source: California County Supervisors Survey, 1988.

A colleague of hers stressed that his original decision to run for city council was prompted by his boredom with his previous work, despite the trappings of success: running his own company, living in a big home in a nice community, driving a red Jaguar, and "doing all the things that should have made me happy." He enjoyed being a council member so much that when he and others became frustrated with the incumbent supervisor over his handling of a land-use matter:

> I didn't have to be encouraged at all to run for the board of supervisors. I was very enthused about it. And very pragmatically, I sat down with my wife . . . and we just decided if that's what made me happy, [we'd do it]. We'd sell the company, and I'd become a full time politician.

There is a relationship, then, between job satisfaction and county supervisors' career choices. However, it is conceivable this relationship is spurious and that both job evaluations and political ambition are a function of the underlying set of political opportunities facing board members. Once the factors stressed by ambition theorists are included in the analysis of office-seeking plans, job satisfaction may be stripped of any explanatory power.

To test this possibility, the relationship between job satisfaction and political careers was re-examined, controlling for county population. Ambition theory suggests a number of reasons to expect that differences in population would explain much of the variance in plans for higher office. The closer the overlap between supervisorial and state legislative or congressional districts, the greater the probability that a supervisor's name will be recognized in a contest for higher legislative office. Supervisors from larger districts also have an opportunity to provide services to a larger portion of their potential constituency, a factor shown to be important in winning elections (see, for example, Jacobson 1987). Additionally, the closer the overlap, the less competition supervisors face from other elected officials at similar levels of government. For example, a board member from the county of Santa Clara in the Silicon Valley (population 1.3 million in 1987) would at most have four other supervisorial rivals in seeking the sixth district state senate seat. On the other hand, a supervisor from rural Plumas County (population 19,000) could receive competition for a first district state senate position from as many as 50 other county board members. Supervisors from larger counties might also be expected to receive more media attention and have a greater potential for raising funds. Thus the decision of one supervisor from a small county not to seek higher office was influenced by the difficulty of raising money in a rural area; "you have to go to the cities" to raise the necessary funds, she said.

Survey data indicate that supervisors from larger counties are indeed more ambitious than smaller county board members. Yet, as shown in Table 5.5, even controlling for population job satisfaction is related to political ambition. When supervisors are grouped by county population, within each category the more satisfied board members tend to be the more ambitious. Job satisfaction appears to affect career choices independently of the opportunity structure that supervisors face.

CONCLUSION

The findings from the California county supervisor study suggest that, in analyzing political career choices, it is desirable and feasible to consider factors other than the opportunity structure facing individual politicians. In particular, it is reasonable to assess legislators' evaluations of present or past positions as lawmakers. The evidence presented suggests that given the same opportunity those legislators who view their positions positively are more likely to be ambitious than those lawmakers

Table 5.5. *Relationship of Job Satisfaction to Political Ambition Among County Supervisors, Controlling for County Population*

I. Supervisors from Small Counties (< 100,000 *Residents*) (N=70)

	Overall Work Satisfaction	
Type of Ambition	High	Low
Progressive	29%	42
Static	52	0
Discrete	19	58

Pearson X^2 = 13, p < .01   Gamma = .232

II. Supervisors from Medium-Sized Counties (100,000 to 499,949 *Residents*) (N=69)

	Overall Work Satisfaction	
Type of Ambition	High*	Low
Progressive	46%	25
Static	46	25
Discrete	9	50

Pearson X^2 = 13, p < .01   Gamma = .566

III. Supervisors from Large Counties (500,000 *or More Residents*) (N=41)

	Overall Work Satisfaction	
Type of Ambition	High	Low
Progressive	51%	17
Static	40	50
Discrete	9	33

Pearson X^2 = 4, p < .05   Gamma = .639

* Column does not sum to 100% due to rounding
Source: California County Supervisors Survey, 1988

who are less satisfied with their work. In effect, lawmakers appear to use evaluations of present positions as clues to their future happiness in elective office.

The above findings would be strengthened by similar evidence from studies of job satisfaction and career choices among lawmakers at different levels of government. Despite the similarities between county supervisors and other types of legislators, there are reasons to be cautious about drawing generalizations from a single study of county board members. For example, variance in job satisfaction may diminish as people move up the political ladder, because the people less enamored of politics have been "weeded out." Hence the political opportunity structure may take on even greater importance among officials at higher governmental levels.[5]

These findings also suggest that our understanding of political career choices would be enhanced by research in which the level of work satisfaction is the dependent variable.[6] Such research could draw upon the findings of industrial and organizational psychologists. A number of factors have been shown to influence work values and perceived rewards, including the actual characteristics of work (e.g., amount of pay, variety of tasks), psychological characteristics of workers (e.g., self esteem), and certain demographic characteristics, such as age. Research is needed on how these factors operate in the political arena to affect lawmakers' job evaluations.

I conducted an exploratory study of the factors that influence job satisfaction in the context of the study of California county supervisors (Lascher 1989). Among the key findings were the following: (1) as anticipated, attitudes regarding specific types of work rewards (e.g., meaningfulness of work, adequacy of pay) influenced overall job satisfaction; (2) at least some specific attributes of supervisorial positions, such as the level of pay provided board members, influence perceived work rewards and, indirectly, overall job satisfaction; (3) some demographic factors (e.g., age) appear to influence job satisfaction, while others (e.g., gender) do not; this is consistent with findings from other studies; and (4) political ideology appears to be an influence; liberal board members appear to be a little more satisfied on the whole than conservative supervisors. Further review and analysis is needed.

---

[5]I am grateful to Thomas Kazee for making this observation.

[6]I am grateful to Linda Fowler for summarizing future research needs in this succinct manner.

Another topic that merits study is the influence of job satisfaction on outcomes other than career choices. In particular, it would be interesting to determine if there is a connection between the level of satisfaction and effectiveness within a legislative body. Making such a determination would be challenging, both because it is often difficult to develop an adequate measure of lawmaker effectiveness, and because the direction of causality would have to be carefully assessed (success may influence job satisfaction, rather than the reverse).

In summary, it seems clear that greater attention should be given to how lawmakers' goals are affected by holding elective positions. Too often political scientists have viewed political office as a "black box," with relatively little scholarly attention given to how people may be transformed by their actual experiences in office, and their perceptions of those experiences. These experiences and perceptions may be crucial to their willingness to continue playing the "great game of politics."

REFERENCES

Barber, James D. 1965. *The Lawmakers: Recruitment and Adoption to Legislative Life.* New Haven and London: Yale University Press.

_____. 1985. *The Presidential Character: Predicting Performance in the White House,* 3d ed. Englewood Cliffs, N.J.: Prentice Hall.

Black, Gordon. 1972. "A Theory of Political Ambition: Career Choices and the Role of Structural Incentives." *American Political Science Review* 66:144-59.

Ehrenhalt, Alan. 1987. "GOP Plight: A Matter of Supply and Demand." *Congressional Quarterly* (October 31):2703.

_____. 1988. "How a Liberal Government Came to Power in a Conservative Suburb." *Governing* 1:50-56.

_____. 1991. *The United States of Ambition: Politicians, Power and the Pursuit of Office.* New York: Harper & Row.

Gruneberg, Michael M. 1979. *Understanding Job Satisfaction.* London: Macmillan.

Henne, Douglas, and Edwin A. Locke. 1985. "Job Dissatisfaction: What Are the Consequences?" *International Journal of Psychology* 20:221-40.

Herrick, Rebekah, and Michael K. Moore. 1990. "Ambition's Influence on Behavior: An Analysis of Congressional Careers." Presented at the annual meeting of the American Political Science Association, San Francisco.

Jacobson, Gary C. 1987. *The Politics of Congressional Elections,* 2d ed. Boston: Little, Brown.

Kelman, Steven. 1988. "Why Public Ideas Matter." In *The Power of Public Ideas,* ed. Robert B. Reich, Cambridge, Mass.: Ballinger.

Koehler, Cortus T. 1983. *Managing California Counties: Serving People, Solving Problems.* Sacramento: County Supervisors Association of California.

Lascher, Edward L, Jr. 1989. "Must One Be Crazy to Do this Job?: Causes and Consequences of Job Satisfaction Among Local Legislators." Unpublished Ph.D. dissertation.

Levine, Martin D., and Mark S. Hyde. 1977. "Incumbency and the Theory of Political Ambition: A Rational-Choice Model." *The Journal of Politics* 39:959-83.

Locke, Edwin A. 1976. "The Nature and Causes of Job Satisfaction." In *Handbook of Industrial and Organizational Psychology*, ed. Marvin D. Dunnette, Chicago: Rand McNally.

_____. 1984. "Job Satisfaction." In *Social Psychology and Organizational Behavior*, ed. Michael Gruneberg and Toby Wall, Chichester: John Wiley and Sons.

Marando, Vincent L., and Robert D. Thomas. 1977. *The Forgotten Governments: County Commissioners As Policy Makers*. Gainesville, Florida: The University Presses of Florida.

Matthews, David R. 1984. "Legislative Recruitment and Legislative Careers." *Legislative Studies Quarterly* 9:547-85.

Mottaz, Clifford J. 1984. "Education and Work Satisfaction." *Human Relations* 37:985-1004.

_____. 1985. "The Relative Importance of Intrinsic and Extrinsic Rewards as Determinants of Work Satisfaction." *The Sociological Quarterly* 26:365-85.

_____, and Glen Potts. 1986. "An Empirical Evaluation of Models of Work Satisfaction." *Social Science Research* 15:153-73.

Payne, James L., Eric P. Veblen, William H. Coogan, and Gene E.Bigler. 1984. *The Motivation of Politicians*. Chicago: Nelson-Hall.

Polsby, Nelson W. 1975. "Legislatures." In *Handbook of Political Science*, 5, ed. Fred I. Greenstein and Nelson W. Polsby, Reading, Mass.: Addison-Wesley.

Prewitt, Kenneth. 1970. "Political Ambitions, Volunteerism, and Electoral Accountability." *American Political Science Review* 64:5-17.

_____, and William Nowlin. 1969. "Political Ambitions and the Behavior of Incumbent Politicians." *The Western Political Quarterly* 22:298-308.

Rohde, David W. 1979. "Risk-Bearing and Progressive Ambition: The Case of Members of the United States House of Representatives." *American Journal of Political Science* 23:1-26.

Rosenthal, Alan. 1981. *Legislative Life: People, Process, and Performance the States*. New York: Harper & Row.

Schlesinger, Joseph A. 1966. *Ambition and Politics: Political Careers in the United States*. Chicago: Rand McNally.

Smith, Patricia Cain, Lorne M. Kendall, and Charles L. Hulin. 1969. *The Measurement of Satisfaction in Work and Retirement*. Chicago: Rand McNally.

Sokolow, Alvin D. 1987. "Legislators Without Ambition: Recruiting Citizens to Small Town Office." Presented at the annual meeting of the American Political Science Association, Chicago.

_____. 1989. "Legislators Without Ambition: Why Small-Town Citizens Seek Political Office." *State and Local Government Review* 21:23-30.

Thierry, Henk, and Agnes M. Koopman-Iwema. 1984. "Motivation and Satisfaction." In *Handbook of Work and Organizational Psychology*, 1, ed. Pieter J. D. Denth, et al., Chichester: John Wiley & Sons.

APPENDIX

Job Satisfaction Questions Used in
Survey of Current California County Supervisors

Notes

Each question gave the respondent four choices: agree strongly, agree, disagree, or disagree strongly. Questions were asked in random order within the job attitude section of the survey.

Questions

Overall Job Satisfaction

1. If I was doing it all over again, I doubt I would seek the position of county supervisor.

2. I am happier in my work than most other people.

3. Generally speaking, I am satisfied with my position as a county supervisor.

Perceived Extrinsic Job Rewards

1. I am satisfied with the amount of pay and fringe benefits I receive.

2. It is difficult for me to put in as many hours as are needed to do an adequate job as supervisor.

3. We supervisors have the number of personal staff we need to do our jobs.

4. I am uncomfortable with the public criticism that comes from being a supervisor.

5. I am concerned about my ability to win reelection.

6. My supervisorial duties have interfered with my time with my family.

Perceived Intrinsic Job Rewards

1. The work I do is very meaningful to me.

2. I usually know when I am doing a good job as a county supervisor.

3. I feel a low degree of personal responsibility for the work I do.

4. I often have difficulty determining if I have made the right decisions.

5. I have little ability to influence the public policy issues that are most important to me.

6. I feel I should personally take the credit or blame for the results of my work.

7. Supervisors make many of the most important policy decisions.

8. Many of the things I do seem trivial.

*Political Careers for
Women and Minorities*

Introduction

Edward L. Lascher, Jr.
Harvard University

Political office in the United States traditionally has been the bastion of white males. Despite important advances over the past 20 years, many ethnic minorities and, in particular, women continue to be significantly underrepresented in elective office relative to their numbers in the general population. This fact has prompted considerable research not only on the political forces and systematic factors that might be working against women and minorities in elective office, but on the circumstances that might be most conducive to advancing the prospects for people other than white males. The chapters by Susan Carroll and Fernando Guerra address these topics (for an overview of issues in this area, see also the introductory chapter by Timothy Prinz).

At a high level of abstraction, it is apparent that many of the factors affecting the political careers of women and minorities are identical to those affecting other politicians. In particular, the structure of opportunities available to women and minority candidates, and the political resources they have at their disposal, influence their ability to obtain elective office. Yet when these factors are examined in more detail, it is evident there are profound differences as well. For example, women and minorities often are not included in the local community organizations (e.g., chambers of commerce) that serve as avenues to elective office. And certain structural characteristics of electoral systems, such as the "first past the post" method of electing legislators that predominates in this country, may reduce the ability of women and minorities to make inroads into offices dominated by white males.

Given that some common factors affect the political careers of both women and minorities, it is tempting to lump their experiences together and apply generalizations equally to both groups. This approach would be mistaken. Leaving aside for the moment the distinct experiences of minority women (an important and too often neglected topic, as Carroll emphasizes), numerous factors cause the career patterns of nonminority women and minority males to diverge. White female politicians are members of a very large, geographically dispersed group, while minority male candidates are members of groups that are often relatively small in relation to the entire polity and physically and culturally separated from the remainder of the population. Potential women candidates encounter different social expectations with regard to mixing work and child raising than do potential minority male candidates. Racism and sexism operate differently in our society. These differences and others have substantial impact on the manner in which underrepresentativeness might be addressed. For example, minority males' concerns about ability to win in situations of racially polarized voting may be addressed through creating new electoral districts that give minorities more influence (see Grofman, Handley, and Niemi 1992); such an approach is not likely to help women candidates.

Basing her arguments on an extensive literature review, Carroll emphasizes that characteristics of the society at large contribute to the lack of parity between male and female officeholders. She stresses the generally greater family responsibilities that are placed on women. She also suggests that American politics is less conducive to traditionally "female" than to traditionally "male" values, and this may discourage potential women candidates from seeking office. On the other hand, some characteristics of the larger society often assumed to work against female politicians are not major barriers. For example, Carroll finds little evidence that the net effect of gender role stereotypes and prejudice works against the election of women who offer themselves as candidates, in part because voters favorably disposed toward female candidates balance those who are inclined to vote against them on grounds of gender alone. She also emphasizes that structural factors (e.g., the staying power of incumbent lawmakers) contribute to the underrepresentation of women.

How might women obtain a larger share of political offices? One possibility is to change the structural features that work against women obtaining parity. But many of the reforms that might facilitate this aim, such as a limitation on the number of legislative terms, would have a multitude of other effects as well and are controversial for that reason. In the absence of changes in the rules of the game, Carroll suggests that women's networks may be one of the most effective ways of assisting female candidates. The strategy of "women supporting women" can partially overcome the other obstacles faced by female candidates.

Guerra focuses less than Carroll on the broader social and political forces explaining the underrepresentation of particular groups among elected officeholders. Instead, he describes the pattern of ethnic recruitment in the nation's largest county, Los Angeles, and analyzes the proximate factors contributing to the success of specific out-group members. He finds that three ethnic groups have made impressive gains in representation since the 1950s: blacks, Jews, and Latinos. These gains have not occurred simultaneously; rather, each subsequent decade has been characterized by the political emergence of one of these groups. His analysis is especially timely given the early 1991 election of Gloria Molina, the first Hispanic to hold a seat on the powerful Los Angeles County Board of Supervisors.

Guerra concentrates on two factors that he argues have been critical to the success of minority candidates in recent years. The first is the development of the position of legislative aide as a launching pad for a career as an elected official. The second is the significance of ethnic group recruitment networks. He provides a number of case studies that demonstrate the significance of minority group organizations, and "sponsorship" of ethnic candidates by existing minority officeholders. He goes so far as to argue that for the right ethnic candidate, election can be "almost automatic" with the backing of a recruitment network.

DIRECTIONS FOR FUTURE RESEARCH

Guerra's focus on recruitment networks provides a key link to Carroll's chapter and suggests an important avenue for future research. Clearly we need to know more about these alternative bases of support for minority and female candidates. Are ethnic recruitment networks significant in communities other than Los Angeles? How do alternative women's networks operate in the crucial preselection phase that, as Carroll indicates, has generally not received adequate attention? Answers to these and similar questions await further study.

REFERENCES

Grofman, Bernard, Lisa Handley, and Richard G. Niemi. 1992. *Minority Representation and the Quest for Voting Equality.* Cambridge: Cambridge University Press.

Chapter 6

The Political Careers of Women Elected Officials:
An Assessment and Research Agenda

Susan J. Carroll
Rutgers University

A sizeable body of literature focusing on the career paths of women elected officials in the United States has developed over the past two decades as growing numbers of political scientists have become concerned with explaining women's continued underrepresentation in political life. This chapter will review the major findings of that literature, identify the gaps that remain, and suggest possible topics for future research.

The vast majority of existing literature focuses on one aspect of the political careers of women elected politicians—the recruitment of women into public office. As late as 1993, women constituted only 9.9 percent of members of Congress and 20.4 percent of state legislators. Only three of the 50 state governors and 18 of the mayors of the nation's 100 largest cities were women (Center for the American Woman and Politics 1993a). Researchers, concerned with explaining this pattern of underrepresentation, have surveyed candidates and officeholders and analyzed the backgrounds of women elected officials (usually in comparison to those of men) in order to identify barriers to candidacy and election for women. As a result, much is now known about the problems women face in running for office as well as the factors that may facilitate their entry into office. Less is known about why so many women in the "eligible pool," who have the experiences and qualifications that would make them potential candidates, do not run for office. Even less is known about the career paths of women after they are elected to office; almost no research has examined women's movement into leadership within legislative institutions or the frequency with which, and conditions under which, women officials move on to higher office or out of politics. This review of research on the career paths of women elected politicians reflects the fact that much greater attention has been devoted to some aspects of women's career paths than to others.

Similarly, reflecting the focus of scholarly literature on public officials more generally, research on women officeholders has more often examined officeholding at state or national levels than at county or municipal levels. Moreover, most studies focus on women who serve in legislative office; little research attention has been paid to women serving in executive positions at any level of government. Because of these tendencies in the literature, the review of research in this paper focuses primarily on women who seek or hold state legislative and congressional offices.

This paper is divided into two sections. The first summarizes the major findings and conclusions of existing research. The second points to important gaps in the literature and suggests several possible topics for future research.

REVIEW OF RELEVANT RESEARCH

This section reviews the major findings and foci of existing research on women's career paths. It begins with an examination of factors related to gender-role socialization and differing societal roles and expectations for women and men. These factors were strongly emphasized in the early research on women and politics conducted in the 1970s, and they continue to present obstacles to women's recruitment and election to office in the 1990s. Also examined in this section are certain fundamental features of the structure and operation of electoral politics in the U.S. as they affect the election of women to public office. Most researchers have come to view these as among the greatest impediments to increasing the number of women elected officials. The section concludes with a review of the efforts of women's organizations and women's networks to assist women's political careers by helping them to overcome the obstacles they face. Three studies figure prominently in this review because they are based on larger and more representative samples than other research. The first is a study conducted by the Center for the American Woman and Politics that surveyed nationally representative samples of women and comparison samples of men serving as state senators, state representatives, county commissioners, mayors, and local council members in 1981; the findings are reported in Carroll and

Strimling 1983. The second is a six-state study of state legislative races during the 1970s, conducted by Janet Clark, R. Darcy, Susan Welch, and Margery Ambrosius and discussed in a variety of publications by these researchers including Darcy et al. 1987. The third is a nationwide study of women candidates for congressional, statewide, and state legislative offices in 1976, reported in Carroll 1985.

Socialization to Different Values

Research on political women conducted in the early to mid-1970s frequently stressed gender-role socialization as the major barrier to the election of greater numbers of women to public office (e.g., Kirkpatrick 1974; Costantini and Craik 1977; Lee 1977). Researchers emphasized that women were not socialized to see themselves as political actors and instead were taught to view active political involvement as inappropriate.

R. Darcy, Susan Welch, and Janet Clark provide several illustrations of common explanations for women's lack of greater political involvement that see differences stemming from gender-role socialization as key:

. . . perhaps women are not ambitious or lack the aggression necessary for political life. Or perhaps women are too naive and really do not understand what goes on in politics. Perhaps women are too concerned with issues relating to their traditional roles, such as child care and education, and not enough concerned with issues more central to the political agenda, such as inflation, the military, the budget, and taxes (1987, 91).

The trend in recent scholarship has been to reject socialization explanations such as these because they tend to "blame the victim" by locating the reasons for women's political underrepresentation in the internalized attitudes and characteristics of women themselves.

Nevertheless, several researchers have concluded that a major factor contributing to women's continued underrepresentation in elective office is the paucity of women candidates (e.g., Karnig and Walter 1976; Welch et al. 1985; Clark et al. 1984, 152; Fowkles et al. 1979; King 1977). While factors other than the attitudes women internalize as a result of their socialization may be sufficient to explain why women are not often recruited to run for office and why they have difficulty winning when they run, any credible explanation for why relatively few women voluntarily put themselves forward as candidates would seem to require some attention to gender-role socialization. Despite the implicit (and sometimes explicit) tendency for socialization explanations to place the burden for change on women themselves, such explanations have pointed to gender differences that are potentially important in helping to account for the paucity of women candidates.

The recent literature on gender difference, produced largely by women's studies scholars outside the discipline of political science (e.g., Gilligan 1982; Chodorow 1978; Ruddick 1983), suggests a way of recasting traditional gender-role socialization explanations so that they no longer blame the victim, but rather place at least some of the burden for change on the political system itself. Many gender difference scholars argue that women and men have different values and perspectives, largely as a result of women's and men's differential relationship to parenting and caretaking. However, the values and perspectives of women are not viewed as inferior to those of men; rather they are viewed as complementary or in some cases even potentially transformative.

The argument is that the public world, largely the province of men and male values, needs female values. Yet women see the political world as one that fails in important ways to reflect their concerns and their experiences, and consequently, a world that is very unappealing to them. According to this line of argument, many women are politically inactive not because their socialization has left them ill-equipped for politics, but rather because politics has not sufficiently incorporated their values and concerns. Consequently, before massive numbers of women present themselves as candidates for political office, the system itself (and not just individual women) may have to change to better reflect women's interests and their values.

Private Life

The political careers of women are influenced to a greater extent by family responsibilities and other private life considerations than are the political careers of men. An important contribution of women and politics research has been to call attention to the fact that men's political careers are affected by families and private sphere considerations to a greater degree than recognized in much of the traditional political science literature (e.g., Blair and Henry 1981; Carroll 1989). Nevertheless, the impact of these factors on the political careers of women is greater.

A number of studies conducted in the early to mid-1970s found that women elective officeholders are older than their male counterparts (Dubeck 1976; Kirkpatrick 1974, 38; Stoper 1977, 324). While a more recent 1981 nationwide study found the median ages of women and men holding various offices to be very similar, women were nevertheless less likely than men to be under 40 or over 60 (Carroll and Strimling 1983, 14-15). The smaller proportion of women over 60 reflects men's longer tenure in office. However, the smaller proportion of women under 40 suggests that women more often than men wait until after the early years of child rearing have passed before running for office. In fact, a number of studies have observed that women wait until their children are grown before seeking office (e.g., Lee 1977; Kirkpatrick 1974, 230; Johnson and Carroll 1978, 16).

This conclusion is further substantiated by the repeated finding in a number of studies that women officeholders are less likely than their male counterparts to have young children (e.g., Carroll and Strimling 1983, 27-28; Johnson and Carroll 1978, 13). Moreover, the fact that the responsibilities of parenthood affect women's political careers more often than men's is reflected in the finding that women officeholders far more often than their male counterparts report that the ages of their children influenced their decisions to run for office (Carroll and Strimling 1983, 28-29).

Just as parental responsibilities seem to have a greater impact on women's political careers than on the careers of men, so too do spousal attitudes. Married women officeholders at various levels of office are significantly more likely than their married male counterparts to report that their spouses are very supportive of their activities in politics and government (Carroll 1989; Carroll and Strimling 1983, 25-26; Mandel 1981, 74; Stoper 1977). This finding suggests that a supportive spouse is almost a prerequisite for a married woman to run for and gain election to office, whereas some married men appear to pursue office with only lukewarm support from, or occasionally against the wishes of, their spouses.

The greater importance that women attach to family responsibilities in making decisions about their political careers is evident in several other findings from research. Virginia Sapiro, in an analysis of data from a study of delegates to the 1972 national party conventions, found that men were just as likely as women to experience conflict between their family commitments and public commitments. However, women and men responded to this conflict differently; men were more likely to pursue their officeholding ambitions anyway whereas women were more likely to forgo political ambitions in favor of their families (Sapiro 1982). In another study Carol Nechemias found that women state legislators on the average live closer to state capitals than do male legislators, suggesting that family responsibilities may deter some women who live far away from state houses from running for office (1985). Finally, Susan J. Carroll found that women state legislators who were married and/or had children were significantly more likely than comparable male legislators to rate the support of their spouses and/or families as one of the three factors most important in influencing their decisions to run for the legislature (1989).

The problem for women is not that they give serious consideration to the likely effects of their political decisions on their families; rather, the problem for women is that men do not weigh family considerations equally as heavily. Until widespread societal change leads men and women to share equal responsibilities for child rearing and weigh equally the effects of their decisions on other family members, private life considerations are likely to continue to have a stronger impact on the political careers of women than men.

Qualifications for Officeholding

Women who seek and hold elective office are as qualified as their male counterparts. Nevertheless, their qualifications differ in some important respects.

Overall, the educational attainment of women does not differ greatly from that of men. However, women state legislators, county commissioners, and local council members are somewhat more likely than their male counterparts to have attended college. Female officeholders at county and local levels are just as likely as their male counterparts to have advanced degrees, but among state legislators, a smaller proportion of women than men have received law degrees (Carroll and Strimling 1983, 17-18). Research on women candidates for congressional, statewide, and state legislative offices has also found women candidates to be well-educated with majorities having college degrees (Carroll 1985, 66-67).

A majority of women officeholders among state legislators, county commissioners, mayors, and local council members nationally have professional or white collar occupations. There are, however, important sex differences in occupations that mirror sex-segregated patterns in the labor force more generally. A sizeable minority of women (about one of every five state legislators) have never worked in paid employment outside the home for an extended period of time.[1] The most common profession for women is school teacher, and substantial minorities of women, especially at local and county levels, are employed as secretaries or clerical workers. Women are also more likely than men to have professions in nursing or health care (excluding physicians). Men, especially among state legislators, are much more likely to be attorneys, the most common professional occupation for men. Men are also much more likely to be employed as managers or administrators, and they more often are farmers (Carroll and Strimling 1983, 18-23). Among members of Congress, men are again more likely than women to be attorneys although the proportion of women lawyers has increased in recent times (Gertzog 1984, 38-40).[2] These occupational differences between women and men who hold office seem to be mirrored in the candidate population (Carroll 1985).

Before seeking office, proportionately more women than men acquire political experience. The only form of political experience in which men surpass women is elective officeholding. Across most levels of office (i.e., state legislatures, county commissions, mayoralties, and local councils), women officeholders are more likely than their male counterparts to have held an appointive position in government, to have worked on the staff of an elected official, and to have worked on a political campaign (Carroll and Strimling 1983, 31-59).[3]

The pattern of sex differences in qualifications apparent among elected officials suggests that women more often than men may use political experience as a way to prepare and qualify themselves for officeholding. While objectively a background in farming or business

---

[1]The proportion of women officeholders who have never worked in paid employment outside the home has dropped during the past two decades as more women have moved into the paid labor force. For example, Kirkpatrick (1974, 61) reported that almost all the women in her study of 50 women state legislators in 1972 were full-time homemakers.

[2]Because increasing numbers of women have attended law school in recent years, the proportion of women elected officials who are attorneys is likely to increase over the next couple of decades.

[3]Among women serving in state legislatures in 1981, more than two-fifths had held an appointive governmental position, about one-fourth had worked on the staff of an elected official, and more than four-fifths had worked on a political campaign before running for office themselves (Carroll and Strimling 1983, 34-40).

may provide no better preparation for officeholding than experience as a teacher, a health-care worker, or even an administrative assistant, nevertheless the fact that most officeholders traditionally have come from male-dominated occupations means that women with occupations in female-dominated fields may have to work harder to prove that they are "qualified." One way they may do so is by becoming active in politics and acquiring political experience.

Political Ambition

Numerous studies of party elites, especially national convention delegates, have found women less ambitious for public officeholding than their male counterparts (e.g., Jennings and Thomas 1968; Costantini and Craik 1977; Kirkpatrick 1976; Farah 1976; Fowlkes, Perkins, and Rinehart 1979; Farah and Sapiro 1980; Jennings and Farah 1981; Constantini and Bell 1984). Since women party activists constitute an important potential pool of people from whom future candidates for office might be drawn, women's lower levels of ambition have been viewed as one of the reasons for the underrepresentation of women in public office.

However, recent research has demonstrated that the gender differences in political ambition found among women party activists do not exist among elective officeholders (Johnson and Carroll 1978, 51-53; Carroll, 1985; Dodson and Farah 1988). Rather, the political ambitions of women in state legislative, county, and local offices equal or exceed those of their male counterparts. Women in these offices are just as likely or more likely than men to want another term in the office in which they serve, to aspire to some other elective or appointive position, and to desire ultimately to be a governor or to hold national office (Carroll 1985). Clearly, women officeholders have overcome the social and psychological barriers that restrict the ambitions of women party activists. Thus, while low levels of political ambition may be one of the reasons why fewer women than men seek political office in the first place, levels of ambition cannot account for the failure of women to move up the political ladder.

Research has also found a clear relationship between feminism and political ambition (Dodson and Farah 1988; Mueller 1982a). Among both delegates and elective officeholders, those women who are sympathetic to feminism are most ambitious. The greater ambition among feminist women may help to account for findings that large proportions of women officeholders support feminist positions on women's issues, identify as feminists, and work on legislation aimed at helping women (Carroll and Taylor 1989; Dodson 1989; Stanwick and Kleeman 1983). Moreover, the greater ambition of feminist women may help to explain why levels of support for feminist policy positions are higher among women who hold state legislative office than among women who serve at county and local levels (Stanwick and Kleeman 1983).[4]

Gender-Role Stereotypes and Voter Prejudice

A number of studies, some based on representative samples of the public and others based on experiments generally using college students as subjects, have demonstrated that voters have a variety of stereotypes about women candidates. However, a number of studies have also found that women candidates fare about equally as well with voters as do male candidates of the same party running in comparable circumstances. In combination, these two sets of findings suggest that while voter prejudice and stereotypes exist, either stereotypes are less important than other considerations in affecting how people actually vote, or alternatively, voters who are prejudiced against women candidates are counteracted by voters who are predisposed to vote for women candidates.

Studies have documented that voters hold strong stereotypes of women candidates, some of which work to women's advantage and some to their disadvantage. Women candidates are perceived, for example, to be better than men at understanding the "human side" of issues, getting things organized, having new ideas, managing details, caring, being effective, having strong opinions, fighting for their beliefs, understanding the needs of voters, being honest, speaking directly to the point, having compassion for the needy, being moral and upright, and working out compromises. Women candidates are perceived as less able than men to handle crises, the emotional demands of public life, the military, big business, large budgets, decisions under pressure, and extensive travel

---

[4]Direct comparisons of the attitudes of women officeholders with the attitudes of women in the general population are difficult because of the lack of direct comparability in question wording. However, the very high levels of support for feminist positions on issues such as the Equal Rights Amendment and abortion found in studies such as Stanwick and Kleeman 1983, suggest that support for feminist positions is greater among women who are officeholders, especially at higher levels of office.

(Sapiro 1981-82; Mueller 1982b; Cooper and Secrest Associates 1984; Yankelovich, Skelly, and White 1984; Hickman-Maslin 1987; Boles 1989; Leeper 1991). Studies have also shown that voter prejudice against women candidates is notably greater when the woman candidate has small children (Hedlund et al. 1979; Yankelovich, Skelley, and White 1984), when the woman is attractive (Bowman 1984), or when the woman is a candidate for executive rather than legislative office or a judicial position as opposed to a seat on a local school board (Adams 1975; Hedlund et al. 1979).

Evidence that these stereotypes really make a difference in election outcomes is lacking. Rather, numerous studies have concluded that women candidates are not significantly penalized at the polls on account of their sex (Darcy and Schramm 1977; Karnig and Walter 1976; Hedlund et al. 1979; Ekstrand and Eckert 1981; Clark et al. 1984; Rosenwasser et al. 1987). Overall, women candidates may fare worse than male candidates, but this seems largely due to the fact that proportionately fewer women are incumbents and proportionately more women challenge incumbents. While some voters may well be prejudiced against women candidates, voters in the aggregate are not a major obstacle to the careers of elected women politicians.

Structural Impediments

Recent research has demonstrated that women are disadvantaged by certain features of the way our political system is structured and operates (e.g., Carroll 1985; Darcy et al. 1987). The existence of these structural impediments is a major reason why the United States lags behind several other western democracies (e.g., Sweden, Norway, Finland, Denmark, Germany, the Netherlands) in the representation of women in elective office at the national level. Two of the most important structural impediments present in the U.S. system are: (1) the advantages that accrue to incumbents in seeking reelection, and (2) the predominance of single-member over multimember districts and elections.

The staying power of incumbents poses a major impediment to women's electoral success, especially at the congressional level. The fact that incumbents often seek reelection and rarely are defeated is a well-known political fact; among incumbents in the U.S. House of Representatives, the rate of turnover is especially slow, with 95 percent or more of incumbents who seek reelection winning. A computer simulation that made (probably unrealistic) assumptions that parties would nominate women at a higher rate and that incumbents would have less of an advantage than has been true in recent elections predicted that only 12 percent of members of the House would be women 40 years from the time of the study (Anderson and Thorson 1984). At the state legislative level the reelection rate of incumbents is also very high, but more vacancies occur because voluntary turnover is greater (Darcy et al. 1987, 151). The power of incumbency and the lack of greater numbers of open seats disadvantage women as a group because most women who run for office have to challenge incumbents, the vast majority of them male, whom they rarely defeat.

At the state legislative level, women run in a greater proportion of multimember than single-member districts, and women who run in multimember districts win at a higher rate than those who run in single-member districts (Darcy et al. 1987, 119; Carroll 1985, 110; Rule 1990). Moreover, evidence suggests that when states change from multimember to single-member districts, as several states have during the past three decades, the proportion of women running and winning election decreases compared to national trends (Darcy et al. 1987, 119-22). Although differences in electoral arrangements are probably less important at the municipal level, there is evidence that women fare slightly better when cities have at-large rather than district elections (Darcy et al. 1987, 117-18; MacManus and Bullock 1989; Welch and Karnig 1979). The explanation that is generally given for women's greater success in multimember districts is that party leaders or others involved in slating candidates are more likely to "balance" the ticket with a woman in a multimember district than to put her forward for the sole seat in a single-member district; in a multimember district her sex may be perceived as an asset in attracting voters to the ticket while in a single-member district her sex may mean that she is viewed as an electoral risk (Darcy et al. 1987, 118-19; Carroll 1985, 28). However, regardless of the explanation for women's greater success in multimember districts, the problems for women candidates are that at the congressional level the U.S. has only single-member districts; at the state legislative level, there are many more single-member than multimember districts, and the recent trend has been in the direction of converting multimember into single-member districts[5]

---

[5]Some of the conversion from multimember to single-member districts, especially in the South, has stemmed from Justice Department intervention or litigation brought under the Voting Rights Act of 1965 and its 1982 amendments. Historically, multimember districts have sometimes been used as a mechanism

(Carroll 1985, 44); and at the municipal level, minority men clearly fare worse in at-large races, suggesting that at-large elections will not in many cases accomplish the goal of increasing representation of women without simultaneously decreasing the representation of men of color (Darcy et al. 1987, 126; Welch and Karnig 1979).

Research has found that some structural features of the political system such as runoffs, size of city council, and length of term seem to have little or no effect on women's electoral chances (MacManus and Bullock 1989; Darcy et al. 1987; Bullock and Johnson 1985; Fleischmann and Stein 1987). However, the representation of women does seem to be inversely related to the desirability of the office and to salary. At both state legislative and local levels, research has found that the less desirable and important the office and the lower its salary, the more likely it is to be held by a woman[6] (Diamond 1977; Carroll 1985; Welch and Karnig 1979).

The fact that women are disadvantaged by the way the U.S. political system is structured and operates is further illustrated by comparison with other countries that elect public officials through proportional representation, awarding shares of legislative seats proportional to the share of votes a party has won. Research has demonstrated that women's representation in national legislatures is greater in countries with

---

to dilute the black vote and to ensure that blacks, who have tended to be concentrated residentially, did not constitute a majority of the voting population. See, e.g., Grofman and Handley 1991; Niemi, Hill, and Grofman 1985. Obviously, one would not want to argue for the preservation of multimember districts designed to prevent the election of black candidates even if they led to greater representation for women. Rather, the challenge would seem to be to create a system of representation that disadvantages neither women of any color nor minorities of either gender.

[6]The extreme example at the state legislative level is New Hampshire, which has the largest legislature (with a lower house of 400 members) as well as the lowest salary of any legislature ($100 per year in 1990) (Council of State Governments 1990, 133-134). New Hampshire has for years been one of the legislatures with the largest proportion of women (33.5 percent in 1993) (Center for the American Woman and Politics 1993b). However, not all state legislatures with relatively large proportions of women have low salaries. For example, in 1993, more than one-third of Arizona's legislators were women (Center for the American Woman and Politics 1991b), but Arizona legislators, who received $15,000 per year (Council of State Governments 1990, 133-34), were by no means at the bottom of the pay scale for legislators.

proportional representation, especially those utilizing party lists, than in countries like the U.S., which elect representatives on the basis of plurality voting[7] (Randall 1987, 140-42; Rule 1981; Norris 1985).

Money

Observers of women's campaigns have suggested that women candidates have a particularly difficult time raising money both because they are not well integrated into male-dominated financial networks and because they find it more difficult than men to ask for money for themselves (Mandel 1981, 181-87; Paizis 1977, 17-24; Tolchin and Tolchin 1976, 189-95). Fund raising clearly is perceived by women candidates as a major problem, if not *the* major problem, they confront (Mandel 1981; Carroll 1985). For example, women candidates in primaries for state legislative, statewide, and congressional offices in 1976 cited money much more frequently than any other factor as the major problem they faced during their primary campaigns (Carroll 1985, 51-52). Moreover, although fund raising is a major concern for many male candidates as well, there is evidence of gender differences in the perception of money as a problem. For example, research on women and men serving in state legislative and local elective office in 1981 found that women officeholders, especially those who ran in races for state senate seats where campaign expenses were greater, were more likely than men holding the same office to report that having financial resources sufficient to conduct a viable campaign was an important consideration in their decisions to run (Carroll and Strimling 1983, 112-13).

Despite the perceptions of women candidates, however, research from recent elections (e.g., 1980 and 1982) indicates that women who are major party nominees for congressional seats raise just as much money overall as do male major party nominees running in similar campaign situations (Burrell 1985, 1988; Uhlaner and Schlozman 1986; Newman et al. 1984). For example, Republican female challengers do just as well

---

[7]The women's movement in the U.S. has devoted little attention to trying to change features of our political system that disadvantage women such as the predominance of single-member over multimember districts, the lack of limitations for most offices on the number of terms for which incumbents can seek reelection, or the plurality method for electing candidates. Yet structural changes are unlikely to come about unless people are mobilized to push for such changes.

as Republican male challengers, and Democratic female incumbents raise just as much money as Democratic male incumbents. Moreover, one of these studies found that women congressional candidates in 1980 were not less likely than men to raise money from big donors (i.e., over $500) or from PACs, although women were somewhat less likely than similarly situated men to receive money from their parties (Uhlaner and Schlozman 1986, 44-45). A similar study of congressional candidates in 1982 again found that women raised as large a proportion of their money from big donors as did men; in addition, women who were challengers, especially Democratic challengers, raised proportionately more money than comparable men from PACs although less from individual contributions (Newman et al. 1984). Unlike the 1980 study, the 1982 study did not find that women received less money from their parties; in fact among Republicans, women received more money from their party than men did (Newman et al. 1984).

Although these studies demonstrate that women party nominees for congressional seats in general elections can raise as much money as their male counterparts, systematic analyses comparing the fund-raising success of female and male candidates in congressional *primaries* are lacking. Moreover, almost no studies compare the fund raising of women and men running for offices other than Congress.[8]

Hopeless Races and the Role of Parties in Candidate Recruitment

Considerable evidence indicates that women candidates for most congressional and many state legislative offices run in "hopeless" races where prospects of victory are very low and that larger proportions of female than male candidates run in such races (Gertzog and Simard 1981; Bernstein 1986; Burrell 1988; van Hightower 1977; Clark et al. 1984; Carroll 1985). Women are more likely to run against incumbents and more likely to run as minority party candidates in districts and states dominated by the other party. While some evidence suggests that the tendency for women to run in hopeless races has declined over time at the state legislative level (Clark et al. 1984), the opposite is true at the congressional level. As Robert A. Bernstein explains, the surge in nominations of women candidates for Congress in recent years:

---

[8]An exception is Darcy, Welch, and Clark 1987, 61, who find that women candidates for the Oklahoma state house in 1978 and 1980 raised more money than their male counterparts.

. . . has failed to lead to a surge in seats because women are getting the wrong types of nominations—nominations to challenge incumbents, rather than nominations for open seats. From 1940 to 1972 women received a slightly higher percentage of open-seat than challenger nominations; however, since 1974, women have been twice as likely to get challenger nominations as open-seat nominations. In 1984 women got thirty-eight nominations to challenge incumbents but only one nomination for an open seat (1986, 155).[9]

It is true that many contests for open seats take place without any woman entering the race; for example, only 15 women ran in primary contests for the 23 U.S. House seats that were open at the primary stage in 1984 (Burrell 1988, 57). Nevertheless, as Bernstein points out, part of the problem is that the women who run in open-seat primaries have had a much lower rate of success than their male counterparts (1986, 156).

To what extent are the political parties to blame for the disproportionate concentration of women in hopeless races, the lack of women candidates in races for open seats, and the low rate of success of those women who have entered open primaries? Political scientists have attempted to answer these questions, but the answers are not completely clear. The literature frequently makes reference to the tendency of party leaders to recruit women as "sacrificial lambs" in hopeless races and has provided evidence that this happens (Diamond 1977, 78; van Hightower 1977; King 1977; Carroll 1985; Stanwick 1983; Gertzog and Simard 1981). Yet most of this research lacks male comparison groups. Consequently, it is not possible to ascertain whether proportionately more women than men are recruited as sacrificial lambs, especially once incumbents are excluded. Systematic research on these questions has also been plagued by definitional and measurement problems. First, who are the party leaders? Clearly, they differ from locality to locality, and the most influential party leaders may not always be people holding formal positions within the party structure. Second, not only does the definition of party leaders vary from one locale to another, but also the extent to which party leaders are involved in candidate selection varies tremen-

---

[9]One development that may contribute to the pattern that Bernstein observes at the congressional level is that in recent years a decreasing proportion of the women elected to Congress (and undoubtedly, a decreasing proportion of women candidates as well) have been widows who ran for seats vacated by their deceased husbands (Gertzog 1984, 13-31).

dously. Does it then make sense to compare women and men running in different districts where the strength of party structures and the role of parties in recruitment may be very different? Finally, there is the question of what constitutes recruitment—simple encouragement, formal endorsement of candidates, arm-twisting, or something else?

Nevertheless, while it is difficult to identify the extent to which party leaders are responsible for the candidacies of the women who run in hopeless races, for the most part political parties have not engaged in affirmative action to end historical patterns of underrepresentation.[10] The national parties have developed PACs to assist women candidates, and they have sponsored campaign techniques training sessions for women (Kleeman 1983; Darcy et al. 1987, 157-58). However, parties do not seem to be making a concerted effort to approach women and encourage them to run in situations where they might have a good chance of winning (Carroll 1985, 22-45). In fact, a nationwide study of women officeholders found that those women who ran in the most adverse electoral circumstances, in which winning was a long shot, were the ones who most often had been recruited by party leaders (Carroll and Strimling 1983, 8, 72-73).

Women's Networks

Although political parties are not practicing affirmative action to bring more women into public office, women individually and collectively are engaged in special efforts to help women overcome the barriers they face and increase the numbers of women in elective office. Research shows that women in elective office have been aided by women and women's organizations and that they, in turn, encourage other women to follow in their footsteps.

---

[10]The one situation historically where the parties seem to have been most willing to encourage women to run where they had a reasonable chance of winning is when the woman's husband died while he was in office. Although the "widow's succession" has until recent years been a major pathway for women into the U.S. House of Representatives, nevertheless, the vast majority of members of Congress who have died in office have not been succeeded by their widows (Gertzog 1984, 16-18). Thus, even the practice of "widow's succession" has not been employed frequently and consistently enough to increase significantly the number of women in Congress.

Although women elective officeholders are much less likely than their male counterparts to be members of groups such as the Rotary or Chamber of Commerce, majorities of women officeholders, at least at higher levels of office, are members of women's groups. In 1988 three-fourths of all women state legislators were members of at least one of three major traditional women's organizations (League of Women Voters, American Association of University Women, Business and Professional Women) and/or a feminist organization (Carroll 1992). Levels of membership in the League of Women Voters were especially high with about two-fifths of women legislators reporting membership in this group. While the League of Women Voters cannot get directly involved in partisan politics, the high levels of membership suggest that the organization serves an important role in stimulating interest in electoral politics and in developing leadership skills. Memberships in feminist organizations were also substantial, with more than one-fifth of all women legislators belonging to the National Organization for Women and almost one-third belonging to the National Women's Political Caucus (Carroll 1992).

Women officeholders not only are embedded in a network of women's organizations, but also receive critical support from women's groups when they run for office. Women and women's organizations have developed a number of political action committees (PACs) to help women candidates. As of 1989, the Center for the American Woman and Politics (CAWP) was able to identify 35 PACs that gave money predominantly to women candidates and/or had a predominantly female donor base. Seventeen of these PACs provided CAWP with information about direct financial contributions made to candidates in 1988; these 17 PACs contributed a total of $1,139,315 to women candidates (Center for the American Woman and Politics, Winter 1989, 16-20).

About one-fourth of women state legislators surveyed by CAWP in 1981 reported that a women's organization actively encouraged them to run for office (Carroll and Strimling 1983, 89-91). Moreover, about three-fifths of state legislators surveyed by CAWP in 1988 claimed to have received formal or informal support during their campaigns from one or more women's organizations. About one-third of women state senators and about one-fourth of women state representatives reported that they received assistance from the National Organization for Women, one of the two feminist organizations most active in electoral politics. Virtually equal proportions of women legislators received support from the Women's Political Caucus, the other major feminist organization that is very active in electoral politics (Carroll 1992). Clearly, women's organizations have played a key role in encouraging and supporting many of the women who have succeeded in contemporary electoral politics.

Women officeholders also have in many cases received special assistance or learned about politics at the side of another woman. Women state legislators in the 1981 CAWP study were notably more likely than men to have worked on the campaigns of other women before running for office themselves (Carroll and Strimling 1983, 38-40). Moreover, those women officeholders who claimed to have had political role models or mentors much more often than their male counterparts had women as their role models or mentors (Carroll and Strimling 1983, 44-50).

In turn, most elected women politicians feel a responsibility to help other women to get involved in electoral politics. For example, among state legislators, a majority reported that they actively recruit women when hiring staff, encourage individual women to become active in politics, and speak to various groups of women urging them to become active (Carroll and Strimling 1983, 135-36).

While the support of other women and women's organizations may not be sufficient to counteract all of the obstacles women confront in deciding to run and winning election to office, this support is nevertheless important. Without the strategy of *women supporting women*, there would undoubtedly be fewer women holding office at all levels of government.

TOPICS FOR FUTURE RESEARCH

This section reviews gaps in current research and indicates general areas where new research is needed. Perhaps as many questions about elected women politicians' career paths remain unanswered as answered.

The Preprimary Selection Process and Primaries

One of the reasons for women's continued underrepresentation in elective office in the United States, which is distinctive in having a primary election system for nominating candidates, is that relatively few women ever become candidates by entering primaries. There are many, many more women in the *eligible pool* from which candidates are drawn than there are candidates. Women are active in politics in sizeable numbers—as party activists, as convention delegates, as staff members for other politicians, as community activists, as leaders in civic and community groups, as members of appointed boards and commissions. Yet, few of these women seek elective public office. Existing research has provided some clues as to why these women might not run for office, but with very few exceptions (e.g., Fowler and McClure 1989), research has focused on women who became candidates for office or who were elected to office, not those who were dissuaded from running or who never considered running despite having the qualifications and experience to do so. To develop a better understanding of why few women run for office, we need to examine what happens *before* primaries, i.e., the preprimary candidate selection process. The role of political party leaders in the preprimary selection process, the extent to which the costs of campaigning discourage potential candidates, and the availability of alternative (most likely women's) networks to encourage and support potential women candidates would seem critical in understanding what happens before primaries. Research focusing on specific state legislative or congressional districts, especially those with open seats, might best illuminate the preselection process. Linda L. Fowler and Robert D. McClure's analysis of Louise Slaughter's decision *not* to run in New York's 30th Congressional District in 1984 is an example of this type of research, but we need more in-depth studies of the preselection process in districts that have strong potential women candidates if we are to develop a comprehensive understanding of why few women even enter primaries.

If what happens before the primaries constitutes the first stage, then the primaries themselves constitute the second stage of the candidate selection process in need of further examination. With few exceptions research has focused on women once they have succeeded in winning their party's nomination. Yet large proportions of women candidates never make it through the primaries (Carroll 1985). Primaries pose an interesting set of questions: Are women hurt by getting started too late as some research has suggested (Carroll 1985)? Do women candidates have particular difficulty raising *early* money? Do they have more difficulty proving that they are credible candidates? Are parties and other organizations involved in supporting female candidates during the primaries, or do they wait until a woman has proven herself by winning a primary before they get involved? Do party leaders treat women candidates the same way that they treat male contenders?

Money

Despite the studies showing that women running for Congress in general elections can and do raise as much money as comparable male candidates, a number of questions remain unanswered about the role of money in women's campaigns and in their political careers more generally. First, is the finding that women candidates in general elections raise as much money as comparable male candidates true for races for offices other than Congress? Second, because women may be taken more seriously as candidates once they have won their party's nomination, how do they fare in raising funds to mount primary contests for the nomination? Do women have more difficulty than men in raising funds for primaries both in congressional races and in races for other levels of office? Third, is the timing of contributions to women's campaigns different? Does the money come in later in women's campaigns, and do they have more difficulty raising the initial money they need to become viable candidates, especially during the early stages of their primary races? Fourth, even when women raise the same amounts of money as men, do they have to work harder to do so? Do they devote more of their own time and the time of staff members to fund raising? Fifth, what can be learned from the experiences of women and men who have been particularly successful in raising campaign funds? Are different models for successful fund raising evident in women's and men's campaigns, or does one model apply to both? Sixth, even if women raise as much or more money from PACs as men, do they raise it from different types of PACs? For example, a number of PACs now exist that target their money mostly or primarily to women candidates (Kleeman 1983); what impact are they having on women's campaigns? Are they, as some research suggests (Wilhite and Theilmann 1986), the reason that women raise as much money from PACs in the aggregate as men do? Finally, to what extent are women dissuaded from running for office in the first place or from trying to move to a higher level of elective office because they fear that they cannot raise adequate funds? Are proportionately more women than men dissuaded? Previous research would suggest that the need to raise large amounts of money to mount a winning campaign is a major deterrent preventing many women from seeking office, particularly at higher levels (Carroll 1985; Mandel 1981).

Media

Little systematic research exists on the relationship between elected women politicians and the mass media. Moreover, the research that does exist does not constitute a well-integrated body of literature examining consistent themes with similar groups of political women. Rather, existing research touches upon a number of different aspects of media coverage.

Some experimental research has looked at the effects of hypothetical political ads portraying women candidates in different settings, finding that women received more favorable ratings in masculine than in feminine settings (Kaid et al. 1984). Other research has found that women candidates for congressional and statewide offices rely more heavily than male candidates on all forms of advertising and that they spend proportionately more on television advertising (Declercq, Benze, and Ritchie 1983). Another study by the same researchers examined the actual content of television ads of female and male candidates for congressional and statewide offices, finding mostly similarities but a few suggestive differences (Benze and Declercq 1984). Kim Fridkin Kahn and Edie Goldenberg have demonstrated both through actual content analysis of print media coverage of U.S. Senate campaigns and through experimental research that media coverage of female and male candidates differs in several respects and overall may disadvantage women candidates (Kahn 1989; Kahn and Goldenberg 1988). Some research has also examined media coverage of the 1984 vice-presidential debate involving Geraldine Ferraro (e.g., Shields and MacDowell 1987; Rosenberg and Elliot 1987).

In short, enough research exists to suggest that gender differences are present in media coverage and that the effect of the media on the political careers of elected women officials is a fruitful area for future research. Nevertheless, so little research exists that the list of potential research topics in this area is very long, and only a few general areas in need of attention will be mentioned here.

More analysis is needed examining possible biases in the placement, extent, content, and tone of coverage of women candidates in newspaper and television news. Analysis of print coverage of candidates in local, county, and state legislative races is especially lacking. However, women's political careers are likely to be affected not only by the coverage they receive during campaigns, but also by the coverage they receive once elected to office. Therefore, systematic studies comparing the coverage of women and men who hold public office also are needed.

Gender differences in political advertising would certainly seem a propitious area for future research, especially given the recent increase in the use of negative campaigning. There are a number of interesting questions about political advertising: do women candidates present themselves through ads in a manner similar to or different from male candidates? Are the media consultants who work for candidates sensitive to the ways in which gender may affect their campaigns? Do women candidates through their ads try to counter gender stereotypes that work to their disadvantage? Similarly, do they try to emphasize gender stereotypes that work to their advantage? Are there differences in the issues female and male candidates emphasize or in the way in which issues are addressed? Finally, are there gender differences in the use and effectiveness of negative advertising? A report based on a meeting of nine Democratic women candidates for Congress in 1988, their managers, and several political experts concluded:

> Women candidates and managers agree that negative media . . . [are] very difficult for women candidates. Some women initially thought it would be more difficult for a man to attack a woman than another man. They were wrong. Women candidates, more than men, had to watch the tone and substance of their media. . . . Most candidates and managers also thought women paid a higher price for negative campaigning. . . . Their negatives went up faster when they put negative spots on the air. . . . Most importantly, women had to spend more time early on building up their positive image . . . before they could go negative (Greenberg-Lake 1989, 26-27).

Research testing these assertions and other possible gender differences in the use and effectiveness of negative advertising would seem particularly timely.

Relationship to Women Voters and Constituents

While research indicates that women's organizations clearly play an important role in women's political careers, the relationship between elected women politicians and women in their constituencies remains relatively unexplored. A few studies have concluded that women voters are not particularly attracted to women candidates (e.g., Darcy and Schramm 1977; Sigelman and Welch 1984). However, other studies have demonstrated that gender-based voting does take place under certain circumstances, for example if the woman is identified as taking feminist positions on women's issues or if she is a liberal (Zipp and Plutzer 1985; Ekstrand and Eckert 1981). Moreover, there is evidence, much of it generated by studies funded through a project of the Center for the American Woman and Politics examining the impact of women in office, that women public officials often feel a special responsibility to represent women and consequently are more active than men in working on public policy to benefit women (e.g., Carroll and Taylor 1989; Dodson 1989; Thomas 1989).

The relationship between elected women politicians and women voters is one that has many aspects and deserves more serious research attention than it has received. One of the questions about the "gender gap" in public opinion and voting behavior that is most frequently asked (but impossible to answer on the basis of existing research) is how, in particular, the gender gap affects women candidates. Clearly, women and men in the aggregate are making different voting choices, but under what circumstances do women candidates receive a disproportionate share of the votes of women? Although women voters have tended to give their votes disproportionately to the Democratic candidate regardless of sex, the answer to this question goes beyond party, as illustrated by counterexamples of Republican women such as former Oregon gubernatorial candidate Norma Paulus or Maryland Congresswoman Connie Morella, who have attracted disproportionate support from women voters.

Other aspects of the relationship between women elected politicians and women voters also need to be explored. Are women more likely to turn out to vote when a woman candidate is in the race? To what extent, under what circumstances, and in what ways do women candidates attempt to appeal to women voters in their constituencies? Do these attempts vary depending on the party and ideology of the candidate and district? Are the appeals different from, or similar to, those used by male candidates? Which groups of women voters are most responsive to gender-based appeals from women candidates? To what extent do women, once elected, cultivate a special relationship with women constituents? Alternatively, to what extent do elected women politicians feel they must deny such a relationship in order to prove that they represent all their constituents? What are the implications for women's political careers of the posture they adopt toward women constituents?

Moving Up and Moving Out

While existing research provides a wealth of information about the special problems and advantages that women confront in gaining election to office in the first place, it provides little insight as to what happens to their political careers thereafter. Under what circumstances do women try to move into leadership positions within the legislative bodies in which they serve, and what obstacles do they face? Do elected women eventually realize the levels of ambition they express in response to questions on surveys? If not, why not? Under what circumstances do elected women politicians make a decision to run for higher office? Why are there not more women who are attempting to move up? What happens to women who lose the first time they run for office? Do they try again? What about the women who lose reelection bids or who lose bids for higher office? Do they run again?

All these questions are central to understanding elected women politicians' career paths. To answer them will require, in part, research tracing the career decisions of a large group of women elected politicians over time.

Women of Color

Women of color are a small, but growing segment of the officehold-ing population. For example, 168, or 12.2 percent, of all women serving in state legislatures at the end of 1990 were women of color. Of the 168, 130 were black, 17 were Asian-Pacific American, 16 were Hispanic, and 5 were Native American (Center for the American Woman and Politics 1992).

Few studies have examined women of color among elected women politicians (e.g., Darcy and Hadley 1988; Carroll and Strimling 1983; Bryce and Warrick 1977; Prestage 1977, 1980; Williams 1982; Greene 1982). For the most part, research on women of color has been concerned with documenting their numbers and describing their back-grounds and experiences.

The literature on African-American women, which is the largest body of literature on women of color, has emphasized the dual discrimination they face. A study comparing African-American and white women officeholders found that African-American women who are successful in gaining office have stronger credentials, experience, and organizational support than white women officeholders, perhaps because overcoming the dual effects of both racism and sexism requires extraordinary effort and backing (Carroll and Strimling 1983). One might expect the same to be true for women who are members of other minority groups, but comparable research is lacking.

We need to know far more about the barriers women of color face in gaining elective office and in building political careers. Because they experience the effects of both racism and sexism, the situation of minority women is distinct from that of both men of color and white women. Because they are a minority of both groups, studies of either women officeholders or minority officeholders will lead to generalizations that inevitably fail to reflect adequately the experiences of women of color. Moreover, mere replication of questions designed to measure the experiences of minority males or white women will also fail to capture all that is distinctive about the experiences of minority women officeholders. For example, Carroll and Strimling (1983) note that in asking African-American women officeholders the same questions designed for a sample of predominantly white women officeholders, they achieved comparability of results but failed to measure some of the factors that might be most critical for African-American women (e.g., the impact of the civil rights movement or the role of black churches and black women's sororities in their political development).

Ideally, any research on the career paths of women (or minority men) should include companion studies of minority women with questions that reflect their distinctive experiences. Because the number of women of color holding office is small, this will require either selecting separate samples or stratifying by race and sex. However, the added ability to separate the effects of race and sex as well as to identify that which is distinctive about the experiences of women of color will be well worth the additional effort.

CONCLUSION

Two decades have now passed since that Center for the American Woman and Politics (CAWP) brought together 50 women state legislators in May 1972 to discuss their experiences as women elected officials. That occasion was momentous not only because it was the first attempt to bring women elected officials from across the nation together to reflect on their experiences in male-dominated political institutions, but also because information gathered from the women who attended the conference led to the publication of Jeane J. Kirkpatrick's *Political Woman*, a landmark book that opened up a whole new area of research.

Since CAWP's 1972 conference and the publication of Kirkpatrick's book, the number of women elected to state legislatures and to other political offices has increased dramatically, and the amount of research focusing on women elected officials has increased just as dramatically. Society has traditionally organized gender relations in such a way that women and men have played different roles, and as this chapter has made clear, we now know a great deal about how traditional gender roles—as manifested in the different values and interests of women and men, the greater responsibility women have shouldered for child rearing and maintenance of family relations, sex-segregation in labor force participation, and the gender role stereotypes held by voters—have posed obstacles for women's involvement in elective politics. Traditional gender roles have been a major impediment to women's achievement in politics, just as they have been to women's achievement in other public institutions such as corporations, academia, and the media.

This chapter has also highlighted a number of aspects of our system of electoral politics that restrict the involvement of women in elective politics. Unlike the obstacles stemming from traditional gender roles, these obstacles—the lack of political opportunities resulting from the staying power of incumbents, the predominance of single-member over multimember districts, the need for substantial financial resources, and the parties' reluctance to recruit women candidates in winnable races—are unique to politics. Research over the past two decades has contributed greatly to our understanding of how these factors restrict women's political careers.

Research over the past two decades has also identified at least one strategy that women have employed to overcome the obstacles they face in elective politics; that strategy is one of *women supporting women*. As research has shown, both individually and collectively through women's organizations, women have attempted to increase the number of women in elected office.

Despite all we have learned during the past two decades, perhaps more questions about women's political careers remain unanswered than answered. A substantial research agenda awaits the next generation of scholars, but three areas, in particular, seem most in need of attention.

First, we need to be especially concerned with the preprimary selection process as it affects women, as well as with the fate of women in primaries. We have learned a great deal about the women who become candidates in general elections and even more about those who are elected to office. However, the political careers of many women may end almost as soon as they begin. In order to understand why more women do not enter primaries and/or never make it through the primaries to general elections, we have to focus our attention on the earliest stages of candidate development and selection.

We also need to focus more attention on the later stages of women's political careers. We know very little about the factors that affect whether elected women are able to move into leadership positions in political institutions or the circumstances under which they decide to seek (or not to seek) higher office.

Finally, we need to learn more about the experiences of women of color who run for elective office and pursue political careers. Without more work on women of color, we risk repeating the error committed by those researchers in the past who overlooked women elected officials, assuming that the experience of the predominant group of officeholders (i.e., men) reflected the experience of all officeholders. Two decades of research on women elected officials has demonstrated how problematic it is to assume that the experience of a group in the majority adequately reflects the experience of a group in the minority. Our goal as researchers should be to understand the diverse array of obstacles, resources, and experiences that confront elective politicians of all backgrounds as they strive to construct political careers and achieve their political objectives.

REFERENCES

Adams, William C. 1975. "Candidate Characteristics, Office of Election, and Voter Responses." *Experimental Study of Politics* 4:6-88.

Anderson, Kristi, and Stuart J. Thorson. 1984. "Congressional Turnover and the Election of Women." *Western Political Quarterly* 37:143-56.

Benze, James G., and Eugene R. Declercq. 1985. "Content of Television Political Spot Ads for Female Candidates." *Journalism Quarterly* 62:278-283, 88.

Bernstein, Robert A. 1986. "Why Are There So Few Women in the House?" *Western Political Quarterly* 39:155-64.

Blair, Diane Kincaid, and Ann R. Henry. 1981. "The Family Factor in State Legislative Turnover." *Legislative Studies Quarterly* 6:55-68.

Boles, Janet K. 1989. "Images of Female and Male Elected Officials: The Effect of Gender and Other Respondent Characteristics." *Journal of Political Science* 17:19-31.

Bowman, Ann O'M. 1984. "Physical Attractiveness and Electability: Looks and Votes." *Women & Politics* 4:55-65.

Bryce, Herrington J., and Alan E. Warrick. 1977. "Black Women in Electoral Politics." In *A Portrait of Marginality*, ed. Marianne Githens and Jewel L. Prestage, New York: McKay.

Bullock, Charles S., and Loch K. Johnson. 1985. "Sex and the Second Primary." *Social Science Quarterly* 66:933-44.

Burrell, Barbara. 1985. "Women's and Men's Campaigns for the U.S. House of Representatives, 1972-1982: A Finance Gap?" *American Politics Quarterly* 13:251-72.

_____. 1988. "The Political Opportunity of Women Candidates for the U.S. House of Representatives in 1984." *Women & Politics* 8:51-68.

Carroll, Susan J. 1985a. "Political Elites and Sex Differences in Ambition: A Reconsideration." *Journal of Politics* 47:1231-43.

_____. 1985b. *Women as Candidates in American Politics.* Bloomington: Indiana University Press.

_____. 1989. "The Personal is Political: The Intersection of Private Lives and Public Roles Among Women and Men in Elective and Appointive Office." *Women & Politics* 9:51-67.

_____. 1992. "Women State Legislators, Women's Organizations, and the Representation of Women's Culture in the United States." In *Women Transforming Politics: Worldwide Strategies for Empower-*

ment, ed. Jill M. Bystydzienski, Bloomington: Indiana University Press.

_____, and Wendy S. Strimling. 1983. *Women's Routes to Elective Office*. New Brunswick, N.J.: Center for the American Woman and Politics.

_____, and Ella Taylor. 1989. "Gender Differences in Policy Priorities of U.S. State Legislators." Paper presented at the annual meeting of the American Political Science Association, Atlanta, August 31-September 3.

Center for the American Woman and Politics. Winter 1989. "News and Notes." New Brunswick, N.J.: Center for the American Woman and Politics.

_____. 1992. "Women of Color in Elective Office 1992." Fact Sheet. New Brunswick, N.J.: Center for the American Woman and Politics.

_____. 1993a. "Women in Elective Office 1993." Fact Sheet. New Brunswick, N.J.: Center for the American Woman and Politics.

_____. 1993b. "Women in State Legislatures 1993." Fact Sheet. New Brunswick, N.J.: Center for the American Woman and Politics.

Chodorow, Nancy. 1978. *The Reproduction of Mothering*. Berkeley: University of California.

Clark, Janet, R. Darcy, Susan Welch, and Margery Ambrosius. 1984. "Women as Legislative Candidates in Six States." In *Political Women: Current Roles in State and Local Government*, ed. Janet A. Flammang, Beverly Hills: Sage.

Cooper and Secrest Associates, Inc. 1984. "Women as Candidates in the 1984 Congressional Elections." Commissioned by the National Women's Political Caucus. Washington, D.C.

Costantini, Edmond, and Julie Davis Bell. 1984. "Women in Political Parties: Gender Differences in Motives Among California Party Activists." In *Political Women: Current Roles in State and Local Government*, ed. Janet Flammang, Beverly Hills: Sage.

_____, and Kenneth H. Craik. 1977. "Women as Politicians: The Social Background, Personality, and Political Careers of Female Party Leaders." In *A Portrait of Marginality*, ed. Marianne Githens and Jewel L. Prestage, New York: McKay.

Council of State Governments. 1990. *The Book of the States*, 1990-91 edition. Lexington, Kentucky: The Council of State Governments.

Darcy, R., and Charles D. Hadley. 1988. "Black Women in Politics: The Puzzle of Success." *Social Science Quarterly* 69:629-45.

_____, and Sarah Slavin Schramm. 1977. "When Women Run Against Men." *Public Opinion Quarterly* 41:1-12.

_____, Susan Welch, and Janet Clark. 1987. *Women, Elections, and Representation*. New York: Longman.

Declercq, Eugene, James Benze, and Elisa Ritchie. 1983. "Macha Women and Macho Men: The Role of Gender in Campaigns Involving Women." Paper presented at the annual meeting of the American Political Science Association, Chicago, September 4.

Diamond, Irene. 1977. *Sex Roles in the State House*. New Haven: Yale.

Dodson, Debra L. 1989. "A Comparison of the Impact of Women and Men's Attitudes on Their Legislative Behavior: Is What They Say What They Do?" Paper presented at the annual meeting of the American Political Science Association, Atlanta, August 31-September 3.

_____, and Barbara G. Farah. 1988. "Political Ambition among Women State Legislators and Convention Delegates." Presented at the annual meeting of the International Society for Political Psychology, July 1-5.

Dubeck, Paula J. 1976. "Women and Access to Political Office: A Comparison of Female and Male State Legislators." *Sociological Quarterly* 17:42-52.

Ekstrand, Laurie E., and William A. Eckert. 1981. "The Impact of Candidate's Sex on Voter Choice." *Western Political Quarterly* 34:78-87.

Farah, Barbara G. 1976. "Climbing the Political Ladder: The Aspirations and Expectations of Partisan Elites." In *New Research on Women and Sex Roles at the University of Michigan*, ed. Marianne Githens and Jewel L. Prestage, Ann Arbor: University of Michigan Center for the Continuing Education of Women.

_____, and Virginia Sapiro. 1980. "New Pride and Old Prejudice: Political Ambition and Role Orientations Among Female Partisan Elites." *Women & Politics* 1:13-36.

Fleischmann, Arnold, and Lana Stein. 1987. "Minority and Female Success in Municipal Runoff Elections." *Social Science Quarterly* 68:378-85.

Fowler, Linda M., and Robert D. McClure. 1989. *Political Ambition: Who Decides to Run for Congress*. New Haven: Yale.

Fowlkes, Diane, Jerry Perkins, and Sue Tolleson Rinehart. 1979. "Gender Roles and Party Roles." *American Political Science Review*, 73:772-80.

Gertzog, Irwin N. 1984. *Congressional Women: Their Recruitment, Treatment, and Behavior*. New York: Praeger.

_____, and M. Michele Simard. 1981. "Women and 'Hopeless' Congressional Candidacies, 1916-1978." *American Politics Quarterly* 9:449-66.

Gilligan, Carol. 1982. *In a Different Voice*. Cambridge: Harvard.

Greenberg-Lake, The Analysis Group, Inc. 1989. "Campaigning in a Different Voice." Washington, D.C.: Greenberg-Lake, The Analysis Group.

Greene, Ghussan Rouse. 1982. "Contributions of Black Women in Politics and Government." In *Contributions of Black Women to America*, vol. 2, ed. Marianna W. Davis, Columbia, S.C.: Kenday.

Grofman, Bernard, and Lisa Handley. 1991. "The Impact of the Voting Rights Act on Black Representation in Southern State Legislatures." *Legislative Studies Quarterly* 16:111-28.

Hedlund, Ronald D., Patricia K. Freeman, Keith G. Hamm, and Robert M. Stein. 1979. "The Electability of Women Candidates: The Effects of Sex Role Stereotypes." *Journal of Politics* 41:513-24.

Jennings, M. Kent, and Barbara G. Farah. 1981. "Social Roles and Political Resources: An Over-Time Study of Men and Women in Party Elites." *American Journal of Political Science* 25:462-82.

_____, and Norman Thomas. 1968. "Men and Women in Party Elites." *Midwest Journal of Political Science* 7:469-72.

Johnson, Marilyn, and Carroll Susan. 1978. "Profile of Women Holding Office II." New Brunswick, N.J.: Center for the American Woman and Politics.

Kahn, Kim Fridkin. 1989. "An Experimental Investigation of Gender and Media Effects in U.S. Senate Elections." Paper presented at the annual meeting of the Midwest Political Science Association, Chicago, April 13-15.

_____, and Edie N. 1988. "An Examination of Coverage Patterns for Male and Female U.S. Senate Candidates." Paper presented at the annual meeting of the American Political Science Association.

Kaid, Lynda Lee, Sandra L. Myers, Val Pipps, and Jan Hunter. 1984. "Sex Role Perceptions and Televised Political Advertising: Comparing Male and Female Candidates." *Women & Politics* 4:41-53.

Karnig, Albert K., and B. Oliver Walter. 1976. "Election of Women to City Councils." *Social Science Quarterly* 56:605-13.

King, Elizabeth G. 1977. "Women in Iowa Legislative Politics." In *A Portrait of Marginality*, ed. Marianne Githens and Jewel L. Prestage, New York: McKay.

Kirkpatrick, Jeane J. 1974. *Political Woman*. New York: Basic.

_____. 1976. *The New Presidential Elite*. New York: Russell Sage.

Kleeman, Katherine E. 1983. *Women's PACs*. New Brunswick, N.J.: Center for the American Woman and Politics.

Lee, Marcia M. 1977. "Toward Understanding Why Few Women Hold Public Office: Factors Affecting the Participation of Women in Local Politics." In *A Portrait of Marginality*, ed. Marianne Githens and Jewel L. Prestage, New York: McKay.

Leeper, Mark Stephen. 1991. "The Impact of Prejudice on Female Candidates: An Experimental Look at Voter Inference." *American Politics Quarterly* 19:248-61.

MacManus, Susan A., and Charles S. Bullock III. 1989. "Women on Southern City Councils: A Decade of Change." *Journal of Political Science* 17:32-49.

Mandel, Ruth B. 1981. *In the Running: The New Woman Candidate*. New Haven: Ticknor & Fields.

Mueller, Carol. 1982a. "Feminism and the New Woman in Public Office." *Women & Politics* 2:7-21.

_____. 1982b. "Nurturance and Mastery: Competing Qualifications for Women's Access to High Public Office?" Working Paper #94. Wellesley: Wellesley College Center for Research on Women.

Nechemias, Carol. 1985. "Geographic Mobility and Women's Access to State Legislatures." *Western Political Quarterly* 38:119-31.

Niemi, Richard G., Jeffrey S. Hill, and Bernard Grofman. 1985. "The Impact of Multimember Districts on Party Representation in U.S. State Legislatures." *Legislative Studies Quarterly* 10:441-55.

Newman, Jody, Carrie Costantin, Julie Goetz, and Amy Glosser. 1984. "Perception and Reality: A Study of Women Candidates and Fund-Raising." Washington, D.C.: The Women's Campaign Research Fund.

Norris, Pippa. 1985. "Women's Legislative Participation in Western Europe." *Western European Politics* 8(4).

Paizis, Suzanne. 1977. *Getting Her Elected: A Political Woman's Handbook*. Sacramento: Creative Editions.

Prestage, Jewel L. 1977. "Black Women in State Legislatures: A Profile." In *A Portrait of Marginality*, ed. Marianne Githens and Jewel Prestage, New York: McKay.

_____. 1980. "Political Behavior of the American Black Woman: An Overview." In *The Black Woman*, ed. La Frances Rodgers-Rose, Beverly Hills: Sage.

Randall, Vicky. 1987. *Women and Politics: An International Perspective*, 2d ed. Chicago: University of Chicago.

Rosenberg, William L., and William R. Elliot. 1987. "Effect of Debate Exposure on Evaluation of 1984 Vice-Presidential Candidates." *Journalism Quarterly* 64:55-64.

Rosenwasser, Shirley M., Robyn R. Rogers, Sheila Fling, Kayla Silvers-Pickens, and John Butemeyer. 1987. "Attitudes Toward Women and Men in Politics: Perceived Male and Female Candidate Competencies and Participant Personality Characteristics." *Political Psychology* 8:191-200.

Ruddick, Sara. 1983. "Maternal Thinking." In *Mothering: Essays in Feminist Theory*, ed. Joyce Trebilcot Totowa, N.J.: Rowman & Allanheld.

Rule, Wilma. 1981. "Why Women Don't Run: The Critical Contextual Factors in Women's Legislative Recruitment." *Western Political Quarterly* 34:60-77.

_____. 1990. "Why More Women Are State Legislators." *Western Political Quarterly* 43:437-48.

Sapiro, Virginia. 1981-82. "If U.S. Senator Baker Were a Woman: An Experimental Study of Candidate Images." *Political Psychology* 1981-82:61-83.

_____. 1982. "Private Costs of Public Commitments or Public Costs of Private Commitments? Family Roles versus Political Ambition." *American Journal of Political Science* 26:265-79.

Shields, Stephanie A., and Kathleen A. MacDowell. 1987. "'Appropriate' Emotion in Politics: Judgments of a Televised Debate." *Journal of Communication* 37:78-89.

Sigelman, Lee, and Susan Welch. 1984. "Race, Gender, and Opinion Toward Black and Female Presidential Candidates." *Public Opinion Quarterly* 48:467-75.

Stanwick, Kathy A. 1983. *Political Women Tell What It Takes*. New Brunswick, N.J.: Center for the American Woman and Politics.

_____, and Katherine E. Kleeman. 1983. *Women Make a Difference*. New Brunswick, N.J.: Center for the American Woman and Politics.

Stoper, Emily. 1977. "Wife and Politician: Role Strain Among Women in Public Office." In *A Portrait of Marginality,* ed. Marianne Githens and Jewel L. Prestage, New York: McKay.

Thomas, Sue. 1989. "The Policy Impact of Increasing Numbers of Women in State Legislatures." Paper presented at the annual meeting of the American Political Science Association, Atlanta, August 31-September 3.

Tolchin, Susan, and Martin Tolchin. 1976. *Clout: Womanpower and Politics.* New York: Putnam.

Uhlaner, Carole Jean, and Kay Lehman Schlozman. 1986. "Candidate Gender and Congressional Campaign Receipts." *Journal of Politics* 48:30-50.

van Hightower, Nikki R. 1977. "The Recruitment of Women for Public Office." *American Politics Quarterly* 5:301-14.

Welch, Susan, Margery M. Ambrosius, Janet Clark, and Robert Darcy. 1985. "The Effect of Candidate Gender on Electoral Outcomes in State Legislative Races." *Western Political Quarterly* 38:464-75.

_____, and Albert K. Karnig. 1979. "Correlates of Female Office Holding in City Politics." *Journal of Politics* 41:478-91.

Wilhite, Allen, and John Theilmann. 1986. "Women, Blacks, and PAC Discrimination." *Social Science Quarterly* 67:283-98.

Williams, Eddie N. 1982. "Introductory Essay: Black Women in Politics and Government." In *Contributions of Black Women to America,* vol. 2, ed. Marianna W. Davis, Columbia, S.C.: Kenday.

Yankelovich, Skelly, and White, Inc. 1984. "Sex Stereotypes and Candidacy for High Level Political Office." Prepared for the National Women's Political Caucus.

Zipp, John F., and Eric Plutzer. 1985. "Gender Differences in Voting for Female Candidates: Evidence from the 1982 Election." *Public Opinion Quarterly* 49:179-97.

Chapter 7

The Career Paths of Minority Elected Politicians:
Resemblances and Differences

Fernando J. Guerra
Loyola Marymount University

The 1989 elections produced the first elected black governor in the history of the United States and the first black mayor of the largest American city. Besides the victories by L. Douglas Wilder in Virginia and David Dinkins in New York City, blacks captured the mayor's office in Seattle, New Haven, Cleveland, and St. Louis.[1] In the 1992 election, the number of black members of Congress elected increased from 25 to 38, and the first black woman U.S. senator, Carol Mosely Braun, was elected. The election of Ilena Ros-Lehtinen in the summer of 1989 to replace Claude Pepper in Miami produced the first Latina member of Congress. In 1992, the number of Hispanic members of Congress elected increased from 11 to 17. These victories are only the latest minority successes in the electoral arena. Since the 1960s, the number of black, Latino, and Asian officeholders at the federal, state, and local level has increased dramatically (Asian American Studies Center 1979, 1982, 1984; Joint Center for Political Studies 1970-1989; National Association of Latino Elected and Appointed Officials 1984-1989). How did this increase in minority officeholding occur?

Most of the analysis of minority electoral success or failure has focused on the characteristics of the minority community, the structure of the political system, or the behavior of the electorate. Studies of community characteristics have typically explored the size or socio-economic condition of the minority community required for one of its

---

[1] Numerous other black officials were also reelected in 1989, such as Los Angeles Mayor Tom Bradley.

members to win public office.   The structural questions typically
addressed the impact of at-large or single-member district elections on
minority representation where district elections are held, and the impact
of the reapportionment process on minority success (Karnig and Welch
1980). Variables measuring the behavior of the electorate have included
the turnout of minority voters, the willingness of white voters to support
minority candidates, and the coalition possibilities along racial, class, and
ideological lines (Murray and Vedlitz 1978).

While all of these questions are crucial, they provide an incomplete
analysis. Taken as a whole, the literature provides a broad profile of the
necessary general conditions for minority electoral success. However,
why a specific minority individual or type of individual won is left
unanswered. This chapter will address this latter aspect by focusing on
successful minority candidates and how they position themselves to win
elections. The specific focus will be on the channels or routes and the
gates and gatekeepers that impact minorities as they attempt to capture an
initial public office and then move up to higher office.

With its diverse population and numerous political offices, Los
Angeles provides the ideal location to examine the increase in minority
officeholding. Minorities holding public office in Los Angeles are a
recent phenomenon. With the rare exception, blacks, Latinos, and Asians
were effectively excluded from holding political office in the first six
decades of this century. This exclusion extended to some white ethnic
groups also, for instance Jews. While Jews are not usually considered an
underrepresented political minority in contemporary America, through a
variety of practices they were excluded from holding public office in Los
Angeles. This was the case even though they were about one-tenth of the
local population and did not share many of the socio-economic
characteristics associated with underrepresented minorities. The history
of Jewish political exclusion and their subsequent inclusion in Los
Angeles provides a useful comparison to the experience of blacks,
Latinos, and Asians.

In 1960, of these four underrepresented groups, only one black, one
Jew, and one Latino held a significant elective position. There was no
Asian holding such a position. By 1989, there were 25 Jews, 16 blacks,
12 Latinos, and three Asians holding significant positions in Los Angeles
County. In terms of officeholding, the political system of Los Angeles
has been dramatically transformed in three decades. Previously excluded
groups have become significant contributors to the pool of public
officeholders.   In addition to the substantial changes in ethnic

officeholding, the political setting and demographic characteristics of Los Angeles make it very useful as a case study of minority recruitment.

THE SETTING: A PYRAMID OF OFFICES

Los Angeles is the largest city in California and the second largest in the United States; Los Angeles County is the most populous in the nation. The Los Angeles Standard Metropolitan Statistical Area (SMSA), which is coterminous with the county, is second in size only to the New York SMSA, which is made up of several counties. Los Angeles has experienced many changes in the last several decades, but none as dramatic as its population growth and increasing diversity. From 1960 to 1990, the city grew by 40 percent, from 2.5 to 3.5 million. From 1960 to 1990, the county grew by 31 percent, from 6.7 to 8.8 million. Most of this increase was due to the growth of the four ethnic communities. The white, non-Latino and non-Jewish population dramatically declined in both the city and the county. From the early sixties to the late eighties, whites declined by 43 percent in the city and by 39 percent in the county. Tables 7.1 and 7.2 illustrate the demographic change that has occurred in both the city and county.[2]

Studies on minority electoral success have typically been confined to a single level of government, usually a city council. Los Angeles County has 88 cities, all with councils of at least five members. The county also has 95 school districts with at least five members on each board. The elective positions available in the county go beyond those at the council and school board level. There are eight elective positions for the county itself. Further, while most counties in the United States are served by one member of the House of Representatives and often share this representative with neighboring counties, Los Angeles County has 13 congressional districts completely within its boundaries and shares five others with neighboring counties. Los Angeles County has more than three times the number of state Senate and state Assembly districts of any of California's 57 other counties. In total, including special district, judicial, and political party positions, there are over 2,000 electoral opportunities available in Los Angeles.

---

[2]Figures for the Jewish category are from the *American Jewish Yearbook*, 1960, 1970, 1980, and 1989. Information for the remaining category is from the U.S. Bureau of Census.

Table 7.1.   *Population of Los Angeles County by Race or Ethnicity, 1960-1990*

	1960		1970	
Latino	629,292	(9.3%)	1,289,311	(18.3%)
Black	464,717	(6.9%)	762,925	(10.9%)
Asian	129,759	(1.9%)	191,619	(2.8%)
Jewish	412,535	(6.1%)	560,200	(8.0%)
Ethnic Total	1,636,303	(24.3%)	2,813,879	(40.0%)
Other	5,106,393	(75.7%)	4,228,101	(60.0%)
Total	6,742,696		7,041,980	

	1980		1990	
Latino	2,066,103	(27.6%)	3,351,242	(37.8%)
Black	943,968	(12.6%)	934,776	(10.5%)
Asian	434,850	(6.1%)	958,296	(10.8%)
Jewish	530,675	(7.1%)	525,000	(5.9%)
Ethnic Total	3,975,596	(53.1%)	5,769,314	(65.1%)
Other	3,501,907	(46.8%)	3,093,850	(34.9%)
Total	7,477,503	(100%)	8,863,164	

Not all of the 2,000 positions can be considered of equal significance. While it is important for minorities to gain elective office at every level, it is especially important for them to gain significant positions. Significant positions control more resources, affect more people, and, due to their strategic location, provide more visibility for the elected officeholder. Holding a significant elective position increases the ability of minorities to articulate, pursue, and protect their interests.

Three measures can be used to identify the most significant positions in Los Angeles County: (1) budget size, (2) constituent size, and (3) prestige of the position—the extent to which it is sought by others

Table 7.2. *Population of Los Angeles City by Race or Ethnicity, 1960-1990*

	1960		1970	
Latino	260,389	(10.5%)	518,791	(18.4%)
Black	334,916	(13.5%)	503,606	(17.9%)
Asian	82,291	(3.3%)	138,855	(4.9%)
Jewish	400,000	(16.1%)	463,000	(16.4%)
Ethnic Total	1,077,596	(43.5%)	1,624,252	(57.7%)
Other	1,401,419	(56.5%)	1,191,809	(42.3%)
Total	2,479,015	(100%)	2,816,061	(100%)

	1980		1990	
Latino	816,076	(27.5%)	1,391,411	(39.9%)
Black	505,210	(17.0%)	454,289	(13.0%)
Asian	212,612	(7.2%)	340,094	(9.8%)
Jewish	503,000	(17.0%)	501,000	(14.4%)
Ethnic Total	2,036,898	(68.7%)	2,686,794	(77.1%)
Other	929,952	(31.3%)	798,604	(22.9%)
Total	2,966,850	(100%)	3,485,398	(100%)

already holding elective office. The first two measures are straightforward and easy to quantify once a uniform source is established (Guerra 1990). The third measure is more complex and needs elaboration.

Using the first two measures, the 100 most significant positions in Los Angeles County were identified and are displayed in Table 7.3. It should be noted that the number 100 was not chosen arbitrarily. The distance between position 100 and 101 was substantial. For the third measure, the political career paths of all those who have held one of the 100 positions was examined. From 1960 to 1989, 283 individuals have held one of the 100 significant positions. In examining their careers two

Table 7.3.   *The 100 Most Significant Elective Positions in Los Angeles County, 1980*

16	U.S. House of Representatives
14	California State Senate
30	California State Assembly
5	Los Angeles County Board of Supervisors
3	Los Angeles County Executives (District Attorney, Sheriff, Assessor)
3	Los Angeles City Executives (Mayor, City Attorney, Controller)
15	Los Angeles City Council
7	Los Angeles Unified School District Board
7	Los Angeles Community College District Board of Trustees

100	Total

questions were asked. First, what elective position, if any, did they hold before gaining one of the 100? Second, where did the individual go after vacating such a position? The answers to these two questions allow a thorough analysis of career movement in both directions, from the less significant, which include some 1,900 positions, to the top 100 positions, and in the reverse direction.

The movement was all in one direction. Of all the individuals who have held one of the 100 positions since 1960, 43 had previously held one of the 1,900 elective positions. No one has vacated one of the 100 to seek one of the 1,900 positions. The career movements of officeholders themselves underscore the significance of the 100 positions.

Using this same method, the 100 most significant elective positions in Los Angeles County can themselves be stratified into a pyramid of significance. Again, budget and constituent size as well as the prestige of the position are the determinants. In tracing the career path of all 283 officeholders within the 100 positions, a clear pattern or pyramid of offices appears. At the top of the pyramid is the position of mayor of the city of Los Angeles; immediately below are the five members of the county board of supervisors and the county district attorney; in the third tier are the 16 members of Congress; the 14 state senators constitute the fourth tier; in the fifth tier are the city attorney, city controller, county sheriff, and county assessor; the sixth tier is made up of the 30 state assembly members and 15 Los Angeles City Council members; the seven Los Angeles School Board members make up the seventh tier; and finally the eighth tier consists of the seven Los Angeles Community College Board members.

In all cases where an incumbent officeholder in Los Angeles County ran for and won a different elective office, the move was up the pyramid. Furthermore, all incumbents who were candidates for another office but failed to win, ran for an office at a higher tier. Between 1960 and 1989, there were no exceptions to this pattern, where incumbents run for an office at a higher tier within the pyramid but never for one at a lower tier. Thus, in Los Angeles there exists a well-defined opportunity structure of elective offices.

The electoral opportunity structure in Los Angeles might appear to be unique, since congressmen are willing to run for county office, but county supervisors do not seek office in Congress. However, there is nothing unique about officeholders seeking more powerful positions. A variety of factors go into making the county board of supervisors the most powerful local legislature in the nation and an attractive position even for members of the House of Representatives. First and foremost, the county budget is larger than that of eight states and affects close to nine million people. Second, with no elected county executive, the board is both the legislature and executive in one. No individual or institution has direct veto power over the actions of the board. Third, the five members of the board defer many decisions to the one member whose district is being impacted, especially in such policy areas as public works. For projects directly affecting his or her district, which comprises about 1.8 million people, in essence the board member is both executive and legislature. Each board member has greater influence over a larger budget impacting more people than do some governors and has that influence without interference from a legislature. In addition, the board members are more visible than members of Congress, receive more local media coverage, and are highly compensated with more perks, without the necessity for cross-country travel, or for maintaining two homes. With the exception of statewide offices, such as U.S. Senate positions, and the mayors of Los Angeles, San Diego, and San Francisco, no other political positions are more powerful in the state, let alone the county, than are the Los Angeles County supervisors.

In some respects the Los Angeles electoral opportunity structure is not unique at all. In other locales as well, there exists a pyramid of significant positions, with the ambitious politicians attempting to move up such a pyramid. The critical question here is not which offices lie at the top of the pyramid, but how this movement occurs, especially as it applies to minorities. In some counties of the country, the lone congressional representative sits on top of the pyramid of elective offices. In other counties, local positions are of greater significance. Thus, in New York, Ed Koch was willing to give up his congressional position to become mayor, as was Harold Washington in Chicago. Los Angeles differs only to extent that there are several local positions that are more significant than being a member of Congress: mayor of Los Angeles, county supervisor, and county district attorney. The significance of the county district attorney is based on the position's high visibility and the expectation that the officeholder will be a candidate for state attorney general, which the last three have been (Ira Reiner, John Van de Kamp, and Evelle Younger); in turn, if successful at advancing to the state attorney general's position, the expectation is that the officeholder will become a candidate for governor, which the last three incumbents have been (John Van de Kamp, George Deukmejian, Evelle Younger).

What is unique about Los Angeles and its electoral opportunity structure, however, is the extent to which the number of significant positions continuously increases. This is in large part due to the increase in California's congressional delegation. For the 1990s, California will have seven more congressional districts. This compares to the eight apportioned after the 1960 census. While California has grown above the average rate of the country, Los Angeles County, until recently, has grown above the average rate of the state. Thus, not only were federal positions being shifted to Los Angeles, but so were state legislative positions. As the number of significant positions expanded, they could be gained by emerging minorities without directly taking representation from existing groups or individual officeholders.

How have minorities done in capturing positions within the different tiers of the electoral pyramid? Before the decade of the 1960s very few minorities held one of these 100 significant positions in Los Angeles County. In the decade of the 1960s, blacks made impressive gains. Black gains outdistanced those of the Jewish and Latino community to such an extent that one can label the decade of the sixties the "Black Emergence" stage. Blacks continued to make gains throughout the 1970s, but black gains in the seventies were not as large as those of the Jewish community. The Jewish communities more than tripled the number of significant positions held by its members. Thus the decade was marked by "Jewish Emergence." In the 1980s, black gains were minimal, Jewish

Figure 7.1.   *Significant Positions Won by Ethnics in Los Angeles County*

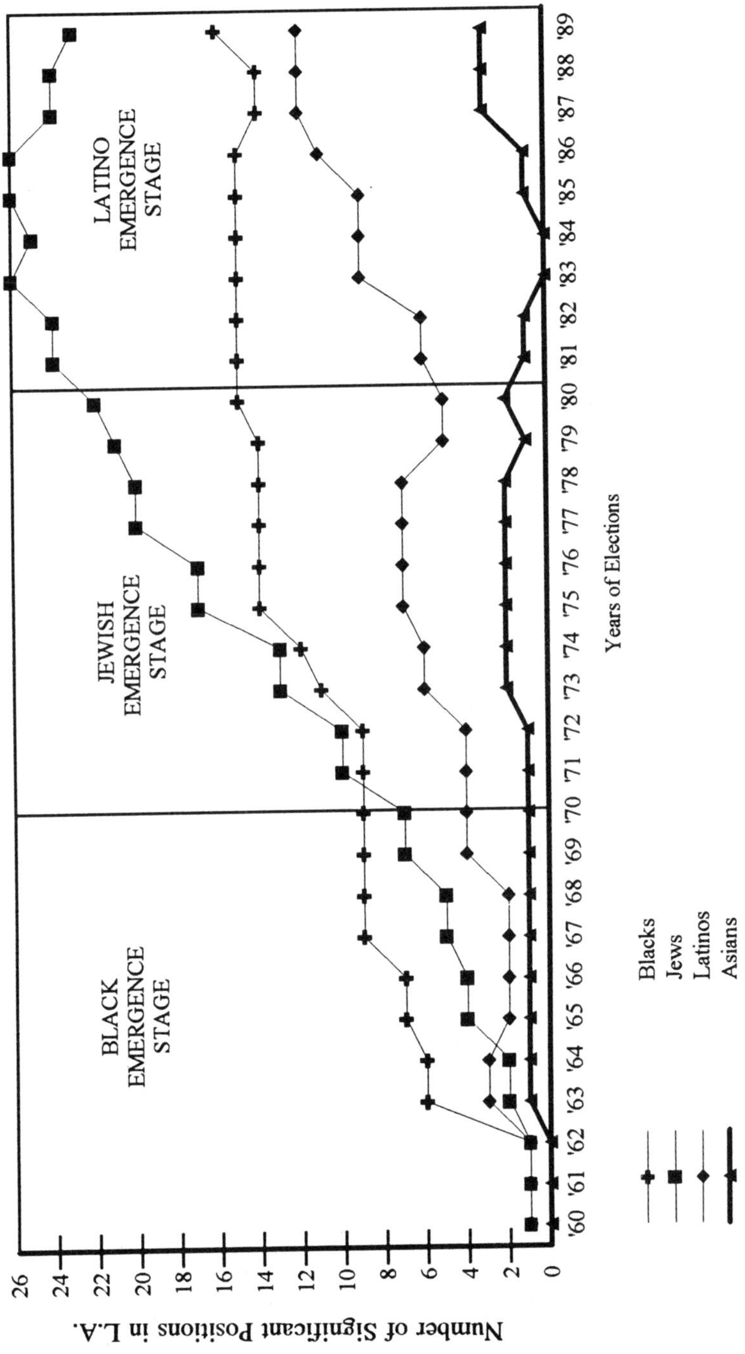

gains continued at a lesser pace, and Latinos more than doubled their gains. "Latino Emergence" defines the third decade being examined. Figure 7.1 illustrates the gains made by blacks, Jews, Latinos, and Asians in capturing some of the 100 significant positions from 1960 to 1989.

Most of the initial gains within the 100 were at the bottom of the pyramid. By the mid-sixties, however, blacks were holding positions in four of the eight tiers, and by the mid-seventies they were holding offices in six of the eight. Latinos were not able to secure representation among the various tiers as quickly. As late as 1982, Latinos did not have representation on the city council, school board, college board, board of supervisors, or any of the executive positions in tiers one and five. But by 1987, Latinos had gained representation at all levels with the exception of the board of supervisors and the executive positions at every level except the mayor's office. Asians had not held more than two significant positions until 1987, when Asians gained three positions, one at each of the three lowest tiers.

The tier on which minorities have had the most difficulty in gaining a foothold is that which includes the board of supervisors and the district attorney. No black, Latino, or Asian had been elected to a position in this tier in the first nine decades of the twentieth century. In large part this was due to the number of positions in this tier not being altered in any way. In contrast, the elective positions in all the tiers below the one containing the board of supervisors have either increased in number, been changed from at-large to single-member districts, been newly established, or gone through a significant reapportionment.[3]

CHANNELS TO OFFICEHOLDING

What channels or routes did those who gained one of the 100 most significant elective positions in Los Angeles County travel? Two preponderant paths emerge. The first is anchored in prior service as an elected official in local government. Forty-three of the 283 had served in elected office before their ascension to the top 100. The second major channel to the 100 is based on service as a legislative aide for an elected

[3]Once the board underwent a drastic court ordered redistricting in 1990, a Latin, Gloria Molina, was elected. This election is not reflected in the data collected for this study, which includes the years 1960 to 1989.

Table 7.4. *Occupational Background of Ethnic Officeholders*

	Lawyer	Business-man	Local Official	Legislative Aide	Civil Service	Educator	Activists	Professional	Corporate	Total
Black	2 (7%)	2 (7%)	1 (4%)	12 (44%)	2 (7%)	5 (9%)	0	3 (11%)	0	27 (100%)
Jewish	9 (26%)	6 (17%)	0	7 (20)	2 (6%)	5 (14%)	4 (11%)	1 (3%)	1 (3%)	35 (100%)
Latino	0	0	4 (22%)	8 (44%)	2 (11%)	2 (11%)	1 (6%)	0	1 (6%)	18 (100%)
Asian	0	1 (17%)	2 (33%)	1 (17%)	0	2 (33%)	0	0	0	6 (100%)
TOTAL	11 (13%)	9 (10%)	7 (8%)	28 (33%)	6 (7%)	14 (16%)	5 (16%)	4 (5%)	2 (2%)	86 (100%)

official. This second route is especially relevant for minority officeholders as shown in Table 7.4.

The emergence of the ethnic officeholders has coincided with the development of the position of legislative aide into a launching pad for a career as an elected official. As ethnic communities grew, incumbent white legislators in ethnic districts recruited ethnic aides to staff their offices. When these incumbents retired or won a higher office, they were often replaced by an ethnic aide.

In retrospect growing population diversity affords a likely explanation for this phenomenon. To begin with, there was a general feeling that it was time to elect an ethnic to represent the district with its increasing ethnic population. Second, once a new position was created, partisan and legislative leaders were in a position to respond to a growing bloc of voters. This response would cost incumbents little, especially if the candidate with the best chance of winning was a known quantity such as a legislative aide. Third, ethnic legislative aides, like legislative aides in general, had several advantages over other potential ethnic candidates. As Charles Price and Charles Bell state, "[They] seem to have the inside track on money, know-how and political connections necessary for a successful run for office" (Price and Bell 1989). Once ethnics began winning office in this manner, nonethnic aides followed suit. Thus, the redefinition of the legislative aide as future winning candidate was begun in large part by ethnics.

Apart from prior service as an elected official or legislative aide, no other specific route to one of the 100 positions is utilized to any significant extent. Robert Putnam identifies other institutions used to channel individuals to significant positions, such as political parties, the bureaucracy, and social institutions, including unions, religious organizations and civic associations (Putnam 1976). While some of the officeholders of Los Angeles County's 100 most significant positions utilized such institutions, it is not frequently done.

A focus on the state Senate and state Assembly indicates that traditional channels to elective office in California as a whole are changing. In 1959, as reported by Bell and Price, 72 percent of the Assembly members had occupations as lawyers or businessmen, while those with prior elective service constituted 4 percent; none had been legislative aides. By 1989, only 51 percent were lawyers or businessmen, while those with prior elective service constituted 16 percent, and former legislative aides 14 percent of the Assembly. The trend is similar for the Senate. In 1959, 66 percent of the members were lawyers or businessmen; only one had prior elective service and none were legislative aides. By 1989, only 45 percent were lawyers or businessmen, while 15 percent had prior elective service, and five percent had been legislative aides (Price and Bell 1989).

Between 1960 and 1989, 41 ethnics, 16 blacks, 12 Jews, 11 Latinos, and two Asians, served in the state Senate and state Assembly from Los Angeles County. Of these 41, 19 were former legislative aides (46 percent), including nine of the 16 black legislators; six of the 11 Latinos, and four of the 12 Jews. Another eight minority lawmakers, 20 percent, were local elected officials, four of them Latino, two black, and two Asian. Of the remaining ethnics who served in the Assembly or Senate, five (12 percent) were practicing attorneys; four (10 percent) were businessmen; three (7 percent) were civil servants; one was an educator, and another a professional. Of the 41 minority elected officials who served in the state Senate and state Assembly from Los Angeles County, six of the 13 elected in the 1960s, (46 percent) were legislative aides; of the 17 elected in the 1970s, seven (41 percent) were legislative aides; of the 11 elected in the 1980s, seven, (67 percent), were legislative aides. Thus, elected officials increasingly serve as legislative aides before their election. This is especially the case for ethnics from Los Angeles County.

The higher the position in the pyramid, the more likely it is to be held by an individual who traveled either by way of prior elective service or as a legislative aide, or both. The more significant the position, the less accessible it is to individuals outside this political network. This is especially the case for minorities.

Focusing on the congressional delegation makes the point. Of the seven minority congressmen and congresswomen who have served on the delegation (three Latinos and four blacks), all but one had prior elective service. These six had held a significant position on average for 11.5 years. All five Jews who served on the delegation had prior elective service, but only for an average of six and a half years. On the other hand, of the 32 whites (non-Latino and non-Jewish) who served on Los Angeles County's congressional delegation, only 17 (53 percent), had prior elective service. It is interesting to highlight the backgrounds of some of the 15 with no prior service. In this group are James Roosevelt, the late son of President Franklin D. Roosevelt; Barry Goldwater, Jr., son of Senator Goldwater; Dan Lungren, son of President Nixon's personal physician; and Alphonzo Bell, president of Bell Petroleum. These backgrounds allowed these individuals to project themselves onto the electoral arena in a manner rarely available to minorities. Thus, it is possible to win a congressional office in Los Angeles County without having prior elective service or having been an aide to an elected official, but such alternative routes are unlikely to be open to minorities.

SPONSORS AND RECRUITMENT NETWORKS

The increase in the number of political staffers, many with an interest in electoral politics, has made it more likely that elected officials will have such backgrounds. This increase has occurred not only at the national level for Congress, in the form of office, district, and committee staff, and at the state level, but also at the local level (Ornstein et al. 1987; Macartney 1987). Staffers make up a large portion of the pool of eligibles for the significant elective positions in Los Angeles County. The institutional locus for the recruitment of officeholders in Los Angeles County has shifted from the political party, local government, and the bureaucracy to the political staff of the elected officeholders themselves. Each officeholder with his or her staff can be seen as constituting an organization from which emerge potential candidates for elective office.

All the significant positions, with the exception of the educational boards, have at least five to 10, and sometimes as many as 20, staff positions that are filled at the discretion of the officeholder. At any one time there are at least 750 legislative aides in the pool of eligibles in Los Angeles County alone. This does not take into account former staffers who have moved on to other public sector positions, usually with the support of the officeholder, and maintain an interest in running for office. Of course being a legislative aide does not guarantee election to a significant position. As Robert Putnam comments about individuals from various institutions that have traditionally channeled political elites to elective office, "recruitment channels do not finally determine who will occupy elite positions, for in the end most party members, most bureaucrats, most local government officials, and most alumni of prestigious schools do not become national political leaders. Recruitment channels provide the pool of eligibles. Choosing among them is a further task" (Putnam 1976). This task often falls to the elected officeholders themselves, who may act as sponsors for selected individuals.

With each officeholder a potential sponsor, the primary group of potential elective office sponsors in Los Angeles County can be said to consist of the 86 individuals holding a significant position other than those on the educational boards. When a position becomes vacant, not all 86 officeholders will have a significant interest in sponsoring a candidate. The degree of interest will depend on whether the vacant position is of geographic, ethnic, or partisan concern, or whether it impacts on the leadership composition of the governing body to which the potential sponsor belongs.

This list of concerns is not exhaustive. Other concerns such as policy preferences can come into play. These concerns are usually from secondary recruitment groups such as labor, developers, the business community, environmentalists, community organizations, and other groups concerned with specific issue areas. These groups may be sufficiently frustrated from time to time to field their own candidates. Most of the time, however, they work through existing officeholders in recruiting candidates.

Most ethnic officeholders are geographically concentrated and belong to the Democratic party. A convergence of interests has created identifiable recruitment regions within the county that determine what kind of sponsors and candidates emerge. Thus, there is a black Democratic recruitment region in South Central Los Angeles; a Latino Democratic recruitment region in East Los Angeles and the southwestern part of the San Gabriel Valley; a Jewish liberal Democratic region in West Los Angeles; and a conservative Democratic Jewish and Republican Jewish region in the San Fernando Valley. The remaining northern and eastern portions of the county are the white Republican regions. These ethnic-political recruitment grounds can be seen as concentric circles. At the core is the inner city, represented by black and Latino officeholders and some long-time white incumbent Democrats. In the ring around this core are liberal Democrats, Jewish on the west side and white non-Jewish in the remainder. The outer ring is dominated by conservatives, who include some Jews, but are mostly white non-Jewish Republicans.

In each region there are established sponsors to whom officeholders from other regions usually defer in recruiting candidates. Competition from other regions usually occurs only when one region expands into the territory of another, due to demographic shifts or when the fourth determinant, leadership battles within a governing body, obtains. Competition usually develops within a region. The development of these recruitment regions is best seen in one black region where rival camps have emerged.

BLACK POLITICAL RECRUITMENT: A CASE STUDY

The election of Mervyn Dymally and Tom Bradley early in the black emergence stage illustrates both the general recruitment of black officeholders and the emergence of rival camps in the black community.

To solidify his hold on the Assembly, Speaker Jesse Unruh utilized the reapportionment of 1961 to create not only safe Democratic districts, but completely new districts that would elect members linked to the speaker. A new congressional district was created for Augustus Hawkins, then an Assembly member. From the core of Hawkins' old Assembly districts two new Assembly districts with black majorities were created. To these recently reapportioned and vacant positions were elected Mervyn Dymally and F. Douglas Ferrell, both recruited by Unruh. From then on, Dymally would be Unruh's point man in the black community. He would, in turn, recruit black candidates just as he had been recruited by the following steps: first, creating a new open position; second, recruiting a loyal aide to run; and third, securing the political endorsements and financial support required.

Bradley was more of a self-starter than Dymally. He was assisted by two organizations with very different views from Unruh. Indeed, one of these organizations, the California Democratic Council (CDC), (Wilson 1962; Mills 1987; Sonenshein 1984) was quite anti-Unruh. The second was an ad hoc organization whose origins lay in the Committee for Representative Government set up to monitor the reapportionment of 1961 at the state and local levels. This organization lobbied the council to appoint a black to a vacancy. When no such appointment was made, the organization turned to a recall. When this strategy also failed, they supported Bradley in a regularly scheduled election (Patterson 1969). Bradley's own ascension to office would thereafter shape the way in which he himself would sponsor other black officeholders.

While Dymally had as a sponsor an individual who had created a favorable election environment (a recently reapportioned and vacant position), Bradley was sponsored by one ad hoc and another undisciplined organization, and faced an incumbent. Given these circumstances, one would have expected Bradley to have greater flexibility than Dymally to sponsor candidates. Bradley was a free agent who did not have to defer to a sponsor and could in fact challenge for a leadership position. On the other hand, Dymally found himself sponsored by the leader of the governing body to which he now belonged. The problem for Bradley, however, was that his election coincided with the election of two other blacks to the city council. Blacks now constituted 20 percent of the council, more than their percentage of the population in Los Angeles. With blacks overrepresented, there was no more room for black officeholders in Bradley's sphere of influence. Furthermore, of the two black council members who already held office, one, Billy Mills, had been sponsored by Unruh, and the second, Gilbert Lindsay, by County Supervisor Kenneth Hahn. In contrast, Dymally was surrounded by allies in Sacramento where blacks were still underrepresented at the Assembly and Senate level. Thus, if Bradley wished to sponsor candidates for office, they would have to take on black incumbents or run for state or federal office, while Dymally candidates would have the advantage because of Speaker Unruh.

With Bradley unable and perhaps unwilling to sponsor candidates for office, the field was left open for Dymally. Dymally once again took advantage of a recently created vacancy when the state Senate was reapportioned under the threat of court action in 1965. In 1966, Dymally relinquished his Assembly seat to run for the state Senate. His legislative aide, Bill Greene, replaced him in the Assembly. The other black Assembly member from Los Angeles, F. Douglas Farrell, retired and was replaced by another Dymally-Unruh aide, Leon Ralph. In 1966, Yvonne Burke was also elected to the Assembly. She received some support from Bradley against an Unruh aide, but most of her campaign was ad hoc and self-sponsored. This was the first time since Augustus Hawkins that a black had won a state Assembly position without the support of Dymally and Unruh.

The only way for Bradley effectively to sponsor blacks for office was to expand the opportunities in his sphere of influence. This Bradley did when he ran for mayor. If he won, his successor on the council would be black. When he was elected mayor in 1973 he hand picked one of his aides, David Cunningham, as his successor. Further, when Billy Mills, a black councilman, resigned to take a judicial position, Bradley sponsored Robert Ferrell, one of his aides, as his replacement. Within a brief time Bradley had sponsored two successful candidates for office. What had prompted Bradley in sponsoring candidates was his need as mayor to have allies in his sphere of influence, the city council. He was willing to let Dymally support candidates unchallenged at the state level, but not at the local level. Thus, there existed a black recruitment region and two camps, one at the local level and the other at the state level.

This tacit bargain, allowing each camp to recruit for the level where it was battling to gain or maintain a leadership position, broke down in

1973 when Unruh, having been defeated for governor in 1970 by Ronald Reagan, ran for mayor against Bradley and was endorsed by Dymally. Unruh came in third to incumbent Sam Yorty and the eventual winner, Bradley. Not only had Dymally and Unruh entered Bradley's sphere of influence, they had run against Bradley himself. In 1974 Dymally was elected lieutenant governor, vacating his state senate seat. Once again, Bill Greene was chosen to replace Dymally. However, this time the Bradley camp ran a candidate, Kenny Washington from the Los Angeles Community College Board, and almost denied Greene the seat (Salzman 1975).

All but three of the black elected officeholders to have held a significant elective position in Los Angeles County could trace some part of their initial support to either Dymally or Bradley. Of those exceptions, two were sponsored by the region's white county supervisor, Kenneth Hahn. One of the Hahn aides to gain a position was city council member Gilbert Lindsay, who had initially been appointed with support from Hahn. Hahn had previously served on the council, and his brother, Gordon Hahn, was serving on the council when the appointment was made. The second Hahn aide to win was Nate Holden, who won a state Senate race against Assemblyman Frank Holoman, a Dymally-Unruh candidate who was from Unruh's old district. Holden then ran for Congress against Julian Dixon, an assemblyman and former Dymally aide, and lost. Later Holden would win a city council seat by defeating Homer Broome, a Bradley candidate and Public Works Commissioner. Thus, both the two major rival camps (and even a third minor camp, headed by Hahn) were all indigenous to the region and autonomous from other regions when it came to recruiting candidates for office in South Central Los Angeles. No candidate has been successful in this region without the support of one of these three camps.

The two major camps had become so effective that they began to exert themselves beyond the region—first, Bradley with his election as mayor and then Dymally as lieutenant governor. Two of the most significant elective positions in the state were held by blacks from Los Angeles. The only position more significant then these is governor of California. If it had not been for Dymally's defeat for reelection as lieutenant governor in 1978, it is quite likely that he would have faced Bradley in the Democratic primary for governor in 1982. As it was, Bradley went on to win the nomination and lose the general election to Deukmejian by the narrowest margin in the state's history.

·CONCLUSION

How important are the recruitment networks to the emergence of ethnic officeholders? Some Latinos and Jews had won before the establishment of such networks in their regions. Some Jews continue to win without the support of any recruitment network, though no black or Latino officeholder was elected in the 1980s without support from such networks. Given the demographic shifts occurring in Los Angeles, it was inevitable that more ethnic candidates would be successful, with or without the recruitment networks, but while this factor set the stage for ethnics to win, it was the networks that determined which individual would be successful.

The ethnic candidate with the best chance of winning was well educated, born in Los Angeles, and employed in the public sector, usually as a legislative aide. These characteristics placed an individual in the pool of eligibles; they did not get such a person elected. What made election almost automatic was the sponsorship of a recruitment network. These networks provided the necessary resources required to run an effective modern campaign. Money, professional campaign expertise, and campaign workers who had previously been mobilized in other campaigns were shifted to the network's sponsored candidate. Only a rival network could compete with such resources.

These recruitment networks went beyond electing ethnics in districts whose ethnic makeup largely predetermined the ethnicity of the officeholder. They made ethnic candidates competitive in districts that were becoming ethnic, but had not yet completed the transition. There are numerous examples of candidates sponsored by secondary recruitment groups, such as community organizations, who were unable to defeat the white incumbent. These campaigns had banked on the shifting demographics alone and failed. Initial efforts of this kind were usually followed by a recruitment network candidate with the necessary resources to win. Recruitment networks therefore helped expand the ethnic-political regions.

Officeholders who emerged from these networks were also protected from any effective challenges to their newly acquired position. No incumbent Latino, black, or Jewish officeholder who emerged from one of these networks was ever defeated for reelection. On the other hand, of the six Latinos who were elected before the establishment of the Latino recruitment network, four were eventually defeated. These networks not only endorse candidates and protect incumbents, but also discipline members and punish challengers.

It would be interesting to see if such recruitment networks have developed in other parts of the United States. While it is apparent that prior elective service is common for minority politicians (Douglas Wilder had served as state senator and lieutenant governor before his election as governor, David Dinkins was borough president before becoming mayor, and Ilena Ros-Lehtinen had been a state senator before winning a House seat), it is not clear whether the position of legislative aide is as important a factor for the election of minority politicians to significant political office outside Los Angeles County. The lack of strong political parties, the professionalization of state and local legislatures, and the large number of elective positions in Los Angeles County provide a conducive environment for legislative aides to flourish and advance in the electoral arena. Such factors may not be as powerful outside Los Angeles.

· REFERENCES

Asian American Studies Center. 1979, 1982, 1984. *The National Asian American Roster.* Los Angeles: UCLA Asian American Studies Center.

Davidson, Chandler, and George Korbel. 1981. "At-Large Elections and Minority-Group Representation: A Re-Examination of Historical and Contemporary Evidence." *The Journal of Politics* 43 (November): 982-1005.

Guerra, Fernando J. 1990. "Ethnic Politics in Los Angeles: The Emergence of Black, Jewish, Latino and Asian Officeholders, 1960-1989." Ph.D. dissertation, University of Michigan.

Joint Center for Political Studies. 1970-1989. *The National Roster of Black Elected Officials.*

Karnig, Albert K., and Susan Welch. 1980. *Black Representation and Urban Policy.* Chicago: The University of Chicago Press.

Macartney John D. 1987. "Congressional Staff: The View from the District." In *Congress and Public Policy: A Source Book of Documents and Readings,* 2d ed., ed. by David C. Kozak and John D. Macartney, Chicago: Dorsey Press, 94-100.

Mills, James R. 1987. *A Disorderly House.* Berkeley: Heyday Books.

Murray, Richard, and Arnold Vedlitz. 1978. "Racial Voting Pattern in the South: An Analysis of Major Elections in Five Cities." *The Annals of the American Academy of Political and Social Science* 439 (September): 29-39.

National Association of Latino Elected and Appointed Officials. 1984-1989. *The National Roster of Hispanic Elected Officials.* Washington, D.C.: NALEO.

Ornstein, Norman, Thomas E. Mann, Michael J. Malbin, and John F. Bibby. 1987. "The Growth of Staff." In *Congress and Public Policy: A Source Book of Documents to Readings,* 2d ed., ed. David C. Kozak and John D. Macartney, Chicago: Dorsey Press.

Patterson, Beeman C. 1969. "The Politics of Recognition: Negro Politics in Los Angeles 1960-1963." Ph.D. dissertation, University of California, Los Angeles.

Price, Charles, and Charles Bell. 1989. "Lawyer-Legislators: The Capitol's Endangered Species." *California Journal* 20 (April): 181-83.

Putnam, Robert. 1976. *The Comparative Study of Political Elites.* Englewood Cliffs, N.J.: Prentice-Hall, 49-52.

Salzman, Ed. 1975. "The Battle Between the Blacks." *California Journal* 6 (March): 72-75.

Sonenshein, Raphael. 1984. "Bradley's People: Functions of the Candidate Organization." Ph.D. dissertation, Yale University.

Wilson Q. James. 1962. *The Amateur Democrat.* Chicago: University of Chicago Press, Ch. 4.

Conclusion

Edward L. Lascher, Jr.
Harvard University

AMBITION THEORY AND BEYOND

Joseph Schlesinger's (1966) work on ambition theory looms large in this volume. Yet the selections in this book indicate that we have moved beyond Schlesinger's pioneering work, albeit sometimes in fits and starts. Timothy Prinz may indeed be correct that "the usefulness of [Schlesinger's] perspective for the study of political careers cannot be overstated." However, those who use the concepts and framework established by Schlesinger find it necessary to criticize, amend, and add to them as well.

There is no mystery in explaining why ambition theory came to dominate analysis of political careers in this country. As Prinz and Linda Fowler indicate, the literature on careers of politicians is far-flung and heterogeneous. Ambition theory provides a coherent and orderly approach to scholarship, which is attractive in a field that may appear chaotic. Ambition theory is simple, conducive to formalization, and conceptually linked to the rational choice approach to political phenomena that has become prominent over the past two decades. Most important of all, it seems to work, at least in some contexts; many political phenomena are explicable using an ambition theory framework.

However, the contributions to this volume as well as other research suggest a number of ways in which Schlesinger's ambition theory framework should be modified, including the following.

Greater Attention to the Actual Characteristics of Political Offices

Schlesinger argued that there is a clear hierarchy of elective positions in the United States, with federal offices at the top of the hierarchy, state offices in the middle, and local offices at the bottom. Yet he failed to explain what makes high office especially attractive and lower offices less attractive. He also gave little consideration to why some politicians in lower level offices seek advancement while others do not.

Greater attention to the actual characteristics of elective positions may produce a more differentiated picture of the hierarchy of political offices, even if it is often true that the incentives are structured in the way Schlesinger envisioned. This is illustrated most vividly by Fernando Guerra's analysis of electoral politics in Los Angeles County. Guerra found that two *local* positions (mayor of the city of Los Angeles and county supervisor) are perched at the top of the political hierarchy. Rather than simply viewing this as an exceptional case, focusing on office characteristics may help us to predict instances in which the structure of incentives does not follow the familiar pattern. For example, some local offices may provide an unusual number of perquisites or may be especially conducive to offering the sense that they are able to make a difference in public policy (on the importance of this incentive, see for example Fenno 1973; Muir 1982, Lascher, this volume). The measures that Guerra uses to evaluate the importance of various offices (e.g., size of the budget) may tap differences in the extent to which positions provide incumbents with the perceived ability to meet their public policy objectives.

Peverill Squire's work provides further evidence of the importance of including information about job characteristics in the analysis of incentives facing politicians. It is striking how much mileage he gets from including information about the monetary compensation available to state legislators in his analysis of career path incentives and their implications.

There is no inherent reason that further analysis in this vein would have to be limited to including information about salaries. As I suggested in my earlier chapter, there is good reason to believe that other characteristics of political positions are important in determining how satisfied politicians are with their positions. Admittedly characteristics other than relative salaries are likely to be more difficult to measure, hence significant effort and imagination will be required to make progress in this area.

Greater Attention to Internal Incentives

As Shirley Williams and I have emphasized previously, John Hibbing's chapter underscores the importance of incentives for advancement within the highly professionalized U.S. Congress, where politicians tend to have long careers. Future studies need to recognize that lawmakers may prefer to rise to more senior positions within the legislative chamber than to attempt to obtain higher-level offices (e.g., governor) elsewhere. Such decisions may be fully rational.

Research on the careers of politicians in other offices could also profit from analysis of internal incentives, or lack thereof. For example, even when they meet the criteria normally associated with professionalism (i.e., full-time status, provision of staff to legislators, high salary for members), some local legislative bodies are too small to offer a differentiated internal structure. Even positions such as chair of the legislative body may be available to first-term members. In these legislatures there is little to "shoot for" by serving multiple terms, and this will be likely to affect the career plans of local officeholders.

Emphasis on Factors That Affect Whether Politicians Can Take Advantage of Structural Opportunities

The contributors to this volume indicate that there can be systematic variation in the extent to which politicians are able to advance their careers, given the same set of structural opportunities. As Fowler argues, ambition theory has tended to underestimate the importance of the social and institutional context in determining the feasibility of obtaining political office. Susan Carroll and Guerra indicate that women and minorities may be particularly disadvantaged by lack of access to important campaign resources and support, although their work and that of Prinz and Fowler suggest that the picture to be drawn with regard to distribution of resources is more complicated than might otherwise be believed. Therefore, a need exists to isolate factors that may contribute to the ability to make the best of opportunities for advancement. Both Carroll and Guerra focus on the availability of interpersonal networks for advancing the candidacies of members of traditionally underrepresented groups.

Differentiating Between Ambition and Opportunity Structure

The most trenchant criticism of ambition theory comes from Hibbing. He demonstrates that much of what passes for analysis of ambition actually constitutes analysis of opportunity structure; the desire for political office is something different. To the extent that there is an implicit view of ambition itself in the literature, it commonly holds that ambition is developed prior to actual experience in elective office. Contrary to this view, both Fowler and I argue that ambition is shaped and changed by politicians' actual experience as candidates and in political office, as well as their evaluation of this experience. Not only may ambition vary among individual politicians, but particular individuals may vary in the strength of their ambition at different points in their political careers. Shirley Williams would add to that external circumstances, which may draw people normally outside political arenas into them, for reasons ranging from the search for national unity to the consequences of revolution or war.

The question remains as to whether and how scholars should approach the question of ambition, separate and apart from the question of political opportunity. Hibbing stakes out one position on this question, arguing that researchers should continue to concentrate on the opportunity structure but be explicit about what they are doing. He is dubious about our ability to determine the impact of ambition given the formidable measurement difficulties.

Hibbing's concerns must be taken seriously. However, my own view is somewhat different. While I acknowledge the difficulties of assessing ambition, it seems possible to make progress by comparing the attributes and attitudes of politicians who are similarly situated with respect to the political opportunity structure. By using interviews and surveys we may be able to develop generalizations about the circumstances and characteristics that promote and sustain political ambition. And by conducting longitudinal research we may be able to isolate factors that produce changes in motivation. Indeed, some interesting hypotheses with respect to the development of political ambition have already been offered and are in need of further testing. For example, Alan Ehrenhalt (1991) has argued that relative to conservatives and Republicans, liberals and Democrats are more likely to be ambitious because they are more supportive of an activist government and hence more comfortable with long-term involvement in politics.

Of course, adding political ambition variables to models of political career choices has costs in terms of loss of elegance and parsimony. But tradeoffs of this type are inevitable in any analytical exercise; the key is to balance gains against losses. Jonathan Bendor and Thomas Hammond (1992, 302) summarize the problem well in a recent article about models of decision making in the public policy arena:

[A] well crafted model must strike a balance between simplicity and complexity. Too simple a model misses key aspects of the problem one is trying to understand; too complex a model is analytically intractable and yields few testable hypotheses.

Albert Hirschman (1985, 7-8) makes a similar argument advocating relaxation of modern economics' basic assumption of the "self-interested, isolated individual who chooses freely and rationally between alternative courses of action." He writes:

Like any virtue . . . parsimony in theory construction can be overdone and something is sometimes to be gained by making things more complicated (Hirschman 1985, p. 8).

Furthermore, it might be argued that scholars already frequently include variables relevant to political ambition in models focusing on the effects of opportunity structure, but do so in an ad hoc fashion. It is common for researchers to include an age variable in their models as a "control." Implicit or explicit in such activity is the view that politicians' age may strongly affect the development of ambition. It would seem preferable to be more systematic about assessing factors that affect political ambition.

AN APPLICATION: LEGISLATIVE TERM LIMITS

It is helpful to highlight some of the implications of the volume by applying them to a political reform that has received a good deal of attention in the 1990s: legislative term limits. While term limits have been widely discussed, there remains a need to analyze in more depth their impact on political careers. The contributions to this book throw some light on this topic.

First, imposition of term limits on the United States Congress or "career legislatures" (to use Squire's terminology) at the state level is likely to have a dramatic impact on the internal career structure, particularly if the limits are stringent. Given their short time horizons and need to make their mark quickly under stringent term limits, lawmakers would be unlikely to accept the highly differentiated stepping stone arrangement that Hibbing indicates is characteristic of the U.S. House of Representatives. If such limits were imposed, the House might come to look more like the California State Legislature in terms of internal distribution of power and influence.

Second, term limits in "springboard legislatures" such as California's may simply enhance the tendency of legislators to view their positions as stepping stones to further office. Casual analysis of the behavior of California state lawmakers since the passage of Proposition 140 (which limited state senators to two four-year terms and state assembly members to three two-year terms) in 1990 is consistent with this view. A recent article indicated that the "largest mass exodus in recent memory" of incumbent state assembly members was occurring in 1992, with 14 lower-house legislators seeking another office (*California Journal* 1992, 249).

Third, it appears improbable that the imposition of term limits will alter the powerful movement toward entrepreneurial, candidate-based politics in the United States described by Fowler (see also her reflections on the term limit movement in Fowler 1992). Term limits are neither likely to strengthen the parties' role in political recruitment nor to weaken the importance of media-dominated campaigns. Term limit proponents who are disturbed by the way modern political campaigns are conducted, and who hope term limits will change them, may be disappointed.

Fourth, term limits are likely to have complicated effects on the representation of women and minorities in legislative bodies. To the extent that incumbency is the key factor in the failure of women seeking legislative office to even approach parity with men, term limits should produce legislatures with a higher percentage of females. But term limits will not address the larger societal factors emphasized by Carroll and therefore may not encourage a greater number of women to seek office. For minority groups the picture is still more complex, given that incumbency itself may not be the major barrier to obtaining greater representation. It is even possible that in some places term limits could reduce the number of minorities in elective positions by lessening the power of influential minority elective officials with considerable seniority (in this regard, it is interesting to note Guerra's finding that minority group politicians with long political careers have acted as key "sponsors" of other minority candidates).

Fifth, if term limits are imposed on state legislators and/or members of Congress but not on those holding local office, there are likely to be partially offsetting effects on the career choices of local elected officials. On the one hand term limits will create more open seats at higher levels of government. There is abundant evidence to indicate that such seats are especially likely to attract ambitious politicians given the difficulty of beating an incumbent. On the other hand local elected officials are likely to perceive higher office as less desirable after term limits are imposed and may thus be more inclined to hold on to their current positions, particularly if they offer substantial benefits and opportunities for policy initiatives. And even upwardly mobile local politicians may be less inclined to *challenge* incumbents than had previously been the case, given that open seats are certain to arise within a specified time period (Fowler 1992).

Finally, the research discussed in this volume underscores the potential variety in the effects of term limits depending on the specific circumstances in which they are imposed (see also Malbin and Benjamin 1992). While some advocates of term limits may be taking a "one size fits all" approach to political reform (e.g., Peter Schabarum, sponsor of the successful voter initiative limiting California state legislators' terms, subsequently pushed for similar limits for other elected officials) our research suggests caution in expecting similar effects across jurisdictions. Among the sources of variety are the attractiveness of positions on which term limits are imposed, the conduciveness of offices to political advancement, the characteristics of officeholders relevant to the development of political ambition (e.g., age, ideology), and the availability of support systems to help potential candidates take advantage of changes in political opportunity.

IMPORTANCE OF FURTHER RESEARCH

I will close by seconding Shirley Williams' emphasis on the work that remains to be done. She highlights a number of topics for further research in her introduction and makes it clear why such research is needed. Each of the other contributors offers additional suggestions. The burgeoning term limit movement only reinforces the importance of understanding the subtleties of the variegated political career structure in the United States. We hope this volume will serve as a useful resource for those who wish to push forward our understanding of politicians' careers.

REFERENCES

Bendor, Jonathan, and Thomas H. Hammond. 1992. "Rethinking Allison's Models." *American Political Science Review* 86:301-22.

California Journal. 1992. "District-by-District Analysis: Assembly." 23: 249-74.

Ehrenhalt, Alan. 1991. *The United States of Ambition: Politicians, Power and the Pursuit of Office.* New York: Random House.

Fenno, Richard F., Jr. 1973. *Congressmen in Committees.* Boston: Little, Brown and Company.

Fowler, Linda. 1992. "A Comment on Competition and Careers." In *Limiting Legislative Terms,* ed. Gerald Benjamin and Michael Malbin, Washington: Congressional Quarterly Press.

Hirschman, Albert O. 1985. "Against Parsimony: Three Easy Ways of Complicating some Categories of Economic Discourse." *Economics and Philosophy* 1:7-21.

Malbin, Michael J., and Gerald Benjamin. 1992. "Legislatures After Term Limits." In *Limiting Legislative Terms,* ed. G. Benjamin and M. Malbin, Washington: Congressional Quarterly Press.

Muir, William K., Jr. 1982. *Legislature: California's School for Politics.* Chicago: University of Chicago Press.

Schlesinger, Joseph A. 1966. *Ambition and Politics: Political Careers in the United States.* Chicago: Rand McNally.